# PROGENY
# OF LIGHT/

# VANISHED
# IN
# DARKNESS

# PROGENY OF LIGHT/

## VANISHED IN DARKNESS

### BY
### EVA BREWSTER

NeWest

© Copyright 1994 Eva Brewster
Revised Edition
All rights reserved. The use of any part of this publication reproduced, transmitted in any form or by any means, electronic, mechanical, recording or otherwise, or stored in a retrieval system, without the prior consent of the publisher is an infringement of the copyright law. In the case of photocopying or other reprographic copying of the material, a licence must be obtained from the Canadian Reprography Collective before proceeding.

Canadian Cataloguing in Publication Data
Brewster, Eva, 1922-
    Progeny of light/vanished in darkness

ISBN 0-920897-75-4

1. Brewster, Eva, 1922-  2. Auschwitz (Poland :
Concentration camp)  3. Holocaust, Jewish (1939-1945)—
Personal narratives. 4. World War, 1939-1945—Prisoners and
prisons, German. I. Title. II. Title: Vanished in darkness.
D805.P7B74 1994    940.54'7243'092    C94-910475-2

Credits
Cover design:  Bob Young/BOOKENDS DESIGN
Interior design:  Brian Huffman
Editor for the Press:  Mort Ross
Financial Assistance: NeWest Press gratefully acknowledges the financial assistance of The Canada Council; The Alberta Foundation for the Arts, a beneficiary of the Lottery Fund of the Government of Alberta; and The NeWest Institute for Western Canadian Studies.

Printed and Bound in Canada by Best Gagné Book Manufacturers

NeWest Publishers Limited
#310, 10359-82 Avenue
Edmonton, Alberta
T6E 1Z9

Cover photo—Eva and mother, 1923

# TABLE OF CONTENTS

# ACKNOWLEDGEMENTS

Neither my travels nor my writing would have been possible without my husband's unwavering support. The antithesis of the "mean" Scotsman, he gave me more than I ever dreamed of throughout our married life. For forty years, he was at the receiving end of, and wakened me from, my recurring violent nightmares to reassure me that I could stop fighting and that I was safe with him. After a long battle with heart and kidney failure, he died peacefully in his sleep on October 18, 1986. It is increasingly hard to face the ongoing battle for human rights and dignity without him at my side to shield me from hurt as he did from the first day we met in 1945, but he left me a legacy of strength and renewed trust in humanity, love, and decency.

To Cleo Mowers, retired publisher of the *Lethbridge Herald*, I owe a debt of gratitude. He never ceased to encourage and promote my journalistic career. When in July, 1979, our twenty-four year old son died in a motor-bike accident and all hope and sunshine had gone out of my life once again, he insisted that I had an obligation to carry on. He persuaded me that, with my writing, I still had something worthwhile and necessary to contribute to our society in general and to a new generation in particular. Only a phone call away, he is still there for me whenever I need his help and advice.

Doug Walker, former editorial page editor of the *Lethbridge*

*Herald* and Joanne Helmer, editorial writer, deserve my sincere thanks. Both encouraged me—perhaps against my better judgement—to relive the most tragic era of this century and devoted many hours to my original *Auschwitz Memoir* for no better reason than their conviction that "everybody must read this book."

My grateful thanks to Lynn Oppolzer for all her help.

My gratitude also to Andy Ogle for editing the manuscript of *Vanished in Darkness* and for his contributions of Prologue and Epilogue, which I believe added to the reader's understanding of my motivation for writing that story.

Since I added new chapters leading up to the Second World War and the early post-war era, Mort Ross, NeWest's long-suffering editor, deserves special acknowledgement. I must have given him a hard time with my frequent doubts and resistance to changes in my manuscript. Yet he always responded with saint-like patience and explained in great detail where and why he had suggested corrections in style, grammar, or expressions.

Last, but by no means least, my eternal love and appreciation to my daughter Joyce and my now seventeen year old granddaughter Tracy Logan, for the renewed sunshine they brought into my life, for their constant active support and their conviction that the hard lessons I have learned since I was Tracy's age must not be forgotten.


Eva Brewster
1994

# INTRODUCTION

Eva Brewster is not a Mother Theresa. Her story is not one of the triumph of good over evil. It is more realistic than that. It tells of courage, of persistence, of stubborn defiance, of being knocked down and carrying on, and being knocked down again and again and always carrying on. She has been called a survivor, but survival has always been by accident of fate, not by her own doings or seeking. Having survived, only God knows why or how, she plods onward, straight into the teeth of more of life's storms.

What pushes her on? She seems bent on paying off a debt, a debt to her revered mother, a debt to the men and women and the children, especially the children, swallowed up by Hitler's death camps. Why was she spared and they were not? She doesn't know, but isn't a debt implied? Can she do no less than speak up, to shout a warning at the least sign of another potential Holocaust? If her parents' generation had spoken up, perhaps the hell of Nazism might have been averted. History is a brutal teacher, and she is an observant student.

The original manuscript for this book was intended only as a bequest to her children and grandchildren, so they would know and remember what she had learned at such frightful cost. When the manuscript and the experiences described in it became known to her friends and book publication was urged on her, she assented.

Why should not that lesson be more widely taught? Why not a larger payment on that bottomless debt?

Her book, published by NeWest Press in 1984 under the title *Vanished in Darkness: An Auschwitz Memoir*, covered only the war years, but the fascinating and challenging Eva Brewster story started earlier and has not yet ended. With *Vanished in Darkness* out of print for the third or fourth time, the publishers wisely and fortunately decided the next printing should cover more years and report more of the story. New chapters were written for the first and last parts of this volume, and we are now left at the start of her new life, her marriage to Ross Brewster in 1947.

I had not even heard of Eva Brewster until the summer of 1971, when she sent a letter to the *Lethbridge Herald* of which I was then publisher and editor. That letter and the controversy attending it were fully in keeping with her dedication to debt repayment and to her purpose in life—to expose, denounce, and, if possible, squelch any first sign of resurgent Nazism or its domestic equivalent anywhere. Quoting her mother, "There will be a new generation happy to be alive who will, I hope, never know the horrors we have seen. If we have one mission in life, a debt to all who have died, you will carry it out. You, Daniella, (her alias in the French Resistance) will see to it that young people will not ever again be persecuted for their race, colour, or beliefs." Daniella's response, as she recalls it: "That day so long ago, I promised my mother, my murdered little family, our six million dead, and myself that, never again, as long as I lived, would a dictatorship rob our children of their birthright, their freedom, and their happiness." And again, a lifetime later, "having failed so miserably to keep my promise to a future generation, it is my last hope that this book may open the readers' eyes to the dangers they refuse to face up to." May your eyes, dear reader, and mine, be always open.

That wish is not rhetorical. No one knows Nazi Germany better than Eva Brewster. On one public occasion she had spoken about Nazism and the Holocaust, and she was asked "Are we here in western Canada that much different from Hitler's Germans? We denounce the hellish evils of Nazism, but can we be sure that if we had been there, we would have withstood the appeals of Hitler?" Her answer: "No, we cannot be sure. The German people who did all those cruel deeds, including the Holocaust, are not different from us here in Canada. What happened there can happen anywhere, and don't you forget it."

(Let me note parenthetically that a highly educated refugee from Bosnia said that she and her friends would never have dreamed, a few years ago, that the evils of "ethnic cleansing," of neighbour slaughtering neighbour, would or could ever happen in that free and happy land. And she said she could observe more potential for ethnic hatred in the Canada of 1994 than in the Yugoslavia of the 1980s.)

Since that first letter to the newspaper I have been awed by Eva's mastery of the English language. She still has an accent, but on paper one might assume that English was her first language. Her French is rusting from neglect, she says. Both she learned at school in Berlin.

Preparing for her frequent trips to Israel, she would ask me what reporting she should do. I would suggest the usual subjects, the water shortage, the health of the kibbutz movement, the Arab situation, and so on. Many doors were opened by her stories in the *Lethbridge Herald*. Several of them were reprinted elsewhere. She was asked to do special work for the Alberta government. She did a CBC Radio series, school broadcasts, a series of television programs, and much other broadcasting and speaking.

This introduction started with the observation that she had

been knocked down so often, and yet always kept going. Her capacity for survival and endurance may be more startlingly obvious by making a partial list: her father's death by heart attack the night the Nazis robbed him of his business; the confiscation of her family's wealth and home; the gradual and reluctant awakening to all the evils of the Nazi movement and especially to the fate of the Jews; the unspeakable horrors of Auschwitz; the murder of her husband and daughter in the gas chambers; her own facing a firing squad; the accidental death of her twenty-four year old son from her second marriage; her own confrontation with cancer eleven years ago, cutting off the debilitating chemotherapy in spite of being told by her doctor that in doing so she had only six months to live, and finally the death of her Scottish husband, her greatest advocate, after 40 years of marriage.

She has been to the edge of the cliff so often that she has no fear of anyone or anything. Defiance is her style. And yet, as her memoir makes clear, there have been interludes of loveliness, tenderness, happiness, even ecstasy. Knowing how good life can be perhaps makes her so intolerant of evil.

Her Auschwitz story has been translated into other languages. She takes special pride in the recently published Danish version, for she has fond childhood memories of Denmark and she harbours such respect and appreciation for the Danish resistance to Hitlerism.

Her many friends marvel at her intelligence, her range of interests, and her tirelessness. She doesn't know how much time she has left, and she doesn't seem to care, but what there is she seems anxious to use well and not to waste. It goes into writing, lecturing, participating in seminars, demonstrating good citizenship via local politics, helping her small family, indulging in good music and good reading. She has pets, hobbies, and a love for adventures of the mind.

Her mother, even more miraculously a survivor of Nazi atrocities, had a long and useful career as a nurse on a kibbutz in Israel. She had endured almost as much hell as Eva, but lived to eighty-seven. Eva visited her many times. Those visits sharpened her interest in Israeli politics. Characteristically she has no patience with those who would persecute or suppress the Arabs.

At the time of writing, a German public-opinion poll had just been published. Of the fifteen hundred Germans over eighteen who had been polled, thirty-nine per cent said "the Jews are exploiting the Holocaust for their own purposes." An American Jewish leader interpreted that to mean "substantial portions of the population do not wish to maintain the memory of the Holocaust." Many would go further; the Jim Keegstras and Ernst Zündels of Canada, the David Irvings of Britain, and innumerable others, deny that there ever was a Holocaust. Many well-intentioned Canadians as well as Germans argue that that bad dream should be forgotten and only happy thoughts accommodated. Eva Brewster's family in pre-war Berlin would have denied with all their strength the remotest possibility of anything resembling the Holocaust. On Eva's arm today there is a scar where her Auschwitz number had been tattooed and then removed. The number had been burned into her arm when she in a transport of a thousand young people was sent to the death camp, and only seven survived. Her Auschwitz number was 51459.

She bears no hatred of the German people. Their fault was in not resisting Nazism. Her concern is that what they did, any other people might also do. Her plea is that everyone practice tolerance and respect, for the potential for another Holocaust is everywhere. We must all be on guard, always.

Many years ago Eva Brewster said "I trust in human nature. In some places a snowstorm is enough for people to become good neighbours. In others it may require an earthquake, but basically, people are good. If just one person comes out of the glasshouse of apathy and indifference, others will surely follow."

This book is intended to bring the reader out of the glasshouse of apathy and indifference. Will it succeed?

Cleo Mowers
March 1994

# CHAPTER 1

On December 28, 1933, I was eleven years old. My parents, Albert and Elisabeth Levy, my ten-year-old brother Stefan, and I lived in the spacious apartment on Nikolsburger Platz 3 in West-Berlin where I was born. Adolph Hitler first came to my attention as a disembodied voice over the radio, then called "wireless". His voice was hoarse, bawling, and aggressive and he spoke in a dialect we could barely understand. It sent my little brother into fits of giggles ending in hiccups and he was dispatched to the care of Christan, our old seamstress who could always calm him.

I was more attentive and tried hard to make sense of what Hitler said because I saw the worried expression in my parents' faces. My father was not an orthodox Jew and we children simply accepted that we were Jewish as our Christian school friends saw themselves as Protestants or Catholics. There was otherwise little difference in our social background or upbringing. I was thus struck and alarmed by Hitler's violent verbal attacks on "Jewish-Communist intellectuals" and on "Jewish-Communist capitalism" which he blamed for the shattered economy of post-World War I Germany.

Our parents had seldom discussed controversial topics in our presence. We were therefore politically ignorant and unbiased. But although barely eleven, I caught the constant contradictions in Hitler's appeals to the whole range of German society.

In one and the same speech, he told workers he'd "wipe out the Jewish-Communist intellectuals" and asked the intellectuals to "use their wonderful brains in their country's service."

He promised small shopkeepers the destruction of "Jewish-Communist capitalistic monopolies". In the next sentence he assured owners and directors of large businesses that he would protect their interests and resources which would guarantee employment, the security and prosperity of a new Germany.

Hitler talked to disaffected youth. He said he would replace "hopelessly antiquated and reactionary old teachers" with young, progressive, and enlightened ones, teachers who would "nurture young people's natural intelligence and dignity." Almost in the same breath, he "entrusted the children to their experienced teachers in the knowledge that their wisdom would guide youngsters into a happier future." Such appeals had already made Hitler so popular that old General von Hindenburg, then president of the German Republic, had found it expedient to appoint the ranting ex-corporal Chancellor even before his National-Socialist party was voted into power.

I remember asking my parents why the radio voice was yelling so harshly at the people he presumably loved and wanted to save. My father gently explained what little he knew of Hitler's background—perhaps unwanted, unloved, and lonely as a boy, frustrated and unsuccessful in later years. He reassured me that the German people would not long be misled by such a man.

My happy childhood, our close, loving family and friends, and the serenity of our homelife had been so different from Daddy's story of young Adolph's past that I felt sorry for Hitler. I cried into my pillow that night, praying that he might find friends and that God might heal his soul. It was to be one of the last prayers of my childhood.

# CHAPTER 2

German adults did not seem to hear the contradictions in Hitler's pre-election speeches. They absorbed only the parts affecting them as individuals. After the Nazis' victory, which was celebrated by endless marches of uniformed SS, SA, and Hitler Youths, by fireworks at night and fights with remnants of left-wing parties, there was a lull. A silence descended upon our gay Berlin. People stayed indoors to avoid street battles with, and mass arrests of, suspected Communists. Cafés and theatres were deserted; and those who had to leave their homes looked at each other with suspicion, avoided talking even to old acquaintances, and quickly moved on.

My parents went to see our principals to find out if it would not be wiser to remove my brother and me from public schools and to educate us privately. Both headmasters happened to be strongly anti-Nazi and assured my father that they would resign before they'd allow a single Jewish child to be discriminated against or hurt. Both were convinced that this craze wouldn't last. The craze lasted; our principals did not. My brother's principal committed suicide and mine was forced to retire.

For a few weeks, however, lessons continued as usual until Fraulein Zachler who had taught us French, entered my classroom. She went up to her desk, clicked her heels, stood to attention, raised her right arm, and shouted: "Heil Hitler!" Her flat bosom was adorned with a swastika and a decoration awarded to long-time members of the Nazi party. We giggled and didn't quite know what was expected. There followed a lecture on future changes of behaviour and veiled threats to those of us who dared remain "reactionaries."

This first Nazi teacher expected the whole class to stand at the beginning and end of each lesson and give the Hitler salute. She, the only Party member on the teaching staff so far, would teach us the "History of the German Race" (Rassenkunde). She informed us that she had also been appointed recruiting officer for the Hitler Youth in our high school and, for this purpose, each student would be required to produce a family tree covering at least four generations. She stressed that four generations must be proved to be of pure Aryan blood for the child to be accepted in the Hitler Youth. To complete this pedigree in good handwriting was to be our homework for the next French lesson.

Speaking for the seven Jewish girls in our class, I asked if we could continue the translation of our current French text since we could prove beyond doubt that we were not Aryans. In her most cutting manner, Miss Zachler said that we were to do the same homework as everybody else. Did we think we could have an easy time while our "Aryan comrades" were sweating over their noses? She added that "it was about time the Jews were made to roll up their sleeves and do an honest day's work." Although I neither regarded translation of French literature as an easy task, nor saw the necessity to roll up my sleeves in order to produce a family tree, I said no more and received friendly digs in my ribs from our "Aryan comrades" who sat on either side of me. To our childish minds, this extraordinary "French lesson" seemed ludicrous, the more so because the other teachers could not resist alluding to the "oldest Nazi" in their midst. They also told us more or less seriously that we better obey the Nazi's instructions if we knew what was good for us.

Zachler's work in our high school quickly multiplied. Our principal warned us that she also represented the Gestapo, the Secret Police, and would thus inform on other teachers, students, and parents alike. She clearly belonged to a legion of frustrated females who idolized Hitler. She collected funds for Nazi organizations which sprang up like mushrooms. Originally an obscure, unpopular spinster, she commanded the attention of the many who now hated and feared her vindictive nature.

That evening, when I told my parents of the "homework," my father produced a huge roll of parchment, a family tree I did not know existed. As we glanced swiftly over names and dates, the ink gradually faded and became difficult to read. When we reached the top of the long tree, having started with our own names at the very bottom of the roll, the date was the third month of the fifteenth year in the thirteenth century and the place of that ancestor's birth was Berlin. My father told me as much as he knew of his forefathers, some of whom were said to have come into Germany with the Romans. Much later, during the Spanish Inquisition, there were fugitives who had made their way through France and their only daughter married into our already long established family. My parents let me take the family tree to school to save me copying names and dates of people who had lived in Germany through seven centuries. They treasured this possession, but valued my eyesight more and were not going to sacrifice it to the whims of my Nazi teacher.

At the start of our next French lesson, Zachler marched into the class: "Heil Hitler, girls!" No response from the students although all stood up politely as was customary in German schools. The teacher collected our homework and glanced quickly through the heap of papers. Mine being by far the bulkiest document, she read some of the entries. "Look at that, children," she cried triumphantly, "here is a family tree any German child could be proud of. One of this girl's ancestors was physician to King Frederic the

Great and another the famous composer Meyerbeer. Whose is it?"

I raised my hand and her face changed color from pasty to bright turkey red. She spluttered and then shouted: "I told you to write out your family tree in your own handwriting. Take it home and copy it twice. I'll teach you lazy Jews!" I did not copy it and the incident was apparently forgotten.

Once more this teacher blundered, much to our delight. One day, she brought her skull measuring instruments which, she claimed, could help her to determine accurately whether a person was of pure Aryan descent. Eager to demonstrate her theory, she stopped in front of a new student's desk. This girl had recently joined my class after spending a year in a private German Language school. She was Russian born and her father owned Nivea and toothpaste factories in Poland and the Baltic States. Her mother had been a dentist in Latvia. They had moved to Berlin before Hitler came to power to give their only child a more cosmopolitan education. The daughter was a beautiful girl; tall, slender with golden hair, she had deep blue eyes, and a most attractive personality. She was by far the loveliest girl in our class.

Miss Zachler led her up to the raised podium in front of the class and announced reverently: "Here, students, is a typical example of Aryan womanhood. Note her proud bearing, her height, her fair hair, blue eyes, straight nose, and perfect teeth. I don't need to measure her skull to be certain of her ancestry. However, just to show you the reliability of these instruments, I shall measure her. . . . What is your name, child?"

"Gertrude," she answered shyly, "but . . ." The teacher interrupted her: "With all the traits of pure nordic blood, you also have a lovely nordic name! 'Ger' is the Germanic word for 'spear' and 'trude' means . . ." We all burst into laughter, but the teacher wouldn't be distracted from her pet theory. She measured Gertrude's head and found the measurements perfect. "You are a member of the

Hitler Youth, Gertrude?" she asked. "No, Madam, I am not," said the girl. "You didn't give me a chance to tell you that I am a Jewess and proud of it. Had you let me finish a sentence, I could have stopped this rigmarole long ago." Shaking her long, blonde curls in disgust, Gertrude walked back to her desk without waiting for permission.

Zachler, our laughter ringing in her ears, shot out of the classroom and, as we heard later, demanded that all Jews be expelled. But at that time, the principal could still overrule the lone Nazi. All the latter achieved was that the Jewish kids were given a free period during her classes on "Racial History" and on the "World Conspiracy of Jewish-Communist-Capitalists and Bankers to take over all countries and to destroy Germany."

My high school was to remain a hotbed for "reactionaries" for a few more years. The teachers were kind and considerate and tried to make our lot bearable. If anything, they demanded more work and expected quicker results from Jewish students. Often, our headmistress took us separately during Zachler's classes, cramming knowledge into us as fast as she could. "You never know, girls, how long I will be allowed to keep you here," she used to say. "I want to give you a good start. Hopefully, you will be able to graduate at least a year earlier than the rest of your class."

We still had a good time at school. There were minor pinpricks: the odd student would explain that she could no longer visit with us or invite us to parties because that would endanger her father's career. But most of our "Aryan comrades" came from good, tolerant homes and did not cave in to pressure.

My younger brother was not so lucky. He was still in elementary school where the older students, at least, were frequently pressured by those who had failed their entrance exams for high school or whose parents could not afford to keep them at school beyond the age of fourteen. Those boys were the early failures, the disgruntled and discontented—easy prey for the Hitler Youth and the incessant indoctrination and brain-washing which produced young Nazi thugs so successfully. Very early under the new regime, these boys began to persecute Jewish children.

My brother's temper tantrums on his return from school became more frequent. He had never been talkative and any trouble he had, he kept to himself. Throwing his satchel at the wall of our entrance hall as soon as the door was opened must have been his safety valve. So far, Christan, our old sewing lady, had always managed to pacify him with a quick snack; but now her theory, that children get bad tempered only when they are hungry, failed. This pleased our cook who had always balked at supplying food just before a main meal. However, Stefan became more silent than ever, seldom smiled, and his face looked pinched, his eyes enormous. He behaved like a hunted animal and we thought he was ill. Yet our doctor soon confirmed that there was nothing physically wrong with him. We didn't find out what upset him until he came home from school one day with a big cut across his forehead and blood on his lips and temples. Then he reluctantly told us that teenage Hitler Youths had thrown him down a staircase and then pelted him with stones, yelling at him to "go to Palestine or die!"

He, our youngest, was the first to suffer physically. Needless to say, he never returned to that school. My parents, who still believed the new government would not last, enrolled him in a very good Jewish school. Although this entailed an hour's journey, my brother was happy again.

# CHAPTER 3

Our two half-sisters and half-brother were not in Berlin during that period. Kathy, the oldest, was training at a teachers' college in Stuttgart to become a gym instructor. Lotte, the youngest, was still in a boarding school in the Harz mountains and Gerhard had been studying law at Heidelberg. Their mother, my father's first wife, had died during the flu epidemic after the first world war. Until my father remarried, the three children had been looked after by a succession of nannies and private tutors. Raised with fairy tales of evil stepmothers by a housekeeper who didn't want to give up her dominating post, they bitterly resented my twenty year old mother at first. She was, after all, only eight years older than Kathy. Only when I was born did they gradually transfer their love for the new baby to their young stepmother. As I grew older, I formed a very close relationship with them that was to last until their deaths.

Now, shortly after our first encounters with Nazis, Gerhard came home from university. Even before Hitler came to power, Heidelberg had a reputation, not only for being the best university in Germany, but also for anti-semitism among its aristocratic and right-wing student corps. Until 1933, my brother had managed to hold his own—probably because he was a brilliant, strong, tall, and good-looking young man who helped the less brainy members of his fraternity to keep up with their studies. But now Gerhard no longer saw any future in Germany. He had long debates with my father about his intentions to give up his career and to become a pioneer in Palestine. He was the first of us to leave the country.

Stefan and I joined a Jewish youth organization, a splinter group which had previously been part of the German Boy Scouts and Girl Guides movement. We went to camps, had occasional fights with Hitler Youths, minor scrapes we could still win. We still travelled abroad during school holidays and, if anything, the occasional insults nettled my pride. As a result, I worked much harder at school and remained among the first five in a class of 40 students, although I was two years younger than the rest of them. Having been ahead of my age group in elementary school, I had passed all tests before a school board and had been allowed to skip two years to enter high school early. To begin with, the age difference had its drawbacks. While my school mates were already dating and going to dances, I was still playing with dolls and sleeping with my teddy bear. Only the fact that I could keep up with the others intellectually saved me from their ridicule. But in dating too, I soon caught up with them.

Barely thirteen, I was introduced to a charming boy of seventeen and fell immediately in love with him. He was tall and full of fun and, as I thought, rather aware of his charms. When he offered to see me home from a friend's birthday party, I decided to prove my independence: "Thank you, I can find my way," and I jumped onto an already moving tram-car. Two of my school pals were horrified when they heard of the encounter the next day: "You mean to say you turned down 'THE F. H. RAPHAEL'? You goose, there isn't a girl in Berlin who wouldn't give ten years of her life if 'F. H.' offered to see her home!"

I could have kicked my thirteen-year-old self. His sparkling brown eyes and teasing laughter haunted my dreams. How could I ever see him again? Being so much younger than my school mates, I did not yet belong to any of their sets, nor did I think it likely that my parents would allow me to join a dancing class he was known to attend. But the next day he phoned me: "Eva, will you give me another chance? Why did you run away yesterday? Did I offend you?" He was so genuinely puzzled, so hurt, that I felt tempted to accept his invitation to go sailing on the weekend. He had a small yacht on a lake close to West Berlin where we lived. But caution prevailed, much as I longed to say 'yes'. Once again, I turned him down.

"Why won't you come?" he asked. "Because you have a reputation." He was indignant: "My dear child, I'm not a baby snatcher!" That cut deep. We exchanged more or less veiled insults and eventually compromised on a date in one of the popular milkshake bars in my neighbourhood. We soon became inseparable, but although I turned to jelly when I only heard his voice, I instinctively avoided the mistakes other girls had obviously made and never ran after him.

Whenever we had one of our quarrels, I never phoned him afterwards although I kept creeping round the telephone like a cat after hot milk. He always made the first move towards reconciliation and never seemed to realize how readily he was forgiven. Any day I didn't see him seemed empty. And, miracle of miracles, my parents allowed me to join his dancing class. It was the most glorious winter of my life. His old flames did everything in their power to entice him away from me, without success. On my fourteenth birthday, when he was just eighteen, he asked me to marry him as soon as I'd be old enough and he gave me a diamond engagement ring.

I didn't tell my parents, but ostentatiously waved my ring around until my father asked me about it. As usual, he listened gravely and said: "F. H. is a very nice boy. If you still feel like marrying him in ten year's time when he is a qualified architect, you have my blessings. In the meantime, darling, I'd suggest you don't wear that ring to school. Other girls might be jealous. And I hope you'll always be as happy and as much in love as you are now." His secretary told me years later about the day my father had mentioned to her that his little girl was already dreaming of marriage and that he thought this was a great and touching joke.

Our once weekly dancing classes finished at 10:00 p.m. Invariably my mother waited for me in the hall. She was terrified our relationship might go beyond that of being dancing partners. But my father trusted us and persuaded her to let us enjoy the loveliest time of our lives; because he trusted us, we behaved. We went sailing every summer weekend on the beautiful lakes near Berlin. The temptation to explore sex was often overwhelming, but after a passionate kiss, Freddy would take my hand and together we'd plunge into the cold water and swim until we ached. We returned to the boat glowing and relaxed. We delighted in the little coves where tall, green reeds sheltered water fowl and fish. We were far removed from the noise and bustle of Berlin, far away from Hitler's marching columns. A sensation of freedom and happiness permeated our times together. The memory of our sailing days was to be with me for years to come and with Freddy for his short lifetime.

In the 1930s, it still seemed to us, in spite of political upheaval, that we had everything in the world: youth and beauty, the best parents imaginable, lovely homes, and wealth. Whether we were walking in the streets, riding our bicycles, sailing, or just talking on a park bench, people turned round to look at us and the grumpiest faces lit up in smiles.

My favourite uncle visited us from Hamburg, took one look at me and sighed: "La beauté du diable!" With the selfishness of teenagers, we lived only for our love and had no eyes or ears for the changes around us. Perhaps because our parents refused to see them, we didn't either. But then the first blows hit our families.

Kurt Raphael, Freddy's older cousin, the only son of wealthy parents, was a playboy. Like many rich boys in the turbulent 20s, he had turned into what my father aptly called a "salon-Communist." His political convictions did not prevent him from enjoying all the privileges his father enabled him to have—his Mercedes-Benz luxury car, a big yacht, and a stable full of horses, but he preached Communism to students at his university and neighbouring colleges. Soon after Hitler came to power, he vanished and was not heard of until a few years later. Then, he and a few other survivors of those early arrests were released from concentration camps to emigrate to England or the United States. In the meantime, his parents died believing him dead.

Ruth Hennig, my mother's cousin, a vivacious concert singer married to a Christian, a well-known violinist—much against her parents' wishes—had one little son before Hitler came to power. Shortly after the change of regime, her husband found his engagements and concert tours cancelled because of his Jewish wife. Hennig divorced her since his career meant more to him than wife and child. She managed to get out of Germany illegally, but had to leave the boy with friends, hoping to get the necessary official visa for him to join her as soon as she reached her destination, somewhere in South America. War broke out before the woman herself was accepted as a genuine refugee in her new country and before red tape allowed her to legitimately sponsor her son. The child, like so many others, was deported and killed. The German father, who could have saved his son, did nothing although he had been informed of the impending deportation. Other fathers in similar situations saved their children by simply acknowledging parentage and taking them into their homes. While these kids were obviously not accepted by the Nazis as equal citizens, they were not harmed.

I didn't know all this at the time and only learned the ghastly details after the end of the war. Little was known about such tragedies in the beginning. If Germans claimed later that they did not know what was going on, they were probably telling the truth although they did learn after mass deportations started that their neighbours vanished and were never heard of again.

# CHAPTER 4

By 1937, only three of us children were at home. My older half-brother Gerhard had left almost four years earlier for Palestine. He had become a pioneer and founder of Hazorea, a communal settlement at the foot of Mount Carmel in the Jezreel valley, now one of the most beautiful villages in Israel. My oldest half-sister Kate was staying with an Italian diplomat's family in Rome, learning Italian, improving her French, and, most seriously, trying to get over her disappointment at not being able to compete in the 1936 Olympic Games in Berlin.

Kate had been an outstanding athlete. Her records in high jumping, discus and javelin throwing, as well as swimming had been among the best in Germany since 1932. To avert a threatened international boycott, the German Olympic Board had promised the world that there would be no racial discrimination, but just before the opening of the games, German newspapers, which had continued to report my sister's record-breaking trial results, mentioned briefly on their back pages that she had sprained or broken her ankle and would therefore be unable to compete. Kate had not, of course, and I'll long remember her on the day of the official opening of the games, sobbing bitterly on her bed. Already twenty-seven, she had struggled to come up to the highest Olympic standards in spite of her age. She knew she would never have another chance to compete. Threatened with imprisonment by the Gestapo should she be seen and recognized in the Olympic stadium or anywhere in Berlin, she was virtually under house arrest. She saw little worth living for now. Only when the Olympics were finally over and after the last foreign visitors had left Germany was she permitted to travel to Italy. She was still only a shadow of her light-hearted former self when she joined us in the Dolomites on our last holiday abroad late in 1936.

During the Easter holiday of 1937, my second half-sister Lotte, then eighteen, came home from boarding school. One day, having promised to be back for lunch, she went to visit a girl friend. She didn't turn up for lunch and didn't appear for dinner in the evening. My father drove to her friend's house to pick her up. He was angry and intended to give her severe censure. Lotte's friend met him with surprise; my sister had never arrived. Papa came home as near to panic as I had ever seen him. He first phoned all the friends Lotte could possibly have visited and then our local police station—without results.

The police chief promised to call us if he got any information, but the night passed and Lotte didn't come home; nor did we get any police or accident reports. Early the next morning, my father went to see a former Freemason, now a high ranking Nazi. This man—my father never revealed his name for fear of endangering his life—had warned my parents long ago to leave Germany. He had close contacts in the Secret Police, the Gestapo, but was still willing to help his old Jewish friends and other former brothers of the now outlawed Lodge. As soon as he heard that Lotte had disappeared, he set the Nazi machinery in motion, asked my father to go home and wait for the results of his enquiries. Barely an hour later, we saw a car park in front of our house and after a few minutes, the elevator stopped on our floor. My father's old friend did not even take off his coat. "Sit down, Albert, and listen," he said putting his hand on my father's shoulder: "Your daughter is in a fix, but it could be worse."

My father paled and his hands trembled, but not a muscle in his face moved. I saw for the first time that he had become an old man. His hair had been silver-white for as long as I could remember, but his face had been strong and handsome. Now there were dark circles under his clear grey eyes. He was fifty-four years old but at that moment he looked seventy.

"Lotte is in prison." Our informant then explained that while she was on the bus, the ticket collector asked her if she was Jewish. When she nodded, he told her to get up from her seat to make room for a young Nazi in uniform. She didn't move and pretended not to have heard. When she got off at her destination, a plain-clothed policeman followed and asked her if she didn't know that Jews on public transport must get up for Aryans. He showed a metal disk, the identification of the Gestapo. Lotte, instead of denying knowledge of this new law, grinned and said: "You'll have to do better than that; anybody could have such a dog tag!" The Gestapo man arrested her and took her to the Alexander Platz jail. The story sounded bad, the former Freemason said, but there was a chance to free her if he used his authority. However it would take time and there would definitely be pre-conditions—one of them a commitment to get Lotte out of Germany within three months.

In 1937 it was already difficult to get entry visas to any country in Europe or North America. We had no relatives in the UK. And Britain made entry into Palestine equally difficult. Boys and girls who wanted to go there had to go through a twelve-months agricultural training course and even if they could complete this, there was no certainty of getting a visa if the number of applicants exceeded the quota.

We had no luck at any foreign consulate. Sympathetic though they were, the ambassadors and consuls, bound by their regulations, saw no way to help. However, the Palestine Office told my father that there was one way of getting around emigration restrictions: If Lotte married a Palestinian, she would have no difficulties joining him. This seemed an impossible and ludicrous suggestion at first. But an old acquaintance, who had just been posted from Berlin to a diplomatic position in Jerusalem, took an urgent message to my brother in Palestine. Within three weeks, Gerhard sent one of his friends, Uri Geismar, back to Germany to marry his sister. It was a sacrifice for the young man who was already engaged to be married and had to postpone his wedding to save a girl he had never met. A week after his arrival in Berlin, they were married by special licence and left for Haifa a few days later. Lotte legally divorced her "husband" as soon as British law permitted, freeing him to marry his fiancée. Lotte went into a large hospital training school to become a nurse and later married a policeman who had immigrated to Palestine from Vienna just before Hitler marched into and annexed Austria.

From then on only isolated incidents are painfully engraved in my memory, one of them a day when the former Freemason, who had helped to get Lotte out of jail, phoned us early in the morning. He warned us not to go out. Some anti-semitic demonstrations were planned, but he wouldn't give us details over the telephone. It became one of those "spontaneous uprisings of the German people" the Nazis were so good at orchestrating. All over Berlin and throughout the whole of Germany simultaneously, Jewish business owners were dragged into the streets and beaten up. There were mass arrests of people who protested or tried to stop the thugs ransacking shops and warehouses. Finally the streets were deserted except for Nazis drunk with power and alcohol, continuing their assaults and looting. Their women suddenly sported gorgeous fur coats and jewelry. In 1938, during the infamous "Crystal Night," they would finish and destroy what was left or had been repaired.

My parents were stunned; I struggled with my fierce pride, my hatred and contempt for the Nazis that surged up in hot waves.

Yet I still felt tied to this country of sheep that followed its leader into crime and murder. Once more we discussed emigration and once again my father refused to leave. By that time he was being bullied into selling his large business. The then Minister of State, Backe, had his eyes on the firm and my father knew that sooner or later the threats, debates, and conferences would cease and his property would be confiscated if he did not sell it quickly. Still, he insisted he was too old to leave Germany. He wanted to die where his forefathers had lived, worked, and prospered. Naively, he thought he could live for the rest of his life on his capital and be left in peace if he gave into the minister and let him have what he wanted.

So great was his love for his home that he was willing to make the ultimate sacrifice: he urged Stefan and me to leave him behind and go. He could still afford to send us to a good boarding school abroad to finish our education. His own roots went too deep, he said, but ours were strong enough to stand transplanting. My mother cried. She was only thirty-five years old, but sixteen years of a very happy marriage to a man who had given her all the love and security she ever desired, had matured her so that the nineteen years of age difference between them seemed non-existent. If he talked and thought of death, she accepted it as an inevitable end to both their lives and she did not protest. Her life had its beginning and its end in him.

My brother had no doubt that his future was in Palestine, but at that stage, he refused to leave without me. My heart shattered, but I couldn't even cry. I still could not see myself leaving behind everything and everybody I had ever known and loved. During the few minutes of silence, while my father looked at me so gravely and waited for a reply, I lived through a lifetime of exile, loneliness and homesickness. The tenderness in my father's eyes, his warm hands holding mine, did the rest. "I can't leave without you!" I almost shouted in despair and then fled the sunny lounge, no longer seeing light or beauty anywhere.

He followed me to my room, and rocked me as he had done since I was a baby, as he had rocked me again every night since I had started sleep-walking a couple of years ago. Night after night he had waited for me, opened all doors and carried me back to bed. I never remembered anything about those nocturnal walks but apparently answered my father's questions sensibly and truthfully. If he thought something was worrying me, he asked about it then and always got the response he needed.

All this was in my mind now and he understood when I pleaded: "Don't send me away, I need you!" "No, my darling, I'll not force you to emigrate, but if you change your mind, please tell me immediately. Don't think I'd be hurt."

Berlin calmed down again. Except for the gutted stores and shop windows boarded up until the businesses were taken over and repaired by "Aryans," there were no signs of the vandalism that had swept through Germany and her capital. At my school, teachers and students were even kinder than before. My father returned to his business as usual. His office building and store houses had not been touched by arson or looters, probably because the Minister of State had a hand in protecting a property which he knew would soon be his.

On January 25, 1938, my father was summoned to have dinner with the minister to finalize take-over conditions. My father knew, of course, that he would be bullied into a forced sale for a fraction of his firm's value, but he was determined to fight for his rights as long as possible.

I had been asleep when he came home that night, but woke up suddenly, shaking with fright. From my parents' bedroom, I heard my mother cry out in agony. I don't know how I reached their door—the long passage between our rooms was dark and seemed endless. I found my father, still in his formal suit, leaning against the marble washhand basin, his face deadly white. My mother sat on the edge of her bed trying to control her sobbing. She was sorry to have wakened me, she said, but Papa had been very sick, had fainted a few minutes ago and scared her terribly.

My father sat down in an armchair somewhat shakily and taking my hand, he drew me towards him with his normal happy grin. "To listen to your mother, one would think it was time to notify the undertaker and order wreaths for my funeral. There's a good girl. Get back to your nice warm bed. I had some oysters tonight which obviously didn't agree with me, but it's nothing to worry about." He turned to my mother: "If it makes you feel better, Sweetheart, go and phone the doctor. But I can tell you now what he is going to say."

Behind my father's back, my mother made frantic signs indicating that she wanted me to stay till she returned. I persuaded him to take his jacket off and lie down on his bed. He closed his eyes for a few seconds and then asked me to get him some very cold water. When I hesitated, he gave me his smile and said: "I'll be quite all right, Eva, till you get back, but I am very thirsty." He seemed tired but comfortable and so I left him to get the water.

Our apartment was huge—fourteen large rooms, and the kitchen was at the far end of a long connecting corridor. In passing, I heard my mother talking to the doctor, asking him to come as quickly as possible. Then she ran back to her bedroom. Just as I filled a glass of water and added ice cubes, I heard her scream, rushed back and found her kneeling beside my father's bed, squeezing and patting his hand. He seemed sound asleep and his face had a look of such peace that I felt a surge of annoyance at my mother for trying to wake him up. I then realized that he was dead and the shock was all the greater because I had never imagined that death could be so sudden, so calm.

My mother cried quietly, had forgotten I was there. I crept

out of my parents' bedroom, oddly at peace, an inner peace that couldn't last. Sorrow would come later. At that moment, I felt my father was still there. I could still see his loving smile and hear his voice: "I'll be quite all right till you get back." A small inner voice seemed to tell me: "God was good to him!"

I tiptoed into my brother's bedroom. He was laughing in his sleep, obviously in the middle of a pleasant dream and his eyelashes threw shadows on his red cheeks. I didn't have the heart to rouse him. Tomorrow would be a dark day for all of us.

January 26, 1938

Stefan was told of his father's death in the morning. All colour drained from his face and his dark eyes filled with tears. Turning his back on us, he walked over to the windows and then wrapped the heavy velvet drapes round himself. Under the folds of the smooth fabric, his small body shook with quiet sobs. We left him alone and he stayed behind his curtains for hours.

The house was unbearably quiet. My mother never left my father's bedside. When I looked in on her, she seemed still in the same position she had been the night before. I put my hand on her shoulder, but she shook herself free. She didn't want me or anybody else. My grandfather had locked himself in his room. In the kitchen, our cook and maids sat with swollen eyes. I wandered from one empty room into the next. When my brother eventually emerged from his hiding place, he seemed taller; the childish softness of his face had gone. Hand in hand we continued our disconsolate walk in silence. Every room was full of memories and we stopped simultaneously in places where our father's voice still seemed to speak to both of us.

Like sleepwalkers, we went out of the front door and stepped into the elevator, pressing buttons that took us down to the basement first and then up to the top floor where Frau von Pritwitz lived. She was the widow of a famous first world war admiral, proud of her blue blood and naval traditions. Every Christmas, she invited children of impoverished seamen and got them to dance round the Christmas tree, lustily singing "Stolz weht die Flagge Schwarz-Weiss-Rot" (proudly waves our black-white-red flag). She despised Jews, gypsies and all foreigners, but like many of the German aristocracy, she had a pet-Jew and that was my father. If she was in trouble with the landlord or the income tax authority, she came to my father for help and advice; she adored him. She used to say to him that she would adopt my brother and me if, God forbid, anything should happen to my parents. During the first wave of arrests, she urged my father to let her hide us in her apartment, an invitation he politely declined.

Now, when the elevator stopped on her floor, she immediately embraced us crying: "My poor children, God looked after your saintly father! He will look after you!" It was as if the message of his death had passed up the ivy covered walls of the house. Frau von Pritwitz wanted us to visit for a while, but we thanked her and said we had to go home. Using almost the same words my father had repeated so often, she said: "You should never ride this elevator all by yourselves, children. It is positively prehistoric. What would you do if you got stuck midway between floors? You might be left there for days if we can't get hold of a mechanic right away." She insisted on seeing us safely back to our floor.

Like visitors, we sat in our own entrance hall on the hand-carved chairs on either side of the marble-topped table where our mail was left every day. The walls were lined with antique book cases, mainly of interest to us because the hollows in the carved crowns of finely chiseled royal faces had hidden so many chocolate Easter eggs over the years, as had the wings of wooden eagles at the back of our chairs. Not so long ago, the hall had an old English fireplace. Because there was no provision for a proper chimney, the fireplace had been filled with artificial logs, illuminated by a concealed electric fire. It looked realistic and we had loved it. But my father abhorred any kind of fake and had replaced it with yet another sixteenth century oak cupboard. A warm, glowing light fell through the stained glass windows on hide-bound volumes of bibles, natural histories, and some illustrated incunabula. It was very peaceful here; the subdued light made it seem a church. We had never before felt the real impact of this hall which had made visitors gasp with delight.

Then my brother and I went instinctively to the only room in the house that didn't seem to mourn. It was a period room of the "Biedermaier" era, long my favourite haunt. Although my father had furnished it with all his love for beautiful things, it was not his in the sense the other rooms seemed to reflect his personality. It was a feminine room, a reflection of a more graceful generation and its enjoyment of a long vanished life-style. There was no pain or sorrow in this place, only sunlight and dreams. My brother and I settled down there, hidden behind doors leading to a balcony where generations of our pets had lived among climbing flowers and plants—home to tortoises and tame hedgehogs, fish and birds, frogs from tadpoles to old age.

My boyfriend's mother called a little later, brought pastries and three cups of coffee out on the veranda, and sat down on the floor beside us. She was a lovely, vivacious woman, tall and graceful and, looking so young, she seemed hardly to be credited with her equally tall son. Freddy, she said, would come to see me as soon as he returned from college.

She had promised my mother that she would take us to buy clothes for our father's funeral. On the way back from the stores, we left Stefan at his best friend's house and Freddy's mother dropped me off at the entrance to our home. My mother met me in the hall and clearly disapproved of my new black coat and wide-brimmed hat. Her voice was cold and distant: "You look like a sophisticated young woman, not at all like a little girl of fifteen." She seemed so upset that I refrained from saying that I was no longer a little girl. But her disapproval was hard to bear; I felt the real impact of loneliness for the first time.

In our lounge, kneeling on the soft carpet and hiding my face in my father's armchair, I cried for him, his love and everything he had stood for in my life. I felt unloved and misunderstood by my mother which seemed doubly hurtful because of the hatred and discrimination we were now experiencing outside of our home. My father had managed to surround us with a sense of security that had made this anti-semitism appear insignificant and no more than a passing shadow. It was not a shadow.

# CHAPTER 5

I did not hear Freddy come in. Blind with tears, I felt myself lifted and embraced. Rocking me gently, as my father had done, he didn't speak. He waited until I had quieted and then kissed me with such passion that my love for him blotted out all other feelings. As on previous occasions when physical tension became almost unbearable, he took my hand like an elder brother. He led me to the bathroom, washed my face and then left me to see my mother. When he returned, his young face was white and his eyes clouded with pity.

We lunched in a small restaurant; although we both merely pretended to eat to please the other, the strange surroundings helped us to regain some inner balance. Afterwards, we walked through the Grunewald, the lovely pine forest in West-Berlin, until dark. That afternoon we made a vow that we would never part, that we would leave Germany together. If possible, we decided, we would honour my father's wish and would wait until Freddy had qualified as an architect and until I had graduated from high school. He left me standing on our balcony under a cold sky; I watched his graceful figure striding along the deserted street. He turned and raised his arms to me in an attitude of so much hope that my spirits soared above my grief and self-pity. I remember forming a small prayer: "Thank you, Papa, for leaving me in such good hands." I now felt strong enough to go and see my father for the last time. But when

I looked at him, surrounded by flowers, the wax-like face was that of a stranger.

The familiar bedroom felt cold. The air was heavy with the sickly-sweet scent of flowers; only my mother was unchanged in her vigil. She seemed to reflect the grief of all the lonely women in the world. Awed and a little frightened, I went over and kissed her, but although she did not shake me off this time, it was as if I had kissed a statue. She was enshrined in her pain and solitude and, for the moment at least, nothing else existed for her.

My father's funeral took place the next day. There was a brief service in the prayer hall of the Jewish cemetery, crowded to overflowing. Apart from the immediate family and friends, there were hundreds of Freemasons from his Lodge, my father's employees and their families, people who had been pensioned off long ago, and relatives of employees who had died and whose families my father had taken care of. My thoughts were mostly of the past until my father's favourite passage of Beethoven's Ninth Symphony—insisted on by my mother over the old Rabbi's objections—brought me back to the present. There was such promise and triumph in this music that it was not a painful return. My father was interred in the family plot beside his first wife. That, too, had been my mother's decision and I admired her for it. Yet I was not mature enough to understand her and felt a kind of jealousy on her behalf. Not being able to see into the future, I could only believe that she had left herself no place to come home to.

Time passed slowly from then on. Outwardly, our home remained the same and for a long time, I felt my father would open its doors any minute. Once more I sleepwalked and knocked my head hard against the closed door of my parents' bedroom—the door which my father had always opened when a sixth sense or perhaps a sound told him I was coming. With that painful awakening, I knew he was never coming back.

Shortly afterwards, my mother sent Stefan to a boarding school in Sweden. He begged me to go with him but I still could not tear myself away; there was my promise to Freddy. So we watched my brother board the train one day, a forlorn little boy in short pants and a navy beret on his dark curls. Would I have gone with him had I known that this young brother of mine would be a man and a father himself when I'd see him again? Now I simply felt lonely without him.

Since my father's death, my mother could neither sleep nor eat. My brother's departure loosened the last tie that had bound her to our home and she now informed me that she had enrolled in a nurses' training school and would live in the student nurses' home. It didn't occur to me to ask: "What about me?" I accepted her decision that I was old enough to look after myself, but after she left, I was not yet adult enough to suppress the thought that she might not love me and that she would have stayed with us had my brother still been here.

My grandfather did his best to look after me, but he, too, was lost without my father on whom he had leaned since my grandmother's tragic death. Now he continued to leave home before I got up in the morning as he had done ever since he moved in with us. He used to walk through the famous "Tiergarten" to my father's office, his pockets full of nuts for the tame squirrels he fed on his way through the park. He seldom returned till late afternoon.

Our cook and maids had to leave us shortly after my father's death. "Aryan" women were no longer permitted to live in Jewish homes where there was a man under 75 years of age. My grandfather was only seventy. The Nazis' widely publicized explanation for enacting this law was that "German women must be protected from being seduced, raped, or racially contaminated by Jews."

Left alone, I missed their cheerful voices and our cook's

rough tenderness. We had a Jewish girl now, but she was not trained nor did she like housework. She did cook for my grandfather and me, but she flatly refused to wash dishes or polish floors. Nor would she take instructions from me, a fifteen year old girl. So, apart from being lonely, I felt like a Cinderella cleaning and polishing when I came home from school, cheered somewhat by occasional help from Freddy, a Prince Charming good at chores. My oldest sister Kate came home from Italy for a while and life was more bearable in her company. She got married to a teacher as soon as the conventional mourning period was over.

On 9 November 1938, my father's old friend warned us of yet another impending "spontaneous uprising" and mass arrests of Jewish males. That was to be a reprisal for the death of a German diplomat in Paris who, presumably, had been shot by a Jew. This day would end in "Crystal Night" when every synagogue in the country was burned to the ground and all remaining Jewish shop windows were smashed again. We had gone into hiding in the small apartment of my half-siblings' maiden aunt. Since only men were targeted, my sister and I could have stayed at home, but we were determined to join our men. In spite of the ghastly reason for being with aunt Hedy, it was cosy sitting round her table under dimmed lights and drawn blinds.

Aunt Hedy, perhaps the kindest person I've known, was the only unmarried sister of my father's first wife. Her fine features, framed by silvery white hair became my persistent image of an angel's face. With an independent income, she dedicated her life to the blind. Day in, day out, she sat copying books she had found worthwhile into braille—hard, exacting labour. She adored us. When my older brother Gerhard studied for his final high school exams, he had moved in with her to avoid the family's distractions. He loved aunt Hedy, but teased her. Once she came to my mother clearly upset. Blushing and stammering she finally confided that she had found a pair of ladies' panties in my brother's bed. "Silk with lace—very expensive—really frivolous! What am I to do, Elisabeth?" My mother's laughter was less at aunt Hedy's expense than at her delighted discovery of the reason—the prank for which her stepson had asked her to lend him some of her nicest undies. Aunt Hedy could laugh at herself, relieved that her nephew was still innocent.

Now she was only too happy to offer us shelter at the expense of her privacy. None of us could foresee how soon her harmless and generous life was to end. A few years later, when elderly people were finally rounded up and deported, she would hang herself rather than face the indignities of arrest and a cruel death.

However, in 1938 as on previous occasions, the mass arrests were stopped a few days later and we returned home. But we all realized at last that we had to get out of Germany quickly if we wanted to survive. My sister and her husband got visas for South America and left within a week. Freddy and I had also applied for visas to Uruguay, one of the South American states that had opened its borders to refugees. It seemed to be our last chance for emigration. We had asked for permission to go to Palestine, but that was hopeless unless we went with an illegal transport on ships which were not seaworthy, often did not arrive at their destination or, if they did, were intercepted by British warships and diverted to concentration camps on Cyprus or Mauritius. We still thought that there was little difference between British and German barbed wire fences.

My mother's oldest sister Edith and her husband, an accountant, had left Hamburg with their two sons long ago. They were now living in Texas and were already American citizens. They were doing everything they could to get us to the United States, but they were not influential enough to speed up immigration procedures. Although a wealthy Quaker family deposited $50,000 in a bank in our names to guarantee that we would not take any jobs from Americans, we were well down on a long waiting list.

At the same time, Jewish school children were sent to, and accepted by the UK. We applied, but this time we were excluded from salvation because we were still financially well off. The transports to Britain, we were told, only took children whose parents could not afford to buy visas to other countries. This was the first we heard about the possibility of bribery, but we were not yet desperate enough to condone corruption.

By then a Jewish administration had been appointed by the German Emigration Department as an official government agency. Its mandate was to speed up emigration, to find countries that would accept refugees and to deal with the paperwork prior to applying for exit visas. This administration genuinely tried to help and did valuable work at first, distributing members of the community into various channels open to them. Later on, its members were mainly—perhaps understandably—concerned with saving their own skins. In the interim, like most bureaucracies anywhere, they were tying themselves in knots with their own red tape. One day, we received a letter from them, something to this effect:

"Although visas to South America for yourself and Mr. F. H. Raphael are now available, we are unfortunately not in a position to issue them to you for the following reasons: There is still considerable incidence of White Slavery in the port where you would have to disembark. We cannot accept the responsibility for a young girl your age to travel alone. We have given this matter serious consideration and are acting in your interest to the best of our belief and conscience. If, however, you and Mr. Raphael decided to get married, we would reconsider your case."

Had I been endowed with prophetic powers, I could have asked whether it was preferable for a young girl to travel alone and unchaperoned to the gas chambers of Auschwitz. The obvious solution to the bureaucratic problem would have been to place me under the care of an adult leaving the country on the same ship. But from previous experience, I knew that bureaucratic authority was as open to argument as the Rock of Gibraltar. What's more, under German law, twenty-one was the age of majority. Nineteen-year-old Freddy Raphael, although allowed to marry me with our parents' consent, did not qualify as adult enough to look after me unmarried.

The same day I was refused my visa, our principal informed us that we had to leave school immediately. The law expelling all Jewish children from public schools had been passed at last. The headmistress was gently regretful, but she could no longer see us through our final high school exams although she was sure we were ready for them. I went home utterly dejected. I phoned my mother at the hospital. She promised to enrol me at the Jewish Domestic Science School, the only secondary education centre still available for my age group. There was a Jewish teacher training college, but I was too young to be accepted there. My mother found out, however, that six months of domestic science and six months practical work with children in a kindergarten or private home would earn me extra credits towards admission to college. Although I still hoped to get out of Germany soon, I felt it was better to get some useful training rather than sit moping.

My mother called back a little later to let me know that I could start at my new school the following Monday. She was on duty and in a hurry to get back to her patients. I therefore did not tell her about the letter from the Emigration Department. That could wait until she came home on her next free weekend. In the meantime, I still had another week ahead of me before I could start school again. The prospect was bleak. Freddy was working and couldn't come to see me till late afternoon or evening. My grandfather was busy winding up the business with my father's secretaries.

The take-over was almost complete and the work yet to be done a farcical formality. The "buyer" was a friend of the Minister of State and the sum he paid was a ridiculously small amount, but there was no redress. Even that pittance was deposited into a blocked account we could not touch. Like all other Jewish property, it was also confiscated later. It was a robbery, only thinly disguised.

My home-help was dull and never talkative; a belated spring cleaning pointless. I tried to read, but could not concentrate, and when I phoned my best friend Elsbeth Kaufmann, her mother told me that she had left Berlin for a week or two. In the end, I decided to do what I should have done long ago: I would spend the week visiting all foreign embassies and consulates to try my luck personally since letters applying for immigration visas had achieved nothing. I visited two or three embassies a day in alphabetical order, starting with the American.

It turned out to be an exercise in futility. Day after day I was asked the same questions and had to give the same answers: "Do you have an appointment?" "No, but I have been expelled from school under the new racial law. I have written to you before and I wondered whether there is a chance now of getting a visa to continue my education in the US, Britain, Canada, Chile, Dutch Honduras," etc, etc. "When did you first apply? What is your name, age, background? Have you parents, brothers or sisters in our country to sponsor you?" "No, I have not." "Sorry, the Ambassador (or Consul) is out, at a conference, on leave, busy. Call back tomorrow, next week, next month." Or: "We'll look into your file and let you know." Once or twice I was told to wait and sat in a crowded waiting room for hours, only to be told that the Ambassador had left and would not be back today.

Freddy came to see me in the evenings and tried to cheer me up. "We'll get married, Darling," he said. "In three months you'll be sixteen. We'll get our parents' permission, and as early as possible in 1939, we'll sail to South America. I'll make sure my little bride doesn't get snatched away by White-Slave-traders." His ideas, I felt, were wishful thinking. His mother had said more than once that we were too young to think of marriage. She was very fond of me and my family and while she had no objections to us leaving Germany together, she saw marriage as out of the question until both Freddy and I had finished school and university education somewhere.

At night I couldn't sleep. Voices in my head repeated: "Too young to go to South America alone!" "Too young to get married!" "Too wealthy to join a youths transport to the UK!" "Too young to enter a teachers' training college! Too young! Too rich! Too young!" When I did doze off, I had a recurrent nightmare. I was alone in the huge hall of a castle. French windows opened into a sunny park where children were laughing and couples walked in the shade of old trees. Music came from a room above and beautifully dressed women and men were floating up a wide staircase towards the orchestral sounds. When I attempted to walk through the French windows into the park, a metal curtain came down. It went up again when I stepped back and the people in the gardens bowed gravely to me as if they were on a stage at the end of a play. Then the curtain came down again, shutting out all light. I went towards the staircase, but before I reached it, all doors were closed by invisible hands and the walls seemed to close in on me. I heard Freddy's voice calling me, but I couldn't see him and woke up with my heart pounding.

A battered dream book our cook had left behind when she got married had no explanation. I did find a psychology book in my parents' library which contained some mention of dreams of closing doors and collapsing walls: "First indication of claustrophobia," I read there and, "if dreams of this kind are recognized as an early symptom and a psychiatrist is consulted immediately, there is a good chance of eradicating this morbid fear of confined spaces by discovery of the underlying causes."

In retrospect, the explanation for this dream seems ridiculously obvious, but at that time I was not even aware of being afraid. Too close to political and social developments, I still did not consciously see an immediate danger. Yet my recurring nightmare made me fear for my sanity and, somewhat morbidly, I looked for mental abberations in our family history. I didn't have far to look.

My mother's young brother, a very intelligent but perhaps somewhat lazy boy of fifteen had submitted an essay his oldest sister had written a few years earlier. He was found out and publicly humiliated. He was reprimanded for cheating and dishonesty in front of his class. He went home and shot himself with his father's hunting rifle. All this happened before I was born. Then, at the height of the great Depression, his mother, my beautiful maternal grandmother, killed herself. In her suicide note, she wrote she could not face my grandfather's bankruptcy. His brewery in Gleiwitz, Silesia, had to be liquidated because he had extended almost unlimited credit to clients who could no longer pay their debts. My grandmother wrote that she could not bear the thought of moving to an apartment too small to accommodate her daughters and grandchildren when they came for a visit. I believe that she ended her life because she never got over her only son's tragic death.

Martin Schweitzer, one of my cousins, the youngest son of my father's sister, had run away from home in search of adventure. He was only seventeen at the time he sailed to America as a cabin boy on a freighter. There, he was lured into volunteering for the French Foreign Legion, presumably while he was "under the influence of alcohol." For that reason and because he had lied about his age when he signed up, his parents' lawyers managed to buy him out just in time. In the desert fort of French Equatorial Africa, where the boy was stationed, he was found to be delirious with fever. Brought home, he recovered—at least physically. A short time later, he also killed himself over a hopeless love affair.

All this in the two preceding and in my own generation, on both my mother's and my father's side depressed me deeply. Towards the end of that week, I could not keep the dream and my fears to myself any longer. Freddy and I were sitting in my favourite room, looking out over the balcony. It had been one of those late Indian summer days and the heat of the day still lingered in the thick stone walls. A White-Russian balalaika orchestra played in the restaurant on the other side of our small park.

I had brought sandwiches and hot chocolate, and, cross-legged on the floor, we talked about everything and nothing. I remember our rather heated debate on the politics of right-wing, militant Zionists and their aims in Palestine. They advocated the use of force to get a Jewish homeland and they trained their youths like stormtroopers. We both admired Jews willing to fight for their rights. Normally, we might have agreed that they were one of the few organizations that could liberate us although, or perhaps because, their ideas, methods, and even uniforms were too similar to those of the Nazis. But now I feverishly opposed everything Freddy said.

He knew me too well. He closed my mouth with a kiss. "Tell me what's worrying you." I told him: the voices I heard when I fell asleep, the ghastly dream, the psychology book, and my fear for my sanity.

Freddy rumpled my hair: "Sweetheart, I'm not going to leave you alone with your bad dreams." With both love and anguish in his voice he promised to look after me from this day on and to dispel my fears. He stood up then and looking up to the oil painting of my father, he seemed to ask forgiveness for breaking the promise made to Papa that we would wait ten years. But I knew Freddy's thoughts: We are still young, but old enough to be hunted and persecuted. We are old enough to fight and die. "Eva's father, I promise that I will treasure and protect your daughter, my first and only real love, until death do us part. So help me God!"

He tucked me in like a child and closed the drapes of my alcove. I heard him on the telephone to his mother: "Don't worry if I don't come home tonight, Mother. I'm going to stay with Eva. She is too depressed to be left alone. We have to get out of this country and I'll marry her as soon as it is legal. . . . I'm sorry, but it doesn't matter how you feel about it. We have to try to build a future for ourselves." I felt tired and exhausted and closed my eyes. And there, almost immediately, was the cold hall in the castle, the curtains and the closing doors. But then I heard Freddy's voice quite close to me: "Eva, my lovely girl!" When I opened my eyes, he was bending over me, his skin glowing with health. He took me in his arms and I felt no more fear, no thoughts of yesterday or tomorrow, past or future. My head cradled in his arm, I slept through a dreamless night for the first time in months.

The following Monday I started my first semester at the Domestic Science school. It was very different from high school: no desks or blackboards, just conference halls, modern kitchens, and sewing rooms. Theoretical lectures were informal and practical lessons in cooking, sewing, and patternmaking were given to small individual groups of students. We were no longer treated like school girls, but like responsible adults.

I soon formed a strong attachment for one of the teachers, Frau Unger. Had I known how tragically this relationship would end, I would have asked for a transfer to another teacher's class, but at that time, she was the first woman in my life for whom I felt an adult friendship. If you asked me why she attracted my attention, I could not tell you. Tall and angular with a pale narrow face and high cheek bones, her face was made even more severe by her straight, black hair drawn tightly into a bun. She was formidable yet had an unfailing sense of humour, tinged with sarcasm. I never got to know her intimately and only found out later that she was married to a dentist and had a little stepson of her husband's previous marriage, but no children of her own. Of all the things we must have been taught at this school, I remember vividly only what this teacher taught me, from the way to fold a brassiere to household economics.

After a few weeks, our principal arranged for me to look after two children every afternoon to earn extra credits towards teacher training. As a mother's help, I was to assist a young woman who was expecting a third baby. My main duties were to take the children out to a park, mend their clothes and wash the baby's diapers. With Judith, a little three-year-old, I got on famously. She was bright and beautiful with that special, though passing beauty you so often find in young Jewish children. But the baby of the family was the most miserable infant I ever knew. She never stopped crying. Looking back, I think her misery might have been caused by a lack of affection from parents and strangers alike; her sister Judith stole everybody's heart.

I looked after these kids for about three months. But then something happened that made me feel so ashamed that I asked to be replaced. One afternoon the baby had been crying for two hours. I had tried everything; I had a splitting headache and was counting the minutes until I could take the children home and leave. Judith kept commiserating with Baby and asked me repeatedly what I was going to do next to quiet her tiny sister. By now I was close to tears myself. "If this was my baby," I cried, "I'd throw it away or put it up for adoption!" I could see her digest this. Alarmed, I said immediately: "No, Judith, I didn't really mean that; but I just don't know what to do anymore. Let's take her home." We did, and I was somewhat relieved to see that the mother couldn't comfort the baby either. Confirming that the child was not sick and had no fever, she became as exasperated as I had been. At least my incompetence was not at fault. The next day, Judith received me at the door and said: "My Mommy says we are not going to throw our baby away or put her up for . . . what did you say we should put her up for?" Her mother said nothing about the incident, but I fancied that she followed me with a reproachful look. In the end, I spoke about it myself, apologized and said that I wasn't mature enough to look after the baby and that my remarks to Judith were unforgiveable. The mother said she was sure I had meant no harm. But the trouble was that I really did mean it and asked to be released. Judith, who missed me, kept visiting me at home for the next two months until one day, the whole family, Jews of Polish origin, was deported. Like so many mothers and children after them, they must have ended victims of the Nazi SS Death Squads in Eastern Europe. My hostile feelings for the baby were added to my long list of sins and I've often cried over it. But Judith's brightness burned like a flame in my memory; I could never imagine that tiny beauty being brutally murdered.

Time passed, I continued to go to my domestic science school, saw Freddy every night and my mother once a week on her day off, and tried to forget that we were sitting on top of a volcano. My aunt and uncle kept writing from Texas that they were sure we would soon be able to join them. The Quakers, who had deposited $50,000 in our names as security, were doing everything to speed up immigration procedures. But nothing happened. More people vanished. All Polish Jews who had fled from pogroms in Polish ghettos after the first world war and had settled in Germany were arrested and deported with their families; and from time to time, yet another girl went missing from school never to return.

In the meantime, we had heard nothing from my older sister and her husband since they had left for South America months ago. But although we were puzzled, we didn't worry unduly. Had there been an accident at sea, the newspapers would have reported the loss of a ship. Once more we tried to persuade the emigration authorities to let Freddy and me have our visas for South America, but they were firm in their refusal and reiterated their previous warning of the danger for a young girl travelling without an adult escort in that part of the world.

And so we were married on 9 February 1939 with the reluctant consent of our parents. It was a glorious day, warm and sunny. After the brief civic marriage ceremony at the city hall, we were married by a rabbi, Freddy's cousin and one of the finest men I have known. Since the synagogues had been burned down, our huge dining-room had been transformed with an improvised altar, masses of flowers, and even an organ. My two best friends and bridesmaids helped me to dress in a white silk gown and adjusted my veil. My grandfather led me to the altar, but I don't remember anything except Freddy in morning coat and striped pants, his dark eyes shaded under a grey top hat. All through the ceremony I was in a dream-like trance and the rabbi, Dr. Leskowitz, had to address me twice before I could stammer: "I do."

There were some hundred and fifty guests. Apart from family and friends, they were mostly my father's loyal employees. Some hundred people stayed behind for lunch and, again, I remember very little other than my own sense of radiance and my Freddy's serene face. Times were such that going away on a honeymoon was out of the question, but we were young and much in love and didn't care. Our home was a luxurious maze of flowers and, surrounded by friends, we forgot once more what was going on in the world around us and were unreservedly happy.

Our apartment's first two adjoining rooms, once our old cook's domain, had been redecorated and the larger of the two was converted into a charming sitting room for our exclusive use. The bedroom with its twin beds and new gold silk-covered eiderdown quilts was full of azaleas in shades ranging from palest pink to deep red, and two little flowering almond trees stood in the window recess. The apartment offered such an illusion of permanence and security that it was quite inconceivable to think of it as a temporary refuge.

That night, after the guests had left, my mother returned to the hospital and my grandfather retired to his room, I stood in the open window of our bedroom. The moon threw patterns over the gold of the eiderdowns and the little almond trees seemed to come alive. My husband had his arms round my shoulders. Again we heard the balalaika orchestra in the distance. Our happiness seemed to make every shadow disappear and I remember saying quite spontaneously: "If, after this night, we had to die, life would have been worthwhile." Freddy gripped my shoulders with unexpected strength, so hard that I nearly cried out with pain: "Don't ever talk about dying! We have only just started to live. You are going to give me children who will be as lovely as you are. Nothing and nobody can destroy me as long as I have you." I did not realize then that his love, a love few women are lucky enough to experience, would expose me to the worst fate man's inhumanity to man can inflict on a woman.

# CHAPTER 6

A few days after our wedding, we went to the emigration office expecting that since we were married, there would be no further obstacles to our leaving for South America. We were admitted to the officer who worked on cases whose names began with L to Z. Crestfallen, he looked up from his file and said laconically: "My dear young lady, you are too late." We can't have looked very intelligent for he elaborated immediately: "The South American states will no longer issue visas to immigrants unless they can deposit thousands of US dollars in a South American bank as security. Are you in a position to do so?" The answer, of course, was no. He continued: "It has been discovered that visas issued lately were forgeries and the money paid for them was going to a gang operating somewhere in Paris where those visas originated. And, what's more, I have to inform you that your sister's ship and all subsequent ships bound for South America have been turned back. Your sister is due to return to Hamburg any day now."

I was speechless; Freddy put his hand under my arm to steady me. He asked the official how my sister and her husband's visas could have been faked since they were not required to pay anything except the usual consular fee of a few German marks. "Your sister-in-law, Mr. Raphael, was probably lucky. Her batch of visas may have been a trial issue to find out if the fraud would be discovered. The only money taken from her and kept by the swindlers were the port and landing taxes she had to pay in advance. But people who left later have been paying considerable sums for their visas. . . . Please believe me," said the harassed official, "we did not intend to keep you in the dark. The Gestapo report of this affair as well as the information that your sister's ship was returning reached us only yesterday." He got up; the interview was over. He mumbled that he would keep us informed of any new openings for emigration and wished us luck.

We went home hardly talking; we were not, however, thinking of our own plight. It was bad enough to have lost yet another chance to get out of this mouse trap, but to have gotten away, to have in fact reached a destination, and then not be allowed to land and to be returned to Germany must have been enough to break the strongest spirit.

Under different circumstances, I would have loved seeing my favourite sister again, but now I dreaded Kathy's return. The days dragged on until a short notice appeared in the Jewish weekly paper announcing the arrival of my sister's ship in Hamburg and giving a list of passengers. To our surprise, my sister's and brother-in-law's names were not mentioned. We waited. A few days later, a young man called on us. He was one of the returned emigrants and he told us the whole story. After an uneventful journey, the ship had landed in Uruguay. There the passengers were told that the ship was scheduled to sail early the following morning and that no landing passes would be issued. As it happened, nobody on board was bound for Uruguay. The majority was heading for Argentina or Chile. Although it was hot and sticky, the passengers didn't mind staying on board for the one night. None of them had been allowed to take much money out of Germany. Not going ashore meant saving the little they had. A few hours after the announcement, Dr. Gunter Ballin, my brother-in-law, was paged over the loudspeaker and requested to report to the captain's cabin. When he returned, he told our visitor, who had shared a table with them at mealtimes, that he and his wife were permitted to leave the ship on a two-hour pass to meet a very good friend who was waiting for them on the quay. They left, the young man said, and that was the last he saw of them.

The ship was held up in Uruguay for over a week and the passengers were getting desperate. Rumours created such a panic that some passengers stormed the captain's cabin. The first five were knocked down and locked up; the rest returned to their families. When the ship finally sailed, they still did not know they were being returned to Germany until the captain had made an unscheduled landing in Cuba where again they were refused landing passes. Only then did the captain inform them that he had been refused entry into ports of Argentina and Chile because, the respective authorities radioed him that he had "illegal immigrants" on board. He was trying everything possible to get his passengers asylum in Cuba, the US or Canada. However, if none of the countries he had begged to take in the refugees responded within two or three days, he had orders to return them to Germany. None of them did accept the unhappy people and, finally, the ship sailed back to Hamburg.

There was no panic or revolt. A few women and children cried bitterly but on the whole the passengers were quiet and seemed resigned. Still, quite a few did not turn up for meals the next day, nor did they appear for breakfast the following morning. As the sea was rough, it was presumed they had lost their appetite. Not until two or three days later did the crew begin to knock on cabin doors and finally used their pass keys to enter. They found and carried out the bodies of whole families who had committed suicide. They were buried at sea. A few jumped overboard the night following the mass burial and a few more before they reached Hamburg. A few passengers had been allowed to get off in England and some were given temporary asylum in Holland and France.

That was all our visitor could tell us. He didn't know what

had become of my sister and her husband except that they had certainly not returned with the ship. Their cabin had been locked and sealed on leaving Uruguay and their luggage had been impounded in Hamburg. The young man had given up his home and sold everything he owned prior to leaving Germany and he had nowhere to go. He stayed with us for a while until he found a furnished room.

It was a relief to learn my sister was safe. At the beginning of May, we had the first letter from a fictitious sender, but unmistakably in Kathy's untidy handwriting. It was composed in the form of a short-story and had somehow passed the censors. It told us that my brother-in-law's influential friend in Uruguay had been informed of the ship's impending return to Germany. In fact, the captain himself had warned him when he issued a two-hour landing pass for my sister and her husband. When they got ashore, their friend provided them with food, money, and a guide who took them to a hiding place where they stayed for a few days. Then, in the middle of a night, the guide swam with them across a narrower part of the river Plate. It was still wide enough to require all their strength and willpower, especially for Kathy's husband. Unlike my athletic sister, he had been a desk-bound scholar and not much of a swimmer. But once they made it, they were safe and given asylum in Argentina. There we had cousins who had moved their cloth manufacturing industry from Berlin to Buenos Aires in the early thirties. They were well off and soon found them a house and helped my brother-in-law to get tenure on the staff of the university. He would be teaching Religious Studies and, somewhat of an irony, German History. They were to live there until my sister's early death in 1951.

However, when we received her letter in May of 1939, the Second World War had not yet started and we still had no premonition how it would all end and that I would never see my oldest half-sister again. Also, at this period, my concern for my sister was mixed with more immediate domestic problems. We had been informed that the German Broadcasting Company had requisitioned our family house and we had two weeks to vacate it. Freddy's parents offered us their home, only too pleased to have us.

The requisition had not come as a surprise. Two laws had been passed by the Nazis in 1938—the first that Jewish-owned homes could be taken over by Aryans at a moment's notice, the second that Jews had to give up or destroy every animal and pet they owned. I had already found homes for our canaries, tropical fish, two tortoises, and tame hedgehogs. Now only one, the dearest of all my pets—a little black cat—was left. She was named "Geistlein" (Little Ghost) because she somehow managed to melt into a background. Two years earlier, I had fished her out of the pond in a park; I had seen bubbles rising in the shallow water under a bridge. I waded in, pulled a sack onto dry land, and found her, the only one of four still alive. Now I would have to find a new home for her too. I could not take the Little Ghost to my in-laws without great risk. Any Jewish family that kept pets after the law was passed was threatened with immediate arrest and deportation. My black cat hadn't been discovered because it never left our apartment. But before we got down to dealing with this and with moving, Freddy and I decided to give a party for twenty-two of our remaining friends. It was to be the last happy affair in my father's house.

The party was a great success. Had anybody looked into the brightly lit windows of the apartment and seen the dining table laden with silver, candles, and flowers, they would probably have envied us. Had they heard the music and laughter, had they seen us dancing, they could not have guessed that we had a care in the world. It was perhaps our greatest gift that we could enjoy each lovely moment and carry its memory in our hearts. What made my young husband so irresistible was his infectious laugh. His utter unconcern for material possessions and his affection for all living creatures were always shining in his eyes.

About midnight, our friends left; we washed and dried the dishes of the priceless old-English dinner set and piled them onto a trolley. As Freddy sped it back to the dining-room, the Little Ghost shot out from under a wine cabinet and tripped Freddy. The heavy trolley turned over with a crash and I sat paralyzed for a moment, then exploded into fits of helpless laughter. The cat didn't need to be told that, in her unorthodox way, she had just saved something from the Nazis clutches. Her amber eyes narrowing into contented slits, she climbed carefully over the debris and vanished into an open ebony sideboard. No doubt she would spend the rest of the night there, not a twinge of conscience disturbing her feline dreams. Freddy and I laughed until we ached.

It isn't easy to pack up the valuable contents of household collections acquired over many generations in just two weeks. Freddy had to go to work, but my mother took leave from her hospital. With the help of a moving firm, we filled two large box containers with the most valuable furniture, fine art, and prized personal items and had them stored in the Free Port of Hamburg, ready to be shipped to America if or when we got our visas. That was something we were still permitted to do as long as we could pay a huge tax for the release of our property prior to storing it. To this day I don't know what happened to the box containers, whether they even reached the port or were destroyed in the air raids on Hamburg during the war.

Packing the containers took a week; that left another week to deal with the rest of our property. Freddy's parents made room for lots of things but by the end of the second week, we had barely touched half of our home's content. We were worn out and, finally, we invited former maids, employees, other old friends, and their families to come along and help themselves to anything they wanted.

Our plight was not an isolated case. One after another

Jewish-owned homes in the better residential districts of Berlin and other German cities were taken over by government officials and government affiliated organizations. That was not really surprising since many of their high-ranking officers were of very humble origin, often from urban slums. They were eager to live in areas representative of their newly acquired social status. Although new housing projects had been started at an unprecedented rate since Hitler's rise to power, it was so much easier to requisition villas and luxury apartments from Jews. By doing so, the Nazis freed money and manpower for the building up of military production. We were luckier than most because we still had a home to go to.

The day I banged our front door for the last time, I shut in a cacophony of voices, leaving behind a crowd of people who had called themselves friends. They were arguing over occasional tables, mirrors, and knick-knacks. Not one of them had asked me where I was going or what was to become of us. The best of luck to them all. Whatever they managed to take away, it would not bring them happiness.

My mother had returned to the hospital and Freddy was working again at a small carpentry shop, well-known in Berlin's Westend for its custom-made modern furniture. He had been apprenticed there, because of his flair for design, as soon as he was expelled from college and before all young Jews were forced into compulsory labour. I was alone then as I left my father's house for the last time. I picked up my cat in its basket, pushed my suitcase like a football to the curb of the road and hailed a taxi. Only when the driver asked me where I wanted to go did I hesitate and told him to drive round our park for a while.

The driver, a tall man with a mouth so permanently turned down at the corners, he seemed unable to smile, looked at me suspiciously and remarked: "It will cost you a bit if you don't know where you are going. Do you have any money?" He suffered from stomach ulcers, I was to learn, and had little faith in human nature. Frivolously, I wondered whether a taxi would make a good home for a cat and whether the man would smile if I offered to buy his cab. Instead, I handed him a few notes and the car moved off. The driver, in spite of his morose appearance, was not an unkindly man. He watched me in his mirror and obviously wondered if his young passenger was running away from home. I didn't wear the by then mandatory yellow star with *JEW* on it since Jews were no longer permitted to use taxis. He therefore couldn't guess what my problem was. But when he saw me bending in sudden tears over the basket on my knees, he pulled up, stopped the meter, and turned round to face me. He didn't ask any questions, but started talking.

His own children had disappointed him, so much so, he said, that he no longer had any liking or hope for the young generation. His son and daughter had denounced him to the Secret Police for a careless, derogatory remark against the Hitler regime. As a result, he had been arrested and spent many days being interrogated, even beaten. Only the fact that he had been the driver of a high-ranking officer during the last war, an officer who now vouched for his good character and patriotism, saved him from destruction. His home life was ruined. He could not bring himself to talk to his children and had to think twice before he made even the most harmless remark to his wife.

He must have noticed my surprise at his revelations to me, a total stranger and of the younger generation he despised. "You," he explained, "are different. You don't show the cruel sarcasm of our goose-stepping young master race. Hitler Youths don't cry over a basket, they trample on it or set it on fire. What's in it?" The driver leaned over and gently put his hand on mine. I couldn't help but respond to this unaccustomed gesture of shy interest and poured out all the pent-up misery of the past two weeks. Somehow I had suppressed the thought of what it meant to lose the home I was born in; and perhaps even worse for me, to have to hawk around my beloved animals, to beg indifferent people to give them a place in their homes and their hearts. My Little Ghost's hopeless mewing in her basket had suddenly opened my eyes to my own helplessness. The taxi driver's solicitude now made me cry enough bitter tears to wash away the last remnants of a happy childhood.

The driver was not an educated man, but his own suffering seemed to have given him an intuition no schooling could provide. He kept silent until he felt I could listen to him again. Then he offered to take my cat and, perhaps to spare me the feeling of accepting charity, he told me more about his experiences with the Gestapo. So far, my problems were nothing compared with this man's ordeals. He deserved the company and affection of the Little Ghost. I gave him my in-laws' address and he drove me there. He stopped just long enough to take my suitcase to their door and left before I could look at the basket again.

My father and mother-in-law made me welcome, as welcome as anyone could be in those hard and dangerous days in Germany just before the war, when any knock at the door could mean a deportation order or the arrest of some member of the household. I resisted the impulse to go back to, or even think of, my home for the sixteen years of my life, my father's for well over twenty-five years. I told myself that we would soon have left to go abroad anyway and once Freddy was home, I knew he was my refuge and that I could be happy anywhere as long as we were together.

The German exploits of 1939 are well documented now. Every child learns about the countries the Nazis overran and occupied before a patient world was patient no longer and war was declared. What they don't fully know and understand is what it was like for the Nazis' domestic victims to live in Germany once the mousetrap closed and all hope for getting out vanished.

Oddly enough, the shock of all-out war came as a relief. It was almost like a first thunder after a period of intense, unbearable heat. For the first time we felt we could breathe again and that there was hope for Germany yet. Surely Hitler and his crazy mobs could not stand up long against the might of a united world.

In the meantime, my husband and I had thought of another way we hoped would lead to a last-minute escape. An elderly aristocratic acquaintance offered to sell us his big cabin yacht in exchange for some fifteen valuable Persian carpets which were stacked in my in-laws' apartment. We had moved them there from my parents' home, but the rooms were smaller and we had nowhere to lay them. In any case, sooner or later, the Nazis would have found and requisitioned them as they gradually did with all valuable Jewish-owned property. So we made the trade with the old gentleman who said his sailing days were over. Once again, we spent every free hour and many nights on the lakes near Berlin learning to cope with the huge sails even in rough weather. Then we plotted an illegal exit through canals to the North Sea. How we would accomplish this undetected and then sail across the English Channel to the UK and freedom was left to luck. It was a lovely dream and we had a wonderful time practicing for our escape. But an early winter put a temporary stop to our sailing days and, by then, I knew I was pregnant. We were sure we'd get back to the boat and out of Germany before the following summer and long before the baby was due in July 1940. It never occurred to us that our child would not be born a free citizen in a free country.

I hugged my secret to myself for a long time. I wanted this baby and I knew my mother would try to persuade me to have an abortion, insisting that our present desperate circumstances made it impossible to bring a new life into the world. Unlike Freddy and I, she didn't believe in miracles anymore. My mother saw nothing but pain and suffering in the foreseeable future. She had been, and still was, nursing the few survivors of Dachau and Sachsenhausen concentration camps who had been released before war was declared because relatives abroad had managed to get them immigration visas to Britain or some other foreign country. Few of them had any hope of recovery from the severe beatings, torture, and starvation they had experienced and since the Nazis wouldn't give them exit visas until they appeared to be healthy, they were trapped too. Many of them had lost their sanity, but in their more lucid moments between attacks of delirium, they would tell the nurses about their ordeals and what might be in store for all of us.

My mother-in-law would have supported my mother in an attempt to terminate my pregnancy. She dreaded the arrival of a baby for a far more frivolous reason. She was young and beautiful and hated the thought of becoming a grandmother. She had said repeatedly that even if we did get out of Germany, she didn't want us to have children for a long time to come since she had no intention to prematurely join the "rocking chair generation." But neither my mother's pessimism nor my mother-in-law's vanity could kill our shortsighted, selfish delight in our budding offspring.

My husband now started to spoil me outrageously. His boss had commissioned him to sketch new lines of furniture and payed him overtime for this work. All extra money he earned in this way, he spent on gifts for me. At first he brought home flowers, out-of-season fruit and my favourite chocolates, then the prettiest maternity clothes he could find. Those we could still hide from his mother, but when he announced that one of his firm's master-carpenters was making a cradle for our baby and that he'd bring it home the following weekend, the time had come to confide in our parents. As anticipated, both mothers were very upset, but in the end they accepted the inevitable and united, as mothers will, to make the remaining months of my pregnancy as easy as possible. In the spring of 1940, Freddy and I went sailing our cabin cruiser again until about a month before the baby was due. Our planned escape was no longer possible. Since war had been declared, German army contingents had started to guard not only the exits to the North Sea, but also all canals and rivers leading to them. Still, the fresh air and exercise and perhaps the excitement of defying Nazi laws kept me fit, strong, and healthy. We still refused to wear the yellow star and sailed and swam in areas which were officially out of bounds to Jews.

Our little daughter Reha was born on the 11 July, 1940, helped into the world by my father's best friend Dr. Paul Mayer, a well-known gynaecologist who had also delivered my brother and me sixteen and seventeen years earlier.

Once again, there was a breathing space of sorts although my husband was forced to leave his furniture designing job. Like all other young Jewish men and women, he had to start work in a large factory. Since all able-bodied "Aryans" of our age group were being called up for army training, industry would have come to a virtual stand-still had they not been replaced by Jews, foreign workers, and prisoners of war. Because I had a new baby, I was still exempted from forced labour for the first year of my child's life. The Nazis must have overlooked or forgotten to change this maternity labour law for Jewish mothers. Our bank accounts had already been blocked by then, which meant that we could not withdraw even the smallest amount without special permission. Nevertheless, we managed. We still had some valuable jewelry we could barter for necessary items and my husband's pay was still adequate for our needs. Theaters, opera, and restaurants were out of bounds for Jews, ironically an automatic money-saver for us. While we had previously ignored and defied racial laws, we now obeyed most of them for the baby's sake. The only time we put the yellow star in our pockets was when we could leave our neighbourhood for the woods and lakes near Berlin where we were not known. That, however, happened quite frequently since even park benches in the city were signposted "Juden verboten" (Forbidden to Jews).

Our daughter was a joy. She was so lovely, healthy and strong that people often remarked: "We should all have had babies when we were teenagers. Only the very young can produce such perfect children!" Spoiled by her grandparents, she was a happy infant, oblivious of the gathering clouds threatening the adult world.

Since the outbreak of war, we were more or less cut off from the outside world. A few lucky people with valid affidavits for America still managed to get out of Germany via Lisbon, Portugal. Some, without even exit visas, escaped on foot across the French Alps in the hope of getting on a ship to the US or on an illegal boat to Palestine. We couldn't risk joining them with our baby. Also, the US government had by then instructed all its embassies not to accept any more emigrants from Germany except parents or children of American citizens. My mother's relationship to her oldest sister in Texas was no longer considered close enough to warrant our admission. But we could still correspond with my family there and send them photographs. Pearl Harbor put an end to that too; letters from my brother and sister in Palestine and from Kathy in Buenos Aires no longer got through. Only mail from Italy, Germany's ally, still arrived regularly.

There, on the Italian Riviera, lived my mother's youngest sister Steffi. She had married an Italian officer after the First World War who, by 1939, was a general stationed in North Africa. My aunt with their two children remained in Latte near Ventimiglia in a villa overlooking the Mediterranean. As a young wife, she had had a hard time before her husband's aristocratic and devoutly Catholic parents accepted her. But now, since his parents were dead, she lived a charmed life boating and swimming from their own beach and raising my cousins Anita and Diego.

Always very outspoken, she wrote as she talked and ignored the fact that her letters would go through German censorship. To this day, I marvel at the censors overlooking her undisguised contempt for Hitler, "the little corporal," and for Mussolini, "the fat, lascivious slob." She even told us in her letters that German officers were going to requisition part of her villa for billets and that she threw them out. She threatened them by pulling her husband's rank and, she wrote, "they crept away with their tails between their legs." She even mentioned that her son intended to join the partisans in the Italian Alps. But she had persuaded him to wait until he was at least seventeen and until he had finished high school. Finally, she begged us to visit her and bring our little girl if or when we would like "a holiday and a break from the Huns!" I can only imagine that the censors were dazzled by her insignia, the crown and her husband's title "Count di Fenoglio" on her envelopes and letter heads. The Fenoglios were a wealthy family whose ancestors had distinguished themselves in the history of Northern Italy as defenders of its coastal cities against invading pirates.

Agostino, aunt Steffi's husband, was ambushed and killed near the end of the Second World War in North Africa by tribesmen his troops had terrorized when Mussolini first invaded Ethiopia. But she remained unmolested in her villa throughout the war. My cousin Diego did join the partisans and fought from his mountain hideout until the last German soldier had left Italian soil. Perhaps Reha, our little daughter, would have been safe there, but by the time we finally realized that there was no way we could escape together, it was too late. By then, Italian Jews and their families were also being deported to German concentration camps. My aunt and her children were saved only because of her husband's army record and his family's wealth and influence in the Catholic Church.

With the wisdom of hindsight, my young husband and I

might be considered totally irresponsible for not heeding my mother's warning, for having a baby at all in that fateful year of 1939. Nor can I understand now why my parents refused to leave Germany at a time when they could still have emigrated and taken us children and all their possessions to safety. The only comparison I can think of is that of people now living in a known earthquake belt or in war-torn areas of the world. They all know that their lives are in mortal danger, but can't bring themselves to move away from all they have ever known and loved. Young people today have to live with the constant threat of nuclear accidents, environmental pollution, the depletion of the ozone layer, diseases like cancer and AIDS. But they still marry and have children though they can't be sure that their babies will have a chance to live out a normal lifespan. Perhaps it is human nature that forces us to pretend normality and to hope for miracles under the most horrible and hopeless of circumstances. Knowing what I know now after more than seventy years of living, it is difficult to combine fear for our children's future with optimism. Still, at the time I started recording the events of the late 30s and early 40s, the real terror was yet to come.

# CHAPTER 7

My baby and I spent the first year of her life in an invisible cocoon, still untouched by the harsh labour laws Jewish mothers with older children had to obey. Since my husband, my mother-in-law, and my remaining school friends were all forced to work long hours in various industries, I was left to my own devices. By then, my father-in-law, a retired pharmacist, suffered from severe angina pectoris and was in such pain that my mother had him admitted to the Jewish hospital. There she could still get him the drugs he needed to control the spasms. A quiet man, much older than his beautiful wife, he had done everything to make me feel at home when we had to leave my parents' house. He adored his grandchild and had spent time with her while I shopped for food, prepared meals, and cleaned up after Freddy and his mother had left for work in the mornings. I missed him badly when he was in the hospital and took my baby to visit him nearly every day when my chores were done. The hospital visits became as rewarding for me and for my little girl as I hope they were for my father-in-law. He died a year later.

Travelling to the Jewish hospital in East Berlin from our West-Berlin home took about an hour by tramcar and only a little less by Underground. I enjoyed those long trips, partly because they got me out of the lonely house, but mainly because it was my only opportunity to meet people and to show off my beautiful baby. I now flaunted my yellow star rather than hid it. For the first time in my life I felt a pride in who I was and contempt for the hateful racists who persecuted others for their religion or the colour of their skin. Those sentiments may have shown on my face and rubbed off on my German fellow travellers. Although Jews wearing the star were forbidden to sit down on public transport, there were invariably people getting up and insisting I take their seat. Sometimes, when I gratefully declined the offer because there were uniformed Nazis on the train who would have pounced on any such friendly German, there'd be somebody quietly asking me to at least let them hold my "little sister." It cheered me to know that there were still so many Germans prepared to ignore Nazi laws and it amused me that they considered me too young to be a mother.

Once I arrived at the hospital, my mother would join me for an hour or two when she was off duty. My father-in-law always seemed to brighten when he saw the baby smiling at him. But he tired easily and my mother or another nurse would then take Reha out in order to let me read or talk to him until he fell asleep. Later, we would play or walk with Reha on the lawns of the hospital grounds if the weather was fine or take her to the play-room of the children's ward. While Reha napped, my mother and I would eat in the nurses' cafeteria. The food there was still good despite food rationing. Having lunch there helped me to save coupons from our ration card, allowing me to cook fairly decent meals for Freddy and his mother when they came home from work. Since I always left the hospital before the rush-hour when factories and businesses closed, their meal was ready and on the table by the time they arrived, tired from a monotonous day's work. Their approval, my husband's love, and the fun I had with my child made me forget the material wealth we had already lost and still made me feel unbelievably rich.

The enclave of the Jewish hospital still provided an illusion of normality and freedom. The doctors and nurses constantly admired my child's health and fast development; it was in sharp contrast to the usual sick, and underdeveloped babies they treated. That made me believe we were strong enough to face any hardship the Nazis could inflict on us.

But that bubble of delusional security, not unlike the cocoon of a silkworm, burst in June 1941. I then received an official notification from the Department of Labour ordering me to report for work at a certain factory on July 12, exactly one day after my baby's first birthday. The letter threatened a warrant for my immediate arrest if I failed to comply.

My hope that the Nazi bureaucracy would forget my existence was dashed, but I was convinced we were safe from further persecution as long as industry needed workers. I started looking for somebody to take care of my child. Baby-sitters were impossible to find since able-bodied women of all ages had already been forced into compulsory labour. Even the slightest cold might have been an excuse to put my daughter on the children's ward of the Jewish hospital in the care of my mother and the nurses who loved her. But there was no way such an obviously healthy, active one-year-old would have escaped the notice and attention of the Gestapo assigned to the hospital. In the end, after a futile search for a better alternative, I had no option but to enroll her in the only remaining, already overcrowded Jewish day-care centre. It was run and supervised by a single sour-faced woman.

When I took Reha there for the first time, some forty preschoolers were packed into a playroom probably designed for no more than ten. About twenty younger ones, one to three- year-olds and a number of babies from about six to twelve months were accommodated in two adjoining rooms. The supervisor explained patiently, but with obvious frustration that, under normal circumstances, she would have refused to add yet another child to her charges. But, she sighed, in order to keep her license and her daycare centre, she had been forced to sign a contract which did not permit her to turn away parents employed in industry; nor was she allowed to hire aides. If I thought she would jump at my offer to bring Reha every day and help her for the remaining two weeks of my comparative freedom, I was wrong. The woman became quite snappy: "I've managed quite nicely without you. Obviously, I can't stop you coming, but don't expect me to thank you!" She looked at my child and then somewhat contemptuously at me and said as a parting shot: "I suspect you are too young to take motherhood seriously, but try to remember that Reha isn't one of your dolls and that she is not coming here to attend a fashion show! And don't forget to brush her teeth and clean her ears before you drop her off. Most children who have children do. Good bye." I was hurt by her remarks and retorted indignantly that I would like her to show me a cleaner, better cared for child and that I had outgrown playing with dolls long ago. But hoping to end the meeting on a friendlier note, I explained that Reha may be too well dressed for kindergarten, but that I had only come to register my child before taking her to visit her sick grandfather in hospital while we were still free to see him. She relented a little and said: "Well, I'll see you tomorrow then. We open at 6:00 a.m. since most parents start work at seven.

Later that day, one of the nurses who knew her well, explained that Ruth was often rude with parents because she was overworked and frustrated, but that she was very conscientious and good with children who loved her in spite of her occasional gruffness. The nurse suggested I ignore her remarks and see for myself how different she was relating to kids. Reha would soon get used to her too and enjoy the company of other toddlers. And if I could help a little, maybe reading to the children or playing with them or even changing the babies' diapers, Ruth would appreciate it.

Although skeptical, I did make an effort the next morning

to arrive at the daycare centre at six o'clock. To me, getting up that early was no hardship since I had always prepared breakfast for my husband and mother-in-law before they left for work. But I never had to wake up my child at such an ungodly hour. I did get her dressed and ready to leave by 5:30 a.m. and packed a very sleepy little girl, a bottle of milk, her breakfast cereal and a banana into the stroller and walked the fifteen minutes to the daycare centre. The sun was already coming up on this June morning and it made me feel better that Reha, snuggling into her fleecy blanket, was sound asleep again, obviously unperturbed by the change in her routine.

The reception we got from Ruth made me feel better yet. She seemed a different person, obviously pleasantly surprised to see me so punctually before her other charges had arrived. She smiled at me, helped to lift the stroller over the door step, then took the sleeping child and put her gently into a cot already made up with brand-new pink sheets and a matching quilt. At the foot of the cot sat an equally pink teddy bear. "I still get donations of bedding and toys from time to time," Ruth explained. "Usually, they come from Jewish families whose children have outgrown them. But the very new ones are often left by Christians in the neighbourhood who want to remain anonymous. Those I try to keep for new arrivals like Reha to make them feel comfortable and at home. You'd be surprised," she added, "what a soothing effect such pretty things have on even very young babies."

We were well into the routine of the day when a few stragglers arrived. To my dismay, Ruth started yelling at them: "If you lazy bums don't get your butts out of bed in the mornings, I swear I'm going to report you. The Nazis have very effective methods of hauling you out from under your warm blankets!"

She didn't even give them the benefit of the doubt when one father mumbled that he did get up, but the electricity had been cut off because he couldn't afford to pay his bill last month.

Ruth continued to berate them: "If you people think you are hard done by and can't cope with one or two children, you can have my job." Only then did she let them go. During the remainder of the two weeks that I brought Reha and helped at the daycare centre, nobody came late again. Still, if I thought the children would be upset by all the yelling and threats they overheard, I was mistaken.

I discovered a phenomenon I would experience with my own child two years later. It would surface again when the "Final Solution" was implemented and whole families were loaded onto long trains of overcrowded cattle trucks. The more desperate and upset the adults became, scared to death, fighting for a little space, a drink of water or a slice of bread, the calmer and more loving became the children. It was almost as if their roles had been reversed. Where parents would normally soothe their children's fears and try to understand unruly behaviour, even very young ones would now attempt to calm their mothers and fathers.

On this occasion at the daycare centre, the children had been like little statues listening to the altercation while I was trying unsuccessfully to distract their attention. As soon as Ruth entered their playroom again, they all came back to life and, surprisingly, flocked around her. Two of the littlest ones brought a smile back to her still angry face by hugging her legs. The older kids behaved like seasoned judicial mediators trying to settle an argument out of court.

"Please, Miss Ruth," said a six or seven-year-old girl, "don't report Danny and Leah's parents. I'm sure they will not be late again, and if they are, we can help them. You don't have to come out at all when you are so busy." Even less articulate children somehow managed to defend the late-comers and at the same time conveyed the impression that they still loved and trusted their care-taker. Ruth, obviously pacified, lifted the two little ones who were still clinging to her legs and carried them back to the adjoining room they had apparently strayed from. Ten minutes later, Ruth came back to say what sounded like an apology: "I wasn't angry with you, children. But if grown-ups can't be punctual, how can we expect you to become reliable, trustworthy people?"

Then she suggested that I look after the babies because it would be less disruptive for the older children when I couldn't come back just when they'd got to know me. I was already at the door when Ruth called after me: "Reha is awake. She is in the playpen. I've warmed her bottle; it's in the pan on the hot-plate in the kitchen beside her cereal on the tray with her name on it. I've changed all diapers that needed changing; but if any of the other babies wake up and are crying, please warm up their bottles too and feed them. Their names are on the cots and on their bottles also."

Ruth had done all that in the short time she had been out of the older kids' playroom. Yet, she had left the door open and there hadn't been a sound from the room Reha was in. I had expected to hear her cry as soon as she woke up in those strange surroundings. But when I got to her, she was happily pushing coloured bricks around in her playpen. The other babies in her room seemed just as contented and hardly ever cried either.

I am sure that Ruth's obvious love for children had a lot to do with it. She seemed to have an instinct for the right time to feed, change diapers, or just cuddle individual babies before they got restless. By the time I had to report to the factory, I had no hesitation about leaving Reha entirely in her care. On my last day as a helper, she gave a first birthday party for Reha. She lit the single candle and cut up a cake she must have baked the previous night. She then said in a brief speech that this was also a farewell "to the best and only help" she had ever had. She handed a small piece of cake to each of the children and added that she had "no doubt Reha would be happy in daycare because she also had a happy home and an always cheerful, courageous, and hard working mother to get back to every night and on weekends." This unexpected tribute made it harder to leave the children. At the same time, knowing now that my baby would be in good hands, it made it easier to face whatever awaited me at the factory I had been assigned to.

The exact location and name of the factory, like most other industries geared to war production by 1941, was kept secret and given a code-name "for security reasons." I was only given instructions on the transportation I had to use as far as the Zoo station. I was then instructed to change to a train and where I had to get off. From there I was to follow a street map with arrows pointing in the direction of, and ending at, a square building marked *FACTORY*. All we could deduce from the plan—my husband helped me to work it out—was that it was considerably further out of city limits than his or his mother's work place. It was apparently not part of the well-known industrial complexes. Allowing for the change from one type of transportation to another, the possible waiting time, and the walk from my final exit to the factory, we estimated at least a one and a half hour's journey. But since I didn't have to report there till 8:00 a.m. that first morning, I could still make it after leaving Reha at the daycare centre at 6:00 a.m. Since I was never very good at reading maps even if the street names were clearly marked, I was afraid I'd get hopelessly lost. For once I was lucky, didn't have to wait long for connections and got to my destination early enough.

The factory turned out to be one of the rare, privately owned small plants; it had been forced to convert from peacetime production of household goods to making heavy black plastic binocular cases for the army. The owner-manager received me very kindly and, pointing to the yellow star on my jacket, said: "You don't have to wear that thing here. Take it off. You are our first and only Jewish worker anyway. As long as you do your job and punch the time-clock with the others, I don't allow any discrimination. In any case, you'll find we have a very decent bunch of people here." He then asked his secretary to call the foreman to take me to the machine assigned to me. To my dismay, the young foreman wore the brown Nazi uniform and the swastika armband. However, I soon found out that he merely used it and his Nazi party membership to keep out of the army and to protect his job security. If he had any racial prejudices, they disappeared when it came to women. They could have been black, yellow, or green and he would have chased them. That I was not only Jewish but also happily married and had a child did not deter him from repeatedly propositioning me, but he was really quite good natured and could take rejection in his stride.

On this first morning, however, he just took me to a store room, told the clerk to give me a pair of overalls and then showed me to the machine floor. There I met my co-workers who, from the start, adopted me like an exotic pet. With an automatic electric drill, I had to punch holes for the attachment of shoulder straps into the hard black plastic of the binocular carry cases. It was a fairly easy but monotonous job. Only keeping up with the speed of production to fill the large order quotas was difficult. The workers on either side of me helped out if I fell behind and introduced me to tricks to speed up operations. The one on my right was an attractive young woman whose long black hair was neatly tied in one pigtail hanging down her back to keep it out of the machines. The machine on my left was operated by a fair, very fit looking young man who soon told me that he was exempt from army service because he had failed his medical tests. Those two were to become loyal friends. Later, when they heard that Jews were taken out of industry and disappeared, both offered to hide me should the Gestapo come for me too. But since the young man lived with his parents and the girl shared a small apartment with two other young women, neither one could have sheltered a whole family or even a mother and child.

Not until they had known me for over a year did they let me

in on their very dangerous secret: Both Peter, the army reject, and the girl—everybody in the plant called her "Tom"—were members of a resistance group. They would eventually take me to their secret meetings which were always held in different places and never in the same district of Berlin. Long before that happened, I was to learn that Tom, at least, had a good reason to hate, fear, and fight the Nazis. Although she was an Aryan, she also belonged to a hunted and persecuted minority which, if discovered, were arrested and sent to concentration camps which few of them survived. Tom was a lesbian.

At the end of my first working day I was simply amazed at the friendliness and lack of prejudice in that small factory, from the owner and office staff down to the workers on the floor. This was not the last time in my life I would become everybody's pet-Jew.

At home that evening, we established a routine we tried to stick to for as long as we worked as forced labour and lived together under the same roof. I went directly from the factory to the daycare centre, picked up Reha and visited the grocer, butcher, fruit and vegetable stores where I, and my mother before me, had shopped long before the war. Since food was rationed and because they all knew me well, the shop owners often kept some illegal staples for me or special treats for my child under the counters. Therefore, although my mother-in-law and my husband came home earlier, they still left the shopping to me.

By the time I got home, my mother-in-law had prepared a meal from leftovers and my husband took over our baby, played with her and gave her a bath to give me time to have a shower and change into more comfortable clothes. I then fed Reha, put her to bed, read nursery rhymes, and sang to her. At the end of this, my first working day, my husband put a record of lullabies on the gramophone next door, came quietly into the nursery, put his arm round me and sang with me to that background music. Reha fell asleep within minutes, a sweet smile on her face. Freddy whispered, afraid to wake our child: "Look at her! I dread the time she'll break men's hearts like you broke mine when you ran away the first time I met you." Everything outside our walls was forgotten.

When we finally sat down for our evening meal, I understood at last why neither my mother-in-law nor my husband had told me much about their working days although they always wanted to hear all I had done during our child's first year of life. They worked in different plants in the huge industrial Siemens empire near Spandau, almost a city within the city of Berlin. I only learned after the war that Siemens had employed more than 80,000 people. Most of the German workers called up for military service were eventually replaced by forced labour, prisoners, and workers from occupied or allied countries. All Freddy and his mother had ever told me was that the Jews were completely segregated. Their monotonous work—mostly producing small electrical components on a conveyor belt, probably for radios—was soul-destroying. Now I was equally reluctant to talk about my first impressions of the factory even though I realized already that I was much better off in my small as yet unsegregated plant than most Jews elsewhere. All I wanted was to squeeze as much and as normal a family life into the few hours and weekends between long working days as was humanly possible. The weather in July 1941 was beautiful, warm and sunny, and it brought our conversation around to planning activities for my first free Sunday. In late April that year, when it was still too cold for the popular Wannsee lake and beaches to be crowded with boats, holiday visitors and Hitler youth, Freddy had already sailed our cabin yacht from our old boat-house to a new mooring. He had taken it to the Havel, a string of beautiful lakes much further from Berlin's Westend. We didn't know anybody there and were not likely to run into anybody who knew us. Since it didn't get warm enough till June, we hadn't gone back to the boat together. In any case, as long as I was free to take my child out to play in the fresh air and sunshine of the Jewish hospital enclave, there was no need to spirit her out of city limits and defy Nazi laws. But now that she would be cooped up in the daycare centre all day and I in the stale air of the factory, the need to get away from it all became an immediate obsession.

My husband agreed wholeheartedly and the two of us spent the rest of the evening planning the best route to get to the boat's new location. We discussed where and when we could safely remove the yellow star and what to take with us. It was harder to convince his mother that we needed to get out and away from restrictions. She accused us of being reckless and irresponsible and warned us of the dire consequences if we were caught. She was right, of course, but we were in no mood to listen to reason. The memory of our early sailing days, the longing to swim and just to feel free was too great a temptation to resist. An old family friend, our pediatrician, visited us that evening and persuaded Freddy's mother to let us enjoy our youth as long as we had the courage.

Dr. Friedlander was a bachelor, madly in love with my mother-in-law which everybody except her seemed to know. He didn't openly court her until after her husband's death. Until then, she just liked his company because he was cheerful and optimistic. He made her laugh and counterbalanced her inherent pessimism. I liked him because I recognized in him a kindred spirit, a man who never gave up hope, was incapable of hating anybody, but had enough self-esteem never to voluntarily knuckle under hateful restrictions imposed on us, especially where they affected children.

On this as on later occasions, he sided with me. He told my mother-in-law about the children he saw in his clinic, most of whom had been in daycare for at least a year. They not only suffered from malnutrition caused by severe rationing of essential food, but also from lack of fresh air and exercise. The single care-takers of overcrowded daycare centres just didn't have the time or means to take so many children for walks, and the parks and public playgrounds had long since been out of bounds to Jewish children. Every park had been signposted "Juden Verboten" (Forbidden to Jews).

"If you saw my patients on a daily basis as I do," Dr. Friedlander said, "if you saw normal children turn into anaemic little ghosts, you too would think it worthwhile to take a comparatively small risk to give your granddaughter every chance to stay as healthy as she still is." Then he pleaded: "Herta, let's all go sailing this weekend. You need some fun too." She finally gave in.

So the two men left home on Saturday after work to get the boat shipshape. They took only a couple of sleeping bags to spend the night on the bunks in the cabin and a few sandwiches for their breakfast. My husband wore under his coat his sailor's uniform which dated back to his early years of membership in the Betar's Marine Corps, the Jewish right-wing organization my father had so detested because its uniforms and paramilitary discipline resembled those of the Hitler Youth. Freddy was going to take off his coat and roll it into his sleeping bag in the washroom of the suburban station where they had to change trains. He would then don his sailor's cap with the gold embossed ribbon bearing the name of our yacht—the *SS EVELYN* (Little Eva). Since the large sailing ships used to train Hitler Youth were also often named after girls, it was a virtual certainty that nobody would give him a second glance.

He phoned from the boat-house near our new mooring as soon as he got there and, as prearranged in case our phones were bugged, simply said: "Who am I talking to?" And when I gave my name, "I'm sorry, I must have a wrong number. I'll try again. I was just going to let my folks know that I'm home if they want to visit tomorrow. Nice talking to you." He hung up and my mother-in-law and I prepared a stew with lots of potatoes, vegetables, and a week's ration of meat in a large pan we could reheat on the one-flame burner in the small galley of our boat.

The next morning, we left at the same time we did on weekdays just in case some nosy German neighbours happened to watch us. They had no idea whether or not we were working on Sundays and would presume I was taking my child to daycare and that my mother-in-law was also on her way to a factory. Only this time we had swimsuits under our dresses and a change of clothes and towels tucked away in my baby's stroller. We caught the first subway train out of the city. As expected, the train ran empty at that early hour and no ticket inspectors came aboard on Sundays either. Since we were the only passengers, we could remove the Star of David as soon as we left our station.

Dr. Friedlander was waiting to take us to the boat, a mere ten minute's walk. After we used a small outboard motor to get us out of the sheltered harbour into open waters, there was just enough of breeze to move at an exhilarating speed, but not fast enough for even our small child to lose her balance; she treated the deck as if it were a large playpen.

About lunch time, we found an isolated sandy beach, inaccessible from any road. There we threw out the anchor and waded onto dry land. We spent hours on that sunny beach, taking turns swimming, playing with Reha, and building sand castles. We had so much fun that day that none of us gave much thought to tomorrow or to anything beyond that. We had successfully escaped reality, gotten away with it and felt so much better for it. From then on, we spent every Sunday on the boat during that summer of 1941 as long as the weather was fine.

I believe that those early flights from the pressures of Nazi persecution were a psychological preparation for all my later attempts to escape life threatening situations. Few Jews, who timidly obeyed all Nazi racial laws then, would have believed that it was even remotely possible to get away. Hardly any would try to escape even if, on very rare occasions, the opportunity presented itself.

For the rest of that summer our situation remained bearable. Because of the long travel time to and from the factory, Reha was always the first at the daycare centre in the morning and the last to be picked up in the late afternoon. Long daylight hours and warm temperatures made this less of a hardship. We also managed to get adequate food supplies thanks to the kindness of the butcher, grocers, fruit and vegetable merchants who, whenever possible, slipped some extras into my shopping bags. Occasionally, we could still buy special treats in the black market with the money my husband had earned the previous winter selling the small tables, book shelves or picture frames he had made at home. The Sundays on the lakes, swimming and playing in the sun also helped to keep us and our little girl fit and healthy.

However, all this stopped as the days got shorter, summer turned into fall and the weather changed. We had to abandon the boat and stay home on weekends. Food rations for Jews were reduced constantly and few extras came my way as both imports and home grown supplies to local shops dwindled. During that winter, it also became increasingly difficult to get an adequate supply of potatoes, even when mashed potatoes with some watery gravy was the best I could offer my hungry family. My husband could no longer get the wood and material to construct and sell his private work. The small furniture factory where he had been employed as a designer before compulsory labour laws were implemented had been closed. It had continued illegally to supply him with his carpentry needs as long as it could. It was put out of business when all its younger employees were called up for army service and the older ones into war industries.

For the next year, 1942, we lived like most other Jews left

in Berlin. We didn't risk going back to the yacht the following summer. We had heard that a few other young Jews who still had boats on the Wannsee had been picked up, arrested, and deported. We later learned through the grapevine that the Gestapo had visited the offices of boat-houses and harbours, scanning their lists of registered boat owners and would lie in wait for suspects on weekends. Although our new mooring on the Havel was much further north than the Wannsee and may not have been included in Gestapo raids, we didn't want to expose our child to additional dangers. My husband had prudently registered our boat under a fictitious name. We had always paid the harbour fees personally and in cash to avoid the yacht being traced back to us through the post office if we mailed the money. When we now had to abandon the yacht and discontinued payments, we presumed it would eventually be auctioned off to recover the mooring fees. However, when I went back after the end of the war, five years later, it was still tied up in our original berth. It had sunk to the shallow bottom of the harbour and only the mast was sticking out above the water. By then, its resting place would mean nothing more to me than a fitting grave of our youthful joys and dreams. The still visible mast became a fragile monument to the past.

Although we lived like most other Jews left in Berlin in the winter of 1941/42, we still had some extraordinary advantages. That year the Nazis expropriated more and more apartments still owned or rented by Jews in many parts of Berlin. The inhabitants were evicted without warning and forced to move in with other Jewish families who had no say as to the number of people or the type of family they had to take in. Under increasingly crowded, ghetto-like living conditions, unwilling landlords and equally involuntary tenants became bitter enemies. Their hostility resulted at best in not speaking to each other, at worst in violent fights over children accused of being too noisy or, simply, over kitchen and bathroom privileges. I didn't know all this at the time because—and I don't know why—we had not been allotted any boarders. Perhaps we were spared because my in-laws' address, 39 Luitpold Strasse in Berlin-Wilmersdorf, was already registered as a two-family dwelling since my husband and I had moved in or perhaps because there were very few Jews left in that district.

Living alone meant that our child could make as much noise as she liked and have the run of the large apartment. Once Reha was asleep, we could listen to records or radio and hear out-lawed foreign news broadcasts without disturbing strangers or risking complaints to the Gestapo. Even "Aryan traitors" denounced for listening to the BBC's German language programs received severe prison sentences. Jews were automatically deported to concentration camps.

Shortly after Reha's second birthday and a year after I had started punching holes into binocular cases at the factory, my Aryan workmates Tom and Peter invited me to one of their Resistance groups' regular monthly Sunday meetings. I had to promise not to tell anyone, not even my husband, where I was going. To make doubly sure that I couldn't accidentally give anything away, they didn't let me know where they were taking me either. They arranged to meet me at my nearest subway station at the Hohenzollern Platz in Wilmersdorf and told me to just follow them. They also warned me that nobody would be introduced by real names and asked me to think of a name I'd like to be called. I chose the name "Daniella," a character from one of my favourite books by Erich Kaestner, "Emil and the Detectives," a juvenile novel I had read over and over again when I was about ten years old. "Daniella," a spunky teenager, had left a lasting impression because of her determination to detect and fight evil and corruption. I had also admired "Daniella," the only girl among the young "detectives," for her ingenuity in extricating herself and the boys from dangerous situations.

I would remain "Daniella" throughout my short-lived association with the Resistance. I would use that alias again in Canada when I finally wrote *Vanished in Darkness: An Auschwitz Memoir* more than 40 years later. I could only relive my devastating past by thinking of "Daniella" as a different person on another continent in another lifetime.

On Sunday afternoon, an hour before the clandestine meeting with my two Resistance sponsors, I told my husband and his mother that I just had to get out of the house for a while. It was the first time I had kept a secret from Freddy, and I felt almost as bad about it as I might have felt had I been cheating on him with another man. There was a grain of truth in my explanation that I was beginning to feel claustrophobic since we couldn't go sailing anymore. I just wanted to walk and walk. I was telling a blatant lie, however, when I said I would have asked Freddy to come with me and taken Reha too had I thought about it earlier. Since it was already afternoon and I might not be ready to come home in time to feed our child, would he please look after her. And if I wasn't home by then, could he or his mom put her to bed at seven o'clock at the latest since I'd have to get her up so early again on Monday morning?

My husband's trusting response made me feel even worse. He remembered the time after my father's death before we were married when I had nightmares of walls closing in on me. He now hugged me again as he had done then and said: "I promised you I'd always protect you from those miserable dreams. If a good long walk is all it takes to make you feel better, you should go out more often." Had I been able to contact Tom and Peter before they came to meet me, I would probably have cancelled the meeting and might never have become involved with the Resistance. Would that have changed our fate?

Still, I did keep our appointment and arrived punctually at the subway station where they were already waiting. As arranged, they did not greet me, but Peter indicated with an almost imperceptible nod when the train they were going to take came to a halt. They boarded it and I followed. Only after we arrived at their destination and they were confident we weren't followed did Peter acknowledge my presence. They then put their arms in mine and led me to the third floor of a nearby tenement house.

That first Resistance meeting I attended was held in Tom's small apartment north of the Alexander Platz, a district mainly inhabited by blue-collar workers. Only some ten people turned up and were introduced to me by first names which, like mine, were not their own. Because Tom and Peter vouched for my trustworthiness, they accepted my presence and explained some of their ground rules.

Only the sponsors of new members and subsequently the central leadership of the Resistance would know the newcomers' background. The reason for adopting pseudonyms was, of course, the danger of some being arrested and interrogated. As long as they didn't know other members' true identity, they couldn't give away names even under torture. Only trusted members who had been with the group since its inception could become sponsors. Their monthly meetings would always be held in different locations to avoid arousing suspicion in any one neighbourhood and there would never be more than ten members present.

The Resistance had similar cells not only in different districts of Berlin but also in other industrial areas across Germany. The only time I might meet delegates from those other groups would be if some joint action was planned by the central leadership or if they wanted to assess the results of individual acts of sabotage. Almost all their members were factory workers and most of them were former Communists. Yes, a few other small Resistance movements did exist. But if we happened to run into any of their members, we were not to reveal the existence of ours under any circumstances because, I was told, "none of them can be trusted!"

At that meeting I learned for the first time since Hitler came to power that there were several active Resistance organizations within German borders. At the same time, I discovered why they would remain so useless and ineffective: I was told then, and it was later confirmed by prisoners who had been members of one or another, that some Resistance workers within the Catholic or Protestant Churches refused to have anything to do with left-wing and Communist anti-Nazis. Intellectuals and student groups had no contact with and didn't trust the blue-collar Resistance. Some Partisans, who later fought in the eastern forests and became one of the strongest and probably best armed groups, would have nothing to do with Jewish freedom fighters. Fragmented, they had little impact on Nazi power. Finally, I was told that only I could decide when I was ready and able to make a commitment to their cause.

After the meeting, Tom explained further that any dangerous and out-of-town assignments were entrusted only to single, unmarried, and experienced volunteers. They had to go through a rigorous training in disguise, memorize a fictitious past to match the false identity papers they were given once they had passed severe tests. She and Peter would see to it that I received the same training although I did not qualify to accept assignments. If I was ever in immediate personal danger, the Resistance could probably spirit me out of Berlin or even out of the country. They had connections and were in constant touch with Resistance groups in France who, occasionally, could help fugitives escape.

Since I still believed I'd be safe as long as slave labour was needed, it seemed unnecessary to consider the question, but I asked anyway: "What about my family if I had to suddenly leave home?" Should that be necessary, Tom said, there was no way I could take my husband and child with me, but she knew of one or two cases where children had been smuggled out separately to join parents who had already managed to get across the border. They would certainly do everything in their power to make that happen should the need ever arise. It did happen much sooner than anybody could have anticipated.

# CHAPTER 8

"Daniella Raphael!" A grey-haired prison wardress with a kind face and sad, old eyes called me from contemplation of the tiny piece of blue sky that could be seen through the high, heavily-barred window.

"Daniella," she repeated, "will you follow me to my office to sign your release papers? I won't keep you long and you can go home as soon as you like. Unless," she added with a smile, "you would rather have some lunch before you go?"

I was speechless. My heart missed a beat and then started racing. I looked at the four girls who had shared the cell with me and saw their startled, doubtful expression. Nobody in my position had ever been released from jail once the Nazis had them in their clutches. Besides, where was I to go? My husband was a prisoner and news had reached me that my mother-in-law had been deported and her house requisitioned. My mind was in such a turmoil that I almost forgot my own mother, who was still nursing the remnants of a fast-dwindling community in the Jewish hospital in East Berlin. Of course, I could go to her.

"Don't look so thunderstruck, girl, and come with me," said the wardress. "To look at you, one might think you were loath to leave this comfortable place. Come on child, you and your type don't belong here. Somebody seems to have realized a mistake has been made."

I followed her to her bare little office, too excited to say goodbye to my fellow prisoners. Right enough, there was my file on her desk. My name was on it, but the details had been left blank. I began to understand why the wardress thought I had been arrested by mistake. I was young, barely twenty years old, and hope surged up inside me like a song. The wardress handed me my pen and the money which had been taken from me when I had been arrested. I signed the release papers; she shook hands with me and, smiling, warned me to keep away from prison in future. She then rang the bell and a young woman in uniform came in to take me to the gate and show me where to get a bus. The policewoman took me past innumerable cells and down staircase after staircase into the yard and through the slowly opening iron gates.

I remember little about this prison in Moabit, Berlin, the last of eleven. All I recollect is the warm sun and the sweet scent and promise of spring in the air. I told the girl I knew my way about Berlin and asked her to leave me. All I wanted was to stand still and savour the sunlight and the freedom after three months' imprisonment.

And so I stood, leaning against a tree, taking deep breaths of fresh air, completely and childishly happy. I did not contemplate my next move but cast my mind back over the past few months. This was the beginning of April 1943. It seemed so long, long ago since I had seen my child the last time.

# CHAPTER 9

My little Reha was only a baby when I was forced to work in a factory and to leave her in a daycare centre. I had an hour's journey each way to and from work. Reha was the first child at the centre in the morning and the last to be collected at night. I remember her forlorn little figure, sitting half asleep in a tiny chair in the huge, deserted playroom, generally dressed to go out, her coat buttoned up and her bonnet the wrong way round on her dark little head.

I remember the delighted shriek when she saw me at last and how I wrapped her up and took her round the shops in her stroller to buy a little food. In winter it was pitch dark. Jews were no longer given scarce milk, butter, eggs, or fruit. Sometimes, a kind woman in a fruit shop would wrap up a few apples if nobody was around but, if Reha saw this, she would cry all the way home for me to give her one. I could not risk letting her eat an apple in the street. We had to wear a large yellow star with *JEW* printed across it, and an apple or a piece of chocolate seen in the hand of a Jewish child had been the excuse for deportation of whole families.

One could get all the forbidden things in the black market at terrific prices but our bank accounts were blocked and we had to live on the pay-packets from the factory. Forced labour wages were barely enough to pay for rent and for the rationed food allotted to us.

My husband occasionally did some private work. Carpentry was his hobby and sometimes he sold a bookshelf, a cabinet, or a set of small tables. Then, for a week or so, we had plenty to eat and Reha got a taste of chocolate, bananas or oranges. Of course, when such luxuries were scarce she would beg me for them. It just about broke my heart if there was nothing but mashed potatoes and some nondescript soup for her supper. All this was bearable when we still lived in our comfortable home. At least we were together in the evenings. My husband played with the baby, bathed her, and put her to bed while I cooked our evening meal, such as it was, swept and cleaned the house, and did our washing and ironing. After the child was in bed and the essential chores done, we could still sit together for an hour or two and talk of the future and what we would do when the Nazis were thrown out and the war over. Or, if we were too tired to talk, we would listen to records or a concert or a play on the radio, or just read.

Even that short spell of small joys and comparative comfort soon came to an end. More and more people were being arrested for trivial or fictitious reasons. Whole families were deported, nobody knew where. Old and sick people were dragged out of their beds to police stations and then vanished. My mother told me of the many, many old people who attempted suicide. Often their attempts were unsuccessful and they were taken to hospital to be nursed back to health only to be arrested and sent to an unknown, terrifying destiny. My mother, who was a senior sister on the emergency ward, chose not to nurse them back to life. They passed out peacefully while she sat at their side. Holding frail, tired hands, she talked to them in her sweet, soft voice of the past and of their children, who were perhaps safely abroad. She talked to them until the drugs they had taken took effect and the old people closed their eyes, no longer afraid of the dark, holding her hand with a tightening grip and, finally, relaxing into peaceful, eternal sleep.

Then, one day she was told by a Gestapo man in charge of sick prisoners at the hospital that a campaign was in preparation to evacuate all Jewish families with young children. As soon as my mother warned me, I decided to hide our child. We did not know what was in store for us but, whatever it was, I was not going to drag a baby into it. A friend, a Christian nurse, proposed to take Reha to her brother in East Prussia and tell him the baby's parents had been killed in an air raid on Berlin.

My mother-in-law vetoed the plan. She said we would all be shot if the Gestapo found out the child had disappeared. We were living in her house by that time as my parents' home had long since been requisitioned by the German Broadcasting Corporation. She was right, of course, but she did not stop to consider that we would probably be killed anyway. My husband backed her up and I decided I would have to leave them. He was so young and I wondered if he could keep a secret if he were tortured. We knew by then of the Gestapo methods of wringing secrets from their suspects and I wanted my husband to be able to swear he knew nothing of the whereabouts of his little daughter. Since I had to leave the house anyway, I was going to take no risks. I explained my motives and he agreed to a divorce, which was much easier than I had thought. We found one of his ex-girlfriends more than willing to spend a night with him and I got a divorce on the grounds of desertion and adultery. After that I moved with Reha into a rented apartment in a house belonging to another Jewish family.

The last two weeks with my child were agony. I had not dared to stay away from work in case the Gestapo became suspicious and arrested me before I got the chance to hide our little girl. The date for her departure was fixed and I knew I would soon see her for the last time. I rushed home at night as fast as I could and often wondered what went on inside that little head when I got to her. She was more affectionate than she had ever been before, kissed and hugged me almost as though I were the child. She never asked for her Daddy or why we had left home for that chilly, impersonal room. Yet she loved her father dearly.

Once more I took her to see him on his twenty-second birthday. We went after dark and sneaked in through the back door. Reha had seen me wrap a present for him and so she had decided to take her most valued possession, a woolly little lamb that had accompanied her everywhere. She handed it to her father and said, "Happy Birthday, Daddy." But the tears in her eyes emphasized more than anything else that there was nothing happy about it. We only stayed for half an hour and before we left, my husband put his arms around me. For the first time since I left him, I broke down and cried, quite unable to control myself. Suddenly I felt a light tug on my coat and the little voice said, "Don't cry, Mommy. I'm going to take my lamb back so we won't be so lonely. You don't mind, Daddy, do you?" She tucked her toy under her arm and sneaked out of the door without looking up, guilt and bad conscience personified in a two and a half year old child.

Margaret, the Christian nurse, was going to take an early train to East Prussia and I was to meet her with Reha just after midnight at the station where trains left for the east, about a forty-five minute walk from my apartment. I had given Reha sleeping pills hoping she would not notice anything until she was on the train. But I was ignorant in those days, and in order to spare my mother's feelings had not discussed this with her. I thought if I gave Reha twice the prescribed dose she would sleep sounder. The overdose had exactly the opposite effect. She cried and cried, became quite hysterical, and by 10:00 p.m. was still wide awake, feverish and restless and I was shaken and at my wits' end. About 11:00 p.m. she was sick, had a drink of water, and at last fell into a deep, exhausted sleep.

I did not dress her, wrapped her in three thick blankets,

tucked her little lamb in as well and crept out of the house. It was a dark night, icy cold and windy but I did not dare take a taxi for fear of drawing attention to us. So I walked. The sleeping child grew heavier and heavier in my arms but this dead weight and the icy wind I had to battle kept my mind off the imminent separation. At last I reached the corner opposite the station. There was no moon and it was so dark I did not see Margaret approaching. When she put her hand on my shoulder, I all but collapsed with fright. "It's all right, Daniella," she said, and the next moment she had taken the sleeping child from my arms and was gone. I tried to run after her, but she was already lost in the dark.

"I have not even kissed her, I have not even kissed her," was all that went through my agonized mind like a broken record as I slowly walked back to my apartment. I don't know how I got home that night. I remember waking up in the morning kneeling in front of the empty cot, my head buried in the small pillow. I was cold and stiff and lonelier than I have been in my life before or since.

# CHAPTER 10

After Reha was gone, I was on the run, always in contact with the Resistance movement which I had quickly joined. This organization, to me, was nothing more than some Christian names, meetings with mysterious people in obscure pubs and street corners in Berlin or under the shade of the Munster of Strassbourg. Off and on, through Resistance contacts, meetings were arranged for my husband and me in equally obscure places. He too was trying to escape arrest, not knowing where he was going or what I was doing. Neither of us stayed for more than a night in any one place and often it was very difficult to find a safe shelter. It would have been a comfort in those dark, cold winter nights to at least walk together, but even that was against Resistance rules and regulations. Within six months, I lost trace of his whereabouts altogether.

At the end of January 1943, the Resistance dispatched me to Dornbirn, a small border village. I was given some documents—technical drawings of I know not what—for delivery to Switzerland. I had been told to lie low until my contact in Dornbirn turned up. His name was Peter and I was to obey his instructions until I was across the border. There, new contacts would meet me, receive the papers, and return me to Germany. I was promised that on completion of three similar missions, I would be allowed to stay in Switzerland where my husband and child would join me.

At midnight on 3 February, my train stopped in Dornbirn.

It was a dark, cold night. Only two other passengers got out at the station, one a young man in fur coat and beaver hat, another in a skiing outfit. They left from different compartments and went straight to the only exit of that little station. I waited till they were out of sight, then followed slowly, wondering where to "lie low" at this time of night. I need not have worried. The two men were waiting for me.

They identified themselves as Gestapo and then offered me the hospitality of the local police station. As each had taken one of my arms in an iron grip, there was no way I could refuse their invitation. At the police station they started to bombard me with questions.

I stuck to my fictitious past, drummed into me day and night during the long weeks of the Resistance briefing. The two Gestapo men were obviously beginners. When they saw no information was forthcoming, they proceeded to search me for identity cards and documents. I had the presence of mind to ask for a woman officer to search me. One could still cling to a moral code in an isolated frontier station. In a larger place, I would have been beaten for impudence and the men would have continued their search. However, the two complied with my demand and locked me in a coal cellar. A messenger was dispatched to rouse the female employed to search women tourists for Customs, while I began to look around for a suitable corner to dispose of my documents.

Barely had I begun, when the door creaked open and in came a uniformed police officer. In a loud voice, holding open the door, he said, "I'm in charge of this border station. Checking to see prisoners are accounted for." Then he shut the door and whispered, "I am Peter. Give me the papers, quickly!" He took the drawings, opened an iron gate leading from the coal cellar to the station's furnaces and burned them on the spot. He said that was all he could do for me at the moment, but he would see me again. "Stick to your story whatever happens," he warned, and with that he left.

Shortly afterwards, I was taken back to the office upstairs. A woman made me undress behind a screen and searched my clothes. Everything she found in my coat pockets she handed to the two officers. She tore open the lining of my coat, the hem of my skirt, belt and collar of my sweater, of course without results. I was then permitted to dress again and my captors called me over to their desks. In front of them were my make-up compact, the mirror torn out and splintered, my lipstick broken out of its case and crumpled, and my necklace unwound and partly broken with beads scattered all over the desk and floor.

"Madam," the older of the men said, "it would be in your interest to make a full confession. While we did not yet find what we were looking for, we did get your description and details of your despicable intentions from headquarters. If you refuse to make a statement, we shall charge you with spying, the intention to unlawfully cross the frontier into foreign territory and the contacting of enemy agents conspiring against the German Reich. You know the penalty for these crimes? We give you ten minutes to think it over."

My reply was that I could not confess to something I knew nothing about. Unless they could produce evidence that I was not the person shown in my passport, I had nothing more to say until they brought me to trial in an open court. I would then do my best to defend myself. That was a last and desperate attempt to bluff my way out of a bad situation. My guess that these two were inexperienced and had not yet been properly trained in methods of inquisition and torture proved correct.

Far from calling my bluff, they attempted to produce evidence in the form of a telegram which they handed to me. The headquarters of my Resistance organization, a business house at the Potsdamer Platz in Berlin, had been raided by the Gestapo and a few people had been arrested. It appeared that, in order to save more important members, they had given the names and details of employment of some insignificant agents like myself who could not do any great damage. Thus I had been trailed all the way from Strassbourg to Dornbirn in order for them to catch my contacts as well. But the two youngsters had bungled the job. They had arrested me prematurely and so failed to meet Peter. They were very angry and disappointed but I must grant them they were polite and never touched me or even raised their voices. Comparing their watches, they waited hopefully for ten minutes and then stood up to formally charge me with my crimes.

The older one spoke again. "We have sufficient proof of your identity. Your refusal to admit it is therefore futile. The penalty for the crimes you have committed or attempted is death. You will be shot at dawn." Once more I tried to demand a trial but was silenced. Hands tied behind my back, I was returned to the coal cellar for the few hours that remained before the break of dawn.

For a short time I leaned against the wall trying to ease my hands where the rope cut into my wrists. Then Peter came in again and said the Gestapo had left the building. He untied my hands, helped me out of my coat, spread it on the floor and advised me to get some sleep. "Don't worry, Daniella," he said. "You'll be all right. I promise to do all I can to get you out of this fix." Again he left. It was kind of him to attempt to ease my mind but I did not see what he could do for me. He was a police officer and, as such, powerless against the Gestapo. Above all, he was an important link in the Resistance and could not afford to risk his position for a lost cause. I did not really care. Very tired now, I felt, oddly enough, a tremendous relief. At last I had reached the end of a long, lonely trail; no longer would I have to keep running; no longer had I to strain every nerve to keep on the alert, to make quick decisions, to keep awake when all I wanted was to sleep. Now others would have to do the thinking for me. Somebody else would shoulder my responsibilities and I was sure I would not be missed. My child was safe and too young to remember me. With that thought, I curled up in my warm, fluffy coat and, breathing in the faint, sweet scent of perfume my husband had given me on my last birthday, I fell into a deep, dreamless sleep.

In the distance, the rhythmic sound of marching feet was audible. They came closer, marched along the passage outside, turned and stopped. I couldn't open my eyes or move. My limbs felt like lead and my mind was a complete blank. Somebody bent over me and a mournful, disembodied voice said, "Sound asleep. She is only a kid. It's a crying shame. Come and see her."

Another voice from the door answered impatiently, "Don't get emotional again, Willy. The sooner you realize you are here to do a job, the sooner we might make a soldier out of you. Hurry up now and get her out of here!"

The man who had spoken first shook me gently and I opened my eyes reluctantly to look up at him. I saw a boy in uniform, hair cut very short, his face flushed. His childish blue eyes seemed panic-stricken. When he spoke again, his voice was barely more than a hoarse whisper, "Get up and come along."

After the bright, unshaded electric light in the coal cellar, the passage outside seemed very dark and I stumbled over my own feet, still very tired and completely numb. The young soldier put his hand under my arm and steered me along. The other soldier preceded us, opened a door and, between them, they led me out of the building. A closed van was waiting and they hoisted me up, got into the van behind me and closed its doors.

I don't know whether we covered a long or a short distance. Sitting on the floor of the vehicle, I dozed off again until it came to a standstill. Lifted out, I found myself close to a wall at the end of what looked like a playing field. The ground was covered in deep snow. It was impossible to find out where I was. It was dawn and the first faint rays of light could be seen on the horizon and on the steep, snowy incline of high mountains.

The two Gestapo men were at my side again. A short distance away, ten soldiers with rifles lined up.

"Take your clothes off," commanded one of the Gestapo. Everything seemed very unreal and I shivered. I will never forget that morning of 4 February 1943. It was bitterly cold. The soldiers had mufflers around their necks and snow helmets. Their noses were blue with frost.

"Get cracking, woman," the man shouted. "We haven't got all day."

I took off my coat, sweater and skirt and was allowed to keep on my pants and brassiere. I no longer noticed the cold and felt no emotion. I was a disinterested observer in a numb body.

"Stand against the wall," somebody commanded and, like a mechanical toy, I stood against the wall.

"Have you anything to say?" I shook my head and even that was difficult. My spine was stiff.

"You will be granted a last wish. What is it? Make it snappy."

"I would like to write to my mother, please."

"Oh no, you won't. Think of something more sensible."

"May I have a cigarette?" I don't know what made me say that. I had never smoked in my life and never had any desire to do so.

The Gestapo man handed me a cigarette, lit it for me and I inhaled slowly and clumsily, coughed and tried again, thinking of nothing except how ridiculous the soldiers looked with their blue noses. I recognized the boy who had wakened me in the coal cellar amongst them. Tears were running down his cheeks and he was trying to catch them with his tongue, pulling the silliest faces. That was all that struck me at the time. I thought neither of my family nor my home, nor the past; I just stood there in my pants, watching everything around me, and smoking my cigarette. Then, something happened.

There was a commotion at the other end of the field. Somebody came running and stumbling across the snowy expanse, waving his arms and shouting something. Everybody was looking in his direction and not a soul took the slightest notice of me. I think I could have run off behind their backs, but I tried to move and was too stiff and frozen to even lift my feet. Anyway, how far could I have gone in my state of undress?

The man came closer, still gesticulating wildly, and at last I could hear him. "Stop it, stop it, you fools!" he yelled. "Is she alive? Stop it at once!" It was Peter. He gave one glance in my direction and ran across to the Gestapo. They were near enough for me to overhear what was said. Peter told them that HQ Gestapo Berlin had just been on the telephone and demanded I be sent back to them for further questioning. He told them the boss was furious about this bungled job of theirs and he had said on the phone he would soon get that little chit to talk.

Peter turned to me and said gruffly, "What are you standing there for? Get your clothes on and be quick about it. I am now responsible for your safe conduct to Berlin and I'll make sure you don't die of pneumonia before your interview." He turned away and waited till I was ready to follow him. The two Gestapo men stood rooted to the ground. They had nothing to say when I crept back into the same van that had brought me to the field, this time in the company of Peter, my secret friend.

At the station he handed me over to one of his men, and once more I found myself locked in the coal cellar. Till then I had not realized how very cold I had been. In this hot place my hands and feet began to itch unbearably and I moved as far away as possible from the gate leading to the boiler room. I took my coat off and rolled up the sleeves of my sweater but that seemed to make little difference to my discomfort. Somebody came in and brought a tray with hot coffee and a few rolls, a basin with water, soap and towel. I had a wash and gulped down the coffee and rolls. It had not dawned on me till then how terribly hungry I was, having had nothing to eat for over twenty-four hours. The man who had brought the tray returned and, at my request, produced a needle and thread. I sat down on the floor to sew up the lining of my coat, the hem of my skirt, and the collar of my sweater.

Vaguely, I wondered what would happen next but I felt on top of the world again, warm, relaxed, fed, and very much alive, ready to cope with anything. Soon, yet another police officer fetched me again and said he was to take me to the station to catch a train to Ludwigshafen, a little place by the Bodensee. I faintly remembered passing through it as a child on my family's travels to Switzerland. Naïvely, I thought I might be put on this train unguarded and wondered which would be the best place to get out and try another escape route. However, at the railway station Peter was waiting with two guards. They put me straight onto the train. A whole carriage had been requisitioned and a guard posted on either exit. Peter pushed me into one of the compartments near the centre, pointed to a seat, and posted himself outside the door, locking it carefully.

About twenty minutes later the train moved slowly out of the station, and shortly afterwards Peter came in and sat down opposite me. He looked at me for a moment and then said quietly, "You are a remarkable girl, Daniella. Were you not frightened at all this morning or are you that good an actress?"

He told me the Gestapo Berlin had not phoned him but that he had taken it upon himself to contact HQ on my behalf. He managed to get hold of the Gestapo chief and informed him of my capture. He had added that no documents or proof whatsoever had been found on me to indicate I was the person the Gestapo was looking for. I might or might not know a lot but the officers attached to his station were too inexperienced to find that out. It was then Peter was ordered to arrange for my transport back to Berlin for further interrogation and that was that. He thought the two idiots who had caught me were not likely to find out who phoned whom. He was now going to hand me over to the prison warder in Ludwigshafen whom he knew as an honest, decent man who had no sympathy for the Nazis. That man would see to it that I was detained in transit prisons for as long as possible, probably until the end of the war if the Nazis were not thrown out before then. Peter was apparently a great optimist.

"The rest I have to leave to your pretty face, courage, and ingenuity, Daniella. Good luck to you." He got up and looked down at me. He was well over six feet tall, his handsome sunburnt face wrinkled with sadness and worry. "Take care of yourself. I'll turn the world upside down to find you when all this is over." He took my hand and kissed it with an unexpected passionate tenderness, turned his back on me and went out into the passage, his head bowed.

He never spoke to me again and I have never seen him since. After the end of the war I heard the rumour that he resigned from the police force shortly after our encounter. Some people who knew him from the Resistance said he had died in a concentration camp, others that he had joined the army and was killed in North Africa; yet another version was that he had volunteered for the Russian front and was taken prisoner there. I will never know the truth now.

# CHAPTER 11

Handed over, as promised, to the prison warder in Ludwigshafen, I heard the warder assure Peter that he would keep me as long as was humanly possible. I was then locked in a tiny cell containing an iron bedstead, a straw mattress, and nothing else. It was the first prison I had ever seen and it seemed pretty grim, but at least it was clean. Not until much later did I realize just how well off I had been there.

For a couple of weeks nobody came near me. In the mornings some gruel and a piece of bread were pushed through an opening in the door; at lunch time there were potatoes, cabbage, or beans swimming in greasy water, and at night some bread, syrup or beetroot jam and a jug of brown liquid, sometimes termed coffee, sometimes tea. There was a bell, however, and on demand the warder came shuffling along and took me to the toilet where I could have a wash in a tiny basin. Once a week, a small wash-tub with hot water was carried into my cell and I had a bath. That was most enjoyable until I noticed an eye looking through the peephole. So much for the warder's decency. Apart from washing and eating, there was nothing to do. No books or writing material were allowed and the solitude and silence nearly drove me mad. My mind kept revolving round the mistakes I had made. All the steps I should have taken to prevent walking straight into this trap were suddenly as clear as daylight.

Then I began to worry about my mother, my husband, and more than anything else, my child. For months I had only thought of her during the odd quiet moments and then only with the reassuring belief she was safe, probably sound asleep in a comfortable little cot in a warm, peaceful farmhouse. There were nine children in the family she had been sent to and she would have plenty of playmates and fun, I told myself. The farmer was well off and his wife loved children and had plenty of help. My child would be better fed and cared for than she had been for a long time.

But as day followed day, the memory of my last weeks with Reha became more and more unbearable and again and again the picture of that last night when I had not even had time to kiss her goodbye came back to me. Everything I had done for my child seemed inadequate and heartless. Surely, there must have been another way out of that mousetrap. Had we just thought about it earlier, I could surely have found a hiding place for both of us instead of sending her to strangers. How long was this nightmare going to last? Would I ever find her again? What if Margaret were killed in the bombing? She was the only one who knew the address in East Prussia. I had never taught Reha her real name. Although she was two and a half years old and talked like a child twice her age, she only knew her many pet names so she could not give herself away. Thus, in the prison, I tortured myself until I could no longer sleep or eat at all. I must have looked a wreck, too, for when the Gestapo turned up one day to verify the warder's statement that I was physically unfit for transport to Berlin, they just took one look at me, nodded and left again.

Then one day the door of my prison cell opened and two girls walked in whom I had known very well in Berlin. They, too, had been caught and arrested somewhere near the Swiss border. They were a bit more fortunate in that they were not married, had no family ties, and had not been connected with any Resistance organization. They were very young, seventeen years old, light-hearted, and seemed to treat jail and everything else as a huge joke, an experience not to be missed. However, they were quite convinced they would soon tire of it all and would then walk out and try some other route to Switzerland. If they were not cracking jokes, they were always hatching some crazy plans for escape. So, the next three weeks were bearable, even though the cell was so small that two of us had to crouch on the bed if one wanted to pass to the door. We had to share the one bed at night, and, as we were all big girls, that was not easy. Eventually, we slept in shifts and that worked out quite well. The two youngsters managed to distract me from my unhappy memories. I felt I had to mother these two children for, although I was only twenty years old, I felt like a hundred. But they did make me laugh, at times so much the warder admonished us to keep quiet, at least until the Gestapo left the building in the evening.

The girls had been with me for nearly two weeks when one night, at some ungodly hour, the warder called me out. I followed him with apprehension and was taken to a washroom. He locked me in, switched on the light from the outside and there, in front of me, stood my husband. It was like a bad dream that must surely end soon. But it was no dream. He was there all right. He, too, had made a beeline for the Swiss frontier, the only chance of escape at that time, had duly been arrested, and was on his way back to Berlin. His clothes were in a pitiable state but he looked strong, healthy, and sunburnt. He seemed older and more mature than I remembered him. Seeing me alive, his spirits rose tremendously and all his exuberance bubbled up. For the next few minutes we laughed and cried in each other's arms and for a few more days the prison warder locked us together for an hour every night after the Gestapo had gone. We continued where we had left off, making plans for the future. And then he was gone again—in a transport, handcuffed to a criminal. We saw him leave when we were in the yard walking round and round for exercise, a privilege recently granted to us for "good behaviour."

He saw me too as he, with eight or nine other men, escorted by armed guards, marched through the prison compound. Handcuffed, he could not wave but nodded his head in my direction, a boyish grin on his face as he tried to keep his unruly, brown hair from falling into his eyes. As he passed, he called over to me, "See you soon, my darling. Keep your chin up." For that, he got a rifle butt in his ribs that would have sent him sprawling had the man to whom he was handcuffed not given a jerk and pulled him up.

I was kept in the prison of Ludwigshafen for six weeks, first because of my alleged ill health, later because scarlet fever had broken out in one of the transit prisons and a quarantine was ordered for all prisoners en route to Berlin. But eventually the ban was lifted and the warder could no longer find any valid excuses for holding me back without risking his job and security. One day, therefore, about the middle of March, the two girls and I were taken to the station and put on a prison train consisting of many carriages, with no windows other than small barred light shafts in the roof.

We passed in transit through eleven different jails before we reached Berlin. Generally, we spent the night in one of them, were put on the train the next morning, travelled an hour or two, were again unloaded and taken to the next prison. There was nothing remarkable about this journey. Some prisons were dirty and we had to sleep on damp stone floors in the company of prostitutes and petty thieves; there were rats and the warders were indifferent to our misery. Other prisons were spotlessly clean with blue and white or red and white gingham sheets and bed covers. In these places there would be a bath or a hot shower, better food, and generally some sympathy for our unusual position. There we would be kept apart from criminals.

I remember Heidelberg particularly because it was such a lovely day when we were unloaded from the smelly train. The sky was a perfect blue and the air was warm and heavy with the scent of spring. Through the barred windows of a police van we could see the bright yellow jasmine bushes, gardens with crocuses and daffodils, and the first primroses. The longing to be free was so great it seemed to burst my heart. There was no hope of escape—we were so heavily guarded—and I just buried my face in the perfume still clinging to my coat and no longer looked out through the window at the glorious spring.

As we travelled further north towards Berlin, we left spring behind and hope for some miracle, the end of the war, or the overthrow of the Nazis, dwindled.

# CHAPTER 12

Now here I was in Berlin again, free, leaning against a tree outside the prison gates, deeply inhaling fresh air and basking in the sunshine. It seemed a miracle had happened. At last I tore myself away and started to walk. I was not quite certain which way to go to get to my mother at the hospital, but what did it matter as long as I could keep walking? I had all the time in the world. I went round the first corner, light-headed and somewhat unsteady as though I had just got up for the first time after a long illness. Then suddenly, I heard echoing footsteps behind me. Before I could turn around, two men got hold of my arms and one put his hand over my mouth to prevent me calling for help. They pushed me into a taxi. Looking around frantically, I realized the street was deserted and there was no point in protesting. One of the men gave the driver the address of Gestapo HQ, an address well-known and dreaded by everyone in Berlin. The cab moved off, silently and speedily.

On arrival, the men took me to a large reception room, full of people, men and women. They all seemed to be waiting for something. Some stood around in groups talking loudly and nervously about football, school, or a dance. Others tried to walk about but never got very far before more people blocked their way. Some stood dejectedly against a wall, their faces white and strained, and if anybody tried to talk to them they turned their heads away or looked right through the speaker and didn't answer. They seemed more dead than alive and only when a name was called did they jump into galvanized attention, just to slump down again if they were not wanted.

In the taxi I had slowly accepted the idea of finding myself a prisoner once more and got over the initial terrible shock. At first I wondered if I might not have escaped had I walked in the opposite direction or had I not waited and day-dreamed so long, but common sense told me the trap had been laid anyway. The reason for this cat and mouse game was obviously to keep prison staff and the general populace ignorant of our fate. It was designed to make them believe young people who had committed some blunder were taken into custody and then sent home to their parents.

By the time I reached Gestapo headquarters, I could, once more, laugh at my own stupidity at having been taken in so easily. In spite of rumours about the activities and cruelty of Gestapo officers, I was not afraid, certain they would know all there was to know about me. They would also know that I was a very unimportant link in the Resistance, small fry, who could not give any information even if I had wanted to do so. In any case, from the time I was recaptured after my short-lived freedom, I no longer gave any thought to either past or future but lived solely in the present, paying attention only to my immediate surroundings. I still believe this detached concentration kept me alive through all that was to follow.

I did not have to wait long. A young man, well dressed in civilian clothes opened the door and smoothing down his wavy blond hair, called my name. When I stepped forward, he said politely with a very cultured voice, "Do you mind coming to my office for a minute! We just want to ask you a few questions relevant to our reports. Do go ahead, please." The door of the waiting room closed behind me and the young man preceded me up the stairs. He took me to an office with two desks. Another man was seated behind one dictating something to a very glamourous secretary. He got up when I entered and I noticed he was tall, dark, and handsome, although not at all the fair, blue-eyed German ideal. His face seemed friendly and honest. He dismissed the secretary and told her he would call her when he had seen this young lady—meaning me. He walked round his desk, offered me a chair, and asked me, ingratiatingly, to sit down. He sat on the edge of his desk and lit a cigarette after offering me one. The second young man who had brought me upstairs, sat down behind another desk and, apparently, looked through its drawers for some papers.

The secretary had left the door slightly ajar and I could hear her high heels clicking down the stairs. There were the usual noises one hears in any office building—a telephone ringing somewhere, somebody calling for a clerk to get some files, typewriters being hammered on steadily, and, downstairs, a low humming of voices, probably coming from the reception room. The fair-haired man got up and closed the door and the world from me.

"Where is your child?" the tall dark man barked. He was towering over me now, his face revealing his true self. It was terribly frightening, this fearful, undisguised, savage brutality. I jumped up from my chair without thinking, but in retrospect it was probably to escape a veritable villain.

He did not give me time to think. His right fist struck me under the chin and I fell back on the chair. His companion, almost immediately, jerked the chair from under me, and as my reactions were too slow after the blow, I found myself on the floor. The fair-haired fellow grinned like a schoolboy playing tricks on somebody, but there was no change in the other man's face.

"Get up you bitch! Get up before I help you," he said in a quiet but all the more dangerous voice. I got up and squared my shoulders, prepared for another blow.

"Where is your child?" Again, I did not have time to think but there was no need to think. Something deep inside me felt elated, singing triumphantly: My child is safe! They can do what they like, but my child at least is safe. I had expected questions about my relations and activities with the Resistance, queries about its members and organization, but this I had not anticipated.

My mother and I had agreed, should we ever be interrogated, we would say we had sent the child to Italy, but Italy was no longer a safe place and any such statement could easily be investigated and disproved by the Gestapo. On the spur of the moment, I said that friends had taken her to Switzerland. Another blow of that hairy, big fist, a kick in my abdomen, another against my knees, a right-handed hook that seemed to close my eyes, another on my nose and mouth and I felt the blood running down my chin.

Flattened against a wall, I stood up straight. Between blows the same monotonous question: "Where is your child?" But no time to answer, more blows, more kicks. The room was reeling around me, faster and faster. No more pain, everything numb. Suddenly a pause, silence, no more beating. My ears were singing, my head was swimming, and I heard my own voice, unnaturally loud:

"You cowards, you terrible, beastly, murderous cowards! Aren't you ashamed? How do you face your mothers or your sisters or your wives if you can treat a woman like this, a woman who has done nothing but try to save her child?"

A sudden, exploding pain in my head behind my eyes and then peace, nothing, darkness and silence, a blissful eternity; something fiercely burning, tearing, hitting my back galvanized me out of unconsciousness. I screamed. "Oh, Mother, help!" The younger of the men got hold of the whip my tormentor was swinging over me.

"Not now," he was saying, "too many people in the building. We'll get her back at night and she can scream the house down."

"All right," they pulled me up by my hair. "You'll tell the truth when we tear the skin off your back strip by strip, gorgeous."

The dark man caressed the knotted leather thongs with an evil grin. "We'll get your mother now. She might not be so tough a nut to crack. Good of you to call for her. I nearly forgot her. She won't be much use to you by the time we have finished with her but she might be useful to us. Take her through the back door, you don't want to frighten newcomers with that apparition."

Through the back door into another police van I went, and after a short drive, found myself in the courtyard of a very familiar building. Previously my domestic science school, it had now been turned into a reception camp for prisoners due to be deported. After the heavy school gate closed behind me, I was met by friendly, clamouring voices in one of the corridors. Somebody eased me gently onto a mattress on the floor and soft hands put a cold, wet cloth on my aching forehead and swollen eyes. A girl pulled my clothes off and bandaged my lacerated back.

Everything seemed unreal and far away, but I was very conscious of having called for my mother when that beast was beating me. I did not keep my mouth shut.

I had reminded him of her existence, betrayed her, and soon she would go through the same ordeal because of my weakness and cowardice.

There were voices, young voices, all around me, trying to talk to me, asking questions, talking to each other. My eyes were too swollen to open, my lips were cracked and I could not talk. But my brain was active now, going over the last few hours, visualizing my mother under the same circumstances, abusing myself, hating myself.

I don't know how long I had been lying there. Somebody poured a drink of cold water through my teeth and placed new cold cloths on my head. A girl was talking quietly. She said I would be all right now, and the transport to the East was due to leave in two days. They were all from camps where young people had been trained in agriculture and forestry, preparing to emigrate to Palestine. She told me she would look after me till I felt better and that we all, young and strong as we were, would survive hard labour in the East. After the war was over, we would go to Palestine together.

She was very kind and I felt her dry the tears that kept running uncontrollably down my face. I wondered whether she would still be so concerned if she knew I had called out for my mother under the first impact of torture.

It seemed like a dream when I heard my mother's voice calling me, but there she was, kissing me and stroking my swollen face. A jab of a needle in my arm and a little later I felt fine, sat up, and carefully opened one eye. My mother was there, unharmed, looking well, and still in her nurse's uniform.

She had been arrested at the hospital, had been taken to the Gestapo headquarters, saw the same two men, and was asked immediately where her grandchild was. She, too, remembered our agreement but, thinking quickly along the same lines I had, replied that friends had taken the child to Switzerland. The two men thanked her for the information and she was sent to the deportation centre without being troubled further.

We were together, alternately laughing and crying. She told me my husband had been taken to the Jewish hospital two days ago with scarlet fever. She had seen him; he was in high spirits despite his illness and sent me his love. He was going to be well looked after by my mother's best friend, a senior sister on the isolation ward. He would be kept there for another month or two. Anything might happen to help him during that time.

Just a few days before her arrest, my mother had managed to buy a Danish passport for herself and my child, but a Jewish boy had been picked up with a similar passport and his own identity card. After that, any Danish identification was automatically suspect and it would not have been safe to make use of it. In any case, there had been no time to bring my daughter back from East Prussia and my mother's dream of disappearing quietly to Denmark came to nothing. We decided therefore to stick to our story if we were asked about the child again.

The days passed quickly and the transport was postponed. I got better, the swelling all over my body subsided, turned black and blue, and then faded. Only shock remained to a certain extent. The days were not too bad. We became very friendly with the boys and girls from the agricultural camps. They were all strong and optimistic and morale was high. Only at nightfall did I become terrified, afraid to sleep, and shaking with fear of being called back to the Gestapo. It happened eventually. I must have been white with terror and lack of sleep. The short trip was agony. Yet when I got to the HQ, there was only an elderly man who was in charge of prisoners at the Jewish hospital, the same man who had warned my mother of the deportation of young women and children.

He spent hours with me, patiently explaining that I could save my mother if I told him where I had hidden my child. He said I would be allowed to take my daughter with me to the East. He guaranteed we would not be separated and that my mother could stay and work at the hospital unmolested. He promised me my mother's life and safety but, he said, "You have to answer to God for what is going to happen to her if you don't answer my question. Her life is in your hands."

Had I not known the experience of a few days earlier, I might have weakened, but as it was I knew our days were probably numbered. We were in the hands of the Gestapo, but my child was not and she had a reasonable chance of being saved. The officer then told me that my tormentors had advocated the deportation of my mother alone and that I be kept until they could make me talk. However, he was their senior and had decided we would be deported together for the sake of my mother of whom he thought the world. He said he would kill me with his own hands if he thought he could thus save my mother's life but, unfortunately, he was not a free agent. It was not in his power to save her, but, he repeated, it was in mine. He informed me we would be deported on 20 April with an extra large transport of young, strong Jews in honour of the Fuehrer's birthday. After that, Germany could be considered free of Jews; the rabble of old and infirm people left behind did not count. They too would soon be eliminated.

And so the day of deportation dawned. It was still dark when we were herded into trucks which took us out of Berlin to a freight train depot. We were unloaded and then started a seemingly endless roll call. Five hundred boys and five hundred girls were there from all the training camps in Germany—strong, healthy, good-looking youths. Truly a proud sacrifice to the Fuehrer! When the roll call was nearly over, another two trucks arrived. Out of them the SS pushed and kicked old men and women, mostly on sticks and crutches, the remnants of two homes for old people. At the last, there were twenty young women with small children. The latter arrivals were not called or counted but loaded straight onto one of the wagons of a long, long cattle train. An SS man came over to us and said to my mother, who was still in the uniform in which she had been arrested, "You better get in with the old people. They might need a nurse."

I tried to follow her but was pushed back into the group of young girls. However, just as my mother was getting into the wagon with the old people, the Gestapo man from the hospital turned up, took her by the arm and led her back to me. To the SS guard he said, "She will be more use to those fit to work." Once more he turned to me and almost pleaded, "Save your mother! Talk.

Tell me where your child is and I'll take your mother back to the hospital in my own car." My mother only shook her head and he turned away and left us.

We were soon loaded into the cattle trucks, fifty boys and fifty girls in each wagon. We sat down on the straw-covered floor, the doors were closed, barred on the outside, and locked. In almost complete darkness, a boy started to play a mouth organ and another a harmonica, first an old Jewish marching song and then the tune that was to become the Israeli national anthem. As the train began to move, we all sang, joined by many young voices in other parts of the train. Rolling east, we sang. It was a sweet and powerful song. We knew we would be free again and show the world that youth would never be defeated, but at what price this future freedom? At what price? We could not have answered that question and we did not ask it then.

# CHAPTER 13

On and on rolled the train; through the day, through the night. When the small toilet bucket in a corner we had screened with straw was near overflowing, we banged against the wooden planks of the cattle truck. To no avail. A giant of a boy battered the wood until it splintered and he managed to break a hole just big enough to empty the bucket. We could thus keep the carriage reasonably clean and aired. In other wagons they were less fortunate and many of the old people suffocated in their own dirt.

Gradually the boys and girls fell asleep. In their youthful health they barely stirred. Nestling against my mother and covered with my warm coat, I too felt drowsy and very tired when I sensed rather than heard the young man next to me shake and sob quietly. He had been so cheerful all day. He resembled a sunburnt Greek god, his profile sharply edged against the gloom. His beautiful voice had carried us from song to song. But now he was crying. I moved away gently from my sleeping mother and put my hand on his curly black head. He started and whispered an apology.

"Tell me why you are crying?" I asked quietly. "Have you left someone behind?"

"That's just it, Daniella, I haven't. For the past three years I have subjected myself to an iron discipline. I was not going to touch a girl until we were settled in Palestine. No girl was going to be tied to me until I could offer her freedom for our children and happiness. And now it is too late. If I had only once kissed a girl. . . . Tell me, what gives you the courage to smile and joke as if you hadn't a care in the world? You have left a husband and child behind and while I felt like crying all day, your voice was so genuinely jubilant. Do you have no regrets because you knew love and fulfillment? Or are you so sure you'll survive and find your family again?" There was no answer to his questions. I could not have explained even to myself why I felt so free and reckless under such hopeless conditions. Perhaps it was because I thought my child safe. Perhaps, because I had been too young for all that heavy responsibility and was now, regardless of outcome, unable to do more. Yet, somehow, I felt responsible even for the despair of this young stranger and had to make an effort to share my peace of mind. So I gently turned his head until his face, wet with tears, touched mine. I kissed his salty tears away and felt his fresh breath on my face. It was no sacrifice to kiss his soft young lips. I imagined it was my husband I was holding and felt him relax like a little boy after a nightmare.

"You darling, darling," he whispered, and his husky voice seemed already far away in the land of dreams. He slept peacefully all night, his curly head on my arm.

He is dead now and I don't even know his name. But does it matter? Dead, too, are all the other four hundred and ninety-nine strong young men of our transport. I wonder how many of them had never kissed a girl, had never lived at all?

The train slowed down and stopped abruptly. Dogs barked, men shouted commands, iron bars screeched, and sliding doors creaked. It seemed an eternity till our wagon was opened. A few boys and girls who had been jammed against the door fell out and the ones next to them were roughly pulled out by SS men. Within seconds we were lined up in blinding sunlight. There was no station, no platform, no houses, no trees; only yellow mud trampled hard by our predecessors. There were a few patches of tough grass and nettles of the most poisonous green I had ever seen. Somebody whispered we were in Poland. My mother stood beside me and held my hand. We noticed suddenly that all men had been taken from our ranks and were standing with the men from the rest of the train some distance away. At the other side of our group were the old people.

An SS guard barked a command: "Stand to attention! The doctor is going to examine you all."

A tall, dark man in the uniform of an SS officer appeared and went slowly through the lines of prisoners. Not until much later did we learn that this young SS officer in his elegantly tailored uniform and shining boots was Dr. Joseph Mengele, chief doctor of Auschwitz-Birkenau concentration camp. He was present at the arrival of every transport from every country in Europe and was in charge of the "selection."

Born into a wealthy family—his father was an industrialist in a small Bavarian town and the farm machine factory is still owned and run by the Mengeles—Joseph was a privileged and gifted child. As a young man, he first studied philosophy and later medicine. Always involved in right-wing politics, he was fascinated by Hitler's oratory and joined the Nazi Storm Troopers in October 1933. He soon adopted the Nazi doctrine of Aryan superiority and got involved in research to find proof that defects of race are inherited in racial genetic make-up.

While he amassed honours in peaceful research, he was not keen to pull his weight when the war broke out. Transferred then from a post as health inspector for the SS to the Viking Division, composed of Scandinavian volunteers, and later to the SS infantry on the Eastern front, he was afraid to fight in Russia. Due to his SS connections and patronage, he managed to get himself transferred to Auschwitz where he was soon appointed Chief Medical Officer. From then on he was entitled to kill or save hundreds of thousands of men, women, and children. Now, at our first encounter, he looked at each girl in turn and said, "Worker—to the left." He stopped in front of a middle-aged woman who, like my mother, held her daughter's hand. "You need an easier life, mother. To the right."

She didn't understand, did not let go of her daughter's hand and pleaded, "I'm only forty. I'm strong and I can work. Leave me with my child!"

"Forty is too old," the doctor said and beckoned to a guard. The tough SS man pushed her into the group of old people who tottered under the impact. The doctor passed on to the crying girl: "Worker—to the left." And on: "Worker—to the left."

Another fifteen or twenty joined the workers. He stopped again and fixed his piercing eyes on an undersized, young girl with a beautiful thin face, huge, dark, luminous eyes, and a slight humpback. "Too weak, needs good, long rest. To the right." She went over to the old people.

He had nearly reached us. I whispered desperately, "Mommy, say you are thirty-five!" She looked younger. The SS doctor had reached my mother. He looked at me. "Is this your daughter?"

"Yes," said my mother. "How old are you?" I kicked my mother lightly. "I am forty-one," she said. He hesitated a moment. "Senior nursing sister?" "Yes," said my mother. "Worker—to the left." He went on and on. Nearly all the young girls from the agricultural camps joined us. All mothers with young children went with the old people. The husband of one of these women had an artificial leg. He went with the old people and young mothers. His wife was sent back to the workers. He lifted his small child and waved with his free hand to his wife. The child laughed and waved too. Then we were told to start marching. I can't remember how long we walked through the desolate country. The most striking feature was the poisonous green grass and a few stunted trees. We passed innumerable watch-towers, all manned by armed guards pointing their machine guns in our direction. All around us were armed SS guards and their huge German Shepherd dogs yapping round our feet.

At last we stopped and were counted in front of an open gate in a barbed wire enclosure, studded with watch-towers. Over the entrance, in large letters, were the words, *Arbeit Macht Frei*— Work Liberates. We passed through the gate and through a neat, clean square of painted wooden barracks, surrounded by beds of struggling, undernourished flowers, and were herded into a huge barrack with a mud floor. The wooden doors closed behind us and, again, we were in semi-darkness.

An SS guard went past and told us to roll up our sleeves and to hand in identity cards and passports. When he took mine, I asked when we were getting them back. With a nasty grin he answered, "You don't need passports where you are going."

There was no doubt about the meaning of his words and there, in the dark, was born my stubborn determination to survive our enemies and torturers. Slowly, we were pushed forward towards a fire in an open grate. Behind it sat a man with a long needle in his hand. He turned the needle in the flame until it was red-hot and then stuck it into the forearm of his victim. Again into the fire and back into sizzling skin. Surprisingly, there was no sound, save a quick intake of breath or a short gasp. Nobody spoke and the silence, darkness, the fire in the grate, and the smell of burning skin reminded me of stories I had read of human sacrifices to ancient gods.

The first girls came past us to take their place at the end of the queue again, and, nursing their sore arms, showed us what the red-hot needle had accomplished: a big, long number across the centre of the forearm and a triangle underneath: a tattoo. My turn came. An SS man immediately twisted my arm back, almost dislocating my shoulder in the process. I became number 51459. Much later I learned what these figures meant: fifty-one thousand prisoners had come here before us and almost forty-five thousand had already died to make room for us. That number did not include the old people, mothers with children, and the weak and the sick who were never tattooed at all. In the meantime, we were branded like cattle.

On either side of us SS guards lined up. "Get ready for delousing! Clothes off!" their officer shouted. Nobody moved. The first SS men advanced menacingly on the frightened girls in the front row and, grabbing their dresses, tore off their clothes until the girls stood naked and shivering with fear and shame.

"I can't face this," my mother whispered. "I'd rather die. Let's get out of it." She pulled a small bottle and a hypodermic syringe from her pocket but before she could get the needle into the bottle an SS man hit her across the wrist with his revolver. The syringe and bottle dropped onto the hard ground and broke. To make doubly sure, the man ground his heel on the splintered glass.

My mother's clothes were torn off, but not before she had withdrawn her hairpins, allowing her long black hair to cover her like a silky coat down to her thighs. I stripped my dress off before the men could get their hands on me and felt no shame. We had to parade through the double line of leering guards to a row of chairs and there the "delousing" began.

Our hair was cut off and our heads shaved so close to the skin that our skulls were grazed. We then had to lift our arms and the hair under the arm pits was shaved. Last and worst indignity of all, we were hoisted on to the chairs and had to submit to the shaving of pubic hair while the guards looked on with sneers and obscene remarks. This went on till late at night.

We were dazed with cold, shock, and hunger. The last sandwiches we had been given by the nurses of the Jewish hospital in Berlin had been shared out and eaten before we were unloaded. Two naked bulbs illuminated our sorry spectacle. I did not recognize any of the girls with shaven heads. I could not find my mother and called out for her, frightened suddenly, like a child alone in the dark. She was right beside me. I had not recognized even her brown, burning eyes in the white face. She looked like death and I turned quickly away to find some consolation in the round, healthy limbs, proud young breasts, and the stubborn, contemptuous faces of the girls of my own age.

At last we were given some clothes. Each girl received a pair of pants, many without elastic, a tattered, faded summer frock, mostly too large and too long. Some even got wooden sandals. Rags though they were, it was something to cover our nakedness and to hide us from the untiring, leering inspection of our guards.

At the end of the barrack, double doors opened and we were marched through a floodlit camp past many wooden huts. Between the huts we could see electric barbed wire fences and watch-towers. Outside the fence, floodlit too, were brick buildings with tall chimneys smoking furiously, often emitting flames that seemed to shoot up to the starry sky. An evil, sickly-sweet smell combined with acrid fumes assailed us from their direction and stung our eyes.

"These are our most productive factories," grinned one of the guards. "Working day and night shifts, and if they don't purify the air here, they certainly clean up the rest of the Fatherland."

Except for the guards talking and laughing, the deadly silence around us was complete. Outside one of the long buildings we were stopped and counted once more. Then, admitted in twos through the entrance, we were met just inside the door by a young woman in a lovely dressing gown, high-heeled slippers, beautifully curled black hair, and carefully made-up face. She had a notebook and pencil in her hands and a stick under her arm. With an amazingly deep voice that belied her feminine appearance, she raved at us to get in quickly and to keep the cold out.

We moved along a narrow passage, almost dark, on either side of which were double-tiered bunks of bricks, some covered with a little straw, most of them bare. We moved a bit further along and heard the doors close behind us and then all hell broke loose. Inhuman voices screeched, whined, and shouted from the bunks around us. Shaved skulls and death-like skeletons shot out and peered at us from all sides. Fleshless claws stretched out and touched our clothes, faces, and arms and an unbearable stench of unwashed, diseased bodies enveloped us. An Inferno! For the rest of my life I have had this vision of hell indelibly imprinted on my mind.

Rapidly we were pushed into vacant bunks, ten of us in each tier where there was barely room for three. My arms round my mother's shivering shoulders, I stretched out as far as was possible on the cold bricks. Ten human sardines lying on our sides, unable to move or turn around, we spent the rest of the night in fitful slumber, interrupted again and again by screams born of nightmares, by hollow coughing along the passage, by cold and by hunger.

# CHAPTER 14

Midway between seconds and eternity we were roused by the deep voice of the house Capo in charge of us: "Roll call! Get up you filthy Bs! Roll call!" She went past the bunks, holding a handkerchief over her nose with one hand and, with the other, hitting immobile backs with her stick. Most of the poor skeletons were galvanized into movement but there were a few who did not respond. Beaten and shoved, they fell off their bunks in untidy heaps, received a last kick from the high-heeled slipper and lay still. A few had escaped the roll call, cold, hunger and degradation. They were quite dead. They were left where they had fallen; the living scrambled over their bodies, out of the hut into a cold, dark April morning just before dawn.

For two hours we stood in lines, clapping our hands and each others' backs in an effort to get warm. At last an SS woman, accompanied by two guards and two dogs, came along and counted our ranks. The woman was very young and fair, her face expressionless. She asked the house Capo for a report. The Capo, or Blockova, as she was commonly known, reported the number of dead with a curious expression of satisfaction as one might expect on reporting a great achievement. The SS woman nodded, marked a list, and called out tattoo numbers. I had to look at my arm before I realized I had been called.

The roll call over, we were allowed back into the hut,

received a chunk of bread each and a chipped enamel bowl containing a lukewarm, black liquid—"tea." The bread was to be the ration for the day but we were so hungry, we wolfed it down there and then. My mother and I shared one bowl of the dark brew and kept the other under our bunk to wash our hands after the old inmates had been marched off to work. So far, we had seen no water.

We sat on our bunks wondering what was going to happen next and tried to understand what we had so far seen. We speculated about the factories, the dead who had been removed, the SS woman, the big, solid crystals in the bread. Many of us were desperate to get to a toilet but didn't know where to go. We were not permitted, under threat of being shot, to leave our hut until the Blockova came back from the gate where she was signing out the workers in her charge. When she did return, she herded us to the lavatories, a long building with frames for doors, but no doors and no roof. The conveniences consisted of rough wooden planks laid over seemingly bottomless pits where rows of women perched precariously like sparrows on telephone wires.

Tripping delicately through mud and puddles, the Blockova next pointed at the washrooms, another long hut with concrete floors and rows of taps. There she left us with the admonition that we were to be back in our barracks in ten minutes "or else." We found to our dismay that in the whole washroom only one tap was working and it was guarded by a huge Polish woman.

The girls had politely made room for my mother to have a wash first, but when she tried to get to the tap, the woman pushed her back forcefully so that she landed in my arms. In Polish, accompanied by violent gestures, the Pole gave us to understand that this was her domain. Nobody used this tap unless they paid first. One bread ration, margarine, or sausage was the privilege of a wash, half a ration for a drink. I tried to reason with her. After all, she was a prisoner like us. However, when she advanced on me, tight fists ready to strike, and when my mother tried timidly to pull me away, all self-control left me and I hit the woman across her broad face with the flat of my hand. She stumbled and slipped on the wet floor and, getting gingerly to her feet, removed herself cowed.

We all had a wash. There was no soap and no towels. We got back into our rags soaking wet but refreshed and I had learned my first lesson: unless you answered violence with violence, you were doomed.

Back in our barrack, we saw the Blockova through the open door of her room preening in front of a mirror, intent on making up her face and pinning up her shiny, black curls. As she paid no attention to us, I decided to have a look around the camp and left my mother with the other girls.

The camp seemed deserted. A warm sun burned the caked mud and, except for the guards on the watch-towers, there was not a soul around, no sound of birds or any other living creature. Absolute silence. Even the factories and their tall, red chimneys were dead. No smoke.

At last, turning a corner, I saw an old woman sitting with her back to the wall of a hut, warming her thin shoulders and claw-like hands in the sun. Her head was shaved, her wrinkled little face seemed almost blind but she could see for she motioned me to sit down. I sat down beside her and introduced myself. She said her name was Ruth and told me she knew what transport I had arrived with. She smiled a little. "We know everything here. Nobody tells us, but we know. We even know when our friends are going to die just by looking in their eyes." I felt uncomfortable and she guessed it immediately. "Don't worry, you'll live. You have the strength and the willpower. In two or three weeks' time you may be a skeleton, but you are a fighter. I can tell you will not lie down and die willingly. Look at me. You wouldn't think I was nineteen years old, would you? But it's true, my nineteenth birthday was two days ago."

I felt myself flush and turned my face away. An "old woman" indeed. What had they done to her here?

"I'm sorry you feel embarrassed. Don't. I am finished with this rotten world. There's no future for me. My mother, father, and little sister were killed and there is nothing for me to look forward to. Don't mind me though. You are so young!" That from a little old woman of nineteen. In spite of myself, tears were welling up, hot and stinging in my eyes.

"I don't want to live, but may I help you and give you some hints that may come in useful?" Ruth had been in Birkenau, the death camp, for three months. On arrival, she had been separated from her parents and little sister and grouped with the workers. Only one woman over forty, a tall and beautiful woman, had been allowed to enter the camp with them. A few days ago, that woman had run from a dog the guard had set on her and was torn to shreds. There was not enough left to bury. Her name was Paula Raphael and, if I ever met her son, would I tell him that she was dead but that she had spoken of him, his young wife, and child.

Paula, my lovely mother-in-law! I swallowed hard, but said nothing. I wanted to know all there was to know.

Lesson No. 1: Don't ever run away if an SS dog is after you. Stand still, even if he has his fangs in you and he'll let go.

The "factories" were gas chambers where whole transports of old people and mothers with children were given a piece of soap and a towel and then driven into huge rooms with innumerable shower heads in the ceiling. When the doors closed, gas instead of water poured in through the sprays. After a few minutes, the bodies were dropped through trap doors into the crematorium and burned. Night after night the chimneys belched forth their black clouds of smoke. A special commando of prisoners served in the gas chambers, removing valuables, rings, gold teeth and the like from the dead, and after a term of service, were gassed themselves and replaced by a new lot of prisoners. Once the commando was chosen, it never came into contact with the rest of the camp again.

The Capos and Blockovas were prisoners like ourselves but after years of concentration camp life, they had learned, if they survived, to be tough, cruel, and thoughtless. Often they were just a shade more cruel than their masters. Thus, they were a privileged class. Most of them were Slovaks, some were German, non-Jewish prisoners who wore a green triangle on their dress, indicating they were criminals. Others were professional prostitutes who had refused to do war work in factories outside. They had been sent to the camp to be "rehabilitated." However, here they played with human lives and at the same time carried on their profession with SS guards and passing German soldiers and, of course, developed all the perversities under the sun.

If the Blockova kept back half your food ration, you had no redress. She was quite entitled to kill you. She could torture you or put your name and number on the list of those no longer able to work and so detail you for the gas chambers.

Although officially you were entitled to nothing but the rags you were given on entering the camp, nobody turned a hair if you were clever enough to "organize" decent clothes as long as they were marked with your number, red triangle (for political prisoners) and a large red cross painted on your back. In fact, if, by stealing, you managed to look clean and well dressed, you were sure to get better and easier work. Ruth did not know how to go about getting new clothes. But she knew that Capos all had friends among the prisoners who worked in the stores where clothes from newly arrived transports were sorted and dispatched to Germany's bombed cities. You could change your rations for clothes on the camp's black market but Ruth had always been too hungry to save as much as a crumb. Now that she was no longer hungry, she also had no desire for a pretty dress. "Does it matter in a mass burial how you are dressed? If your clothes are worth looking at, they are stripped before your body is cold anyway."

Ruth told me that the SS woman who had taken our first roll call this morning was Irma Grese who was only seventeen years old. She had been recruited by her lover, an SS officer of unusual cruelty and perversity. Irma was getting a thorough training in the art of torture and killing.

I also learned that the crystals in the bread were a chemical which, given in quantity, completely suppressed any normal sex instincts and menstruation in women, and made prisoners dull and easier to handle.

Ruth closed her eyes and her head sunk forward. I felt she had, for my benefit, spent her last energy talking. I got up and apologized for tiring her out. "I better get back to my hut now, but I'll be back tomorrow with some bread for you," I said optimistically.

She smiled a sweet, tired smile. "You have to eat all the bread you can get merely to exist. Thank you just the same, but I won't be here tomorrow.

"Where are you going?" I asked foolishly. Ruth grinned happily but did not reply. Instead she said in a voice so low I had to bend down to hear her at all:

"Goodbye, good luck, and my love to your mother. She must be a wonderful woman. You are so lucky to have her around to keep you alive." Not until much later did I realize I had not mentioned my mother. But there was much I had to learn before I knew from experience all the things one understands when one is about to die.

As I turned the corner to our barrack, I saw the girls were lined up and a big, fat SS officer was strutting up and down in front of them. The Blockova jumped at me like a cat pouncing on a mouse, grabbed me by the shoulders and propelled me forward. She was much smaller than I, but it did not occur to me to resist. Just as she was going to shove me into the last row, the SS man called to her to bring me to him. He looked me up and down and rumbled, "Are you one of this transport?"

"Yes."

"Hm, from Berlin?"

"Yes."

"Is that so? I'm from Berlin myself. Have a soft spot for girlies from our great capital. What were you doing? Playing truant already?"

"No, I just walked around to have a look at the camp."

"Adventurous type. Liked what you saw?"

"Of course not. It's the most evil place I ever dreamed could exist!"

"Well, at least you are honest. Tell you what," he said jovially, "made up my mind to give the girls from Berlin a chance. You are a good-looking healthy lot. I'll make you a special working commando, an example to the rest of the camp, with uniforms—say, striped dresses, aprons, headscarves, blue or red—and double rations. How would you like to be a Capo?" he asked me.

I said I'd hate it. "From what I have seen and heard of Capos and Blockovas so far, they are a despicable lot." Our Blockova turned as red as a turkey's neck.

The officer gave a deep, rumbling laugh. "That's enough of your cheek. One day in camp and no respect yet? I'll teach you. You are the Capo of the Berlin Commando and you better do well. Keep fit, clean and healthy and you won't regret it. By Jove, if you don't make these girls work, you'll have to answer for what's coming to you. Off with you now! Get deloused, new clothes, double rations and tomorrow morning you'll collect vegetables for the camp kitchen. That's your first assignment and then we'll see again." He turned to the Blockova. "If you don't treat these girls well, you'll go digging trenches. I'll ask if they have any complaints. So you better behave. They are under my protection." He explained he was the labour leader and repeated unnecessarily that he, too, came from Berlin. He flicked his whip and disappeared. I have forgotten his name now, but he was as good as his word.

We were led to the sauna. Only nothing here worked as, I presume, it works in Finland. The steam was so hot it scalded our skins. Fortunately, this ordeal was of such short duration no serious damage was done. The water after the steam was icy and, as we had each been given a piece of soap, we made the most of it and covered our bodies with a rich, if peculiar smelling, lather. That done, we discovered the water had ceased to run. Probably a little practical joke of the sauna Capo. We had no towels and our old rags had been removed. All we could do was to scrape the soap off as best we could and leave the rest to dry and cake on our skins. At last, prisoners brought in heaps of grey, blue-striped dresses of a heavy, warm material, blue-checkered headscarves, aprons, and a pair of leather sandals for all of us.

Back in our barrack, we were given a bowl of soup, an extra bread ration with a piece of margarine, a spot of beetroot jam, and a piece of sausage. The soup was the most peculiar dish I had ever eaten in my life, but one got used to this conglomeration of potato peelings, greenery, odd pieces of Turkish delight or caramels, and even sodden rolls of bank notes swimming in it at times. We felt heaps better, warm now, adequately, even neatly dressed, and no longer hungry. For the rest of the day we were left in peace except for another roll call after the return of the workers.

The Blockova was now ingratiatingly friendly and told us of her early days in the camp. She had arrived in winter before there were any huts. The whole of Auschwitz and Birkenau were nothing but vast fields of deep, yellow mud, fenced in by barbed wire.

Just before her arrival it had been a camp for Russian prisoners of war and she still found innumerable bodies half-buried in the mud. For days she existed and slept in the open. During the day, she and others of her transport collected and buried the dead, decaying bodies. Later they carried stones, bricks, and timber many miles to build our huts. The barracks were then built in record time by male prisoners, none of whom were now alive. Of her transport only she and two of her sisters survived. She made no secret of the fact that they had achieved this by stealing the clothes and the bread rations of their unfortunate fellow prisoners who were too weak to fight. I tried to imagine what she had gone through to find extenuating circumstances for what she had done, but it was impossible. The sight of her well-fed, well-groomed, self-satisfied face made me shudder with horror.

Just before dark she distributed horse blankets, one to every two or three girls. There were a few more bunks available and we spent a slightly better night than the one before.

The following morning after roll call, we were marched off to the gate where a yellow armband with "CAPO" printed in large, black letters was pinned to my right sleeve. We were then given baskets and an escort of four guards with the inevitable German Shepherd dogs at their heels. After being counted, we left through the gate with the words *Work Liberates* above it. We were marched into a fresh, sunny morning, through poisonous green fields and the illusion of a certain freedom, to collect "vegetables," that is, nettles for the camp kitchen. There was no scarcity of nettles in that area. In fact, I have never known of any other place in the world where there was such an abundance of nettles growing to man's height. All day we picked nettles, and in no time were covered with irritating, burning blisters all over. It was agony at first but one got used to nettle stings, too, in time.

The guards did not trouble us. They had been told we were

under the special protection of the labour leader. They teased us for a while, calling us the "Berlin Elite" or the "Beauties of the Kurfuerstendamm," but they soon got bored and gave it up when we didn't respond.

In the afternoon we returned to camp, roll call, a wash, and double rations, but before we had to turn in for the night, I took my extra ration and walked round the block to find Ruth. She wasn't where I had met her the previous day and I went into her hut where I was met by a dragon of a Blockova. Just as she was going to turn on me, brandishing a stick, she saw the *CAPO* on my sleeve. So she checked herself and listened to my question. "Ruth, Ruth? Oh, do you mean that useless B that was always sitting in the sun? She kicked the bucket last night. Buried her this morning, good riddance! Had her on my hands far too long. She was always moping about and refused to work from the very beginning. No interest in anything. Well, she'll rot in her grave now for long enough."

I turned on my heels and ran back to our barrack, shaken to the core. But I didn't mention Ruth even to my mother who knew me so well; she understood without my saying a word that I had seen a ghost. Nor could I bring myself to enlighten the others about the "factories" or anything else I had learned. They'd find out soon enough. Just now, they were so happy about the apparent consideration of the SS labour officer and his order to our Blockova—the woman in charge of our barrack—to be friendly "or else," they were laughing and fooling around. I knew that we would not laugh again for a long, long time. A few more hours or days without that dreadful knowledge of realities would therefore not hurt the girls of my transport. So I wiped away the tears surreptitiously and listened to their excited chatter, to somebody aping the labour officer's sonorous voice, "I'm from Berlin myself. Have a soft spot for the girlies from our great capital . . . " and to their uninhibited laughter.

# CHAPTER 15

A few more days passed, one like the other. Sometimes the roll call took hours and, on one occasion, we stood lined up all through the night because somebody had tried to escape and didn't return from outside work. However, no escape was successful in those early days. The prisoner was always tracked down by the dogs or, if she got far or even managed to get beyond the radius of guards and watch-towers, the Polish population invariably handed her over to the SS and Gestapo. The runaways were, at that time, always Jewish prisoners. German inmates were too placid and well-fed to bother, conscientious objectors and Bible students believed in the inevitability of their martyrdom, and gypsies were too frightened. The Polish population could recognize a Jew or Jewess no matter how well disguised, and if they hated the Germans, they hated the Jews more. They were most helpful in the total elimination of their Jewish problem. Thus, sooner or later, the culprit was returned dead or alive, and if the latter, was publicly tortured and hanged.

The whole camp had to look on and SS guards went through our ranks to make sure nobody turned their eyes from this ghastly spectacle. I got into the habit of standing with my eyes staring straight ahead but seeing nothing. My brain refused to take in what I must have seen. The roll call ended when the hanging was over. During this night-long roll call, my mother collapsed. She had not been well for days, was white as a sheet and very weak. There was no medicine unless one went to the camp hospital, but once there, there was little or no chance of surviving. The patient might, on occasion, be treated but even if she recovered, she was generally sent to the gas chambers at the weekly selection from the sick bay. Knowing this, we bullied and threatened the Blockova into concealing my mother in a bunk the next morning and reporting her as essential for cleaning work in the barrack so that she would not have to go out to work.

When we returned that night, she came out for roll call but was too weak to stand up and we carried and held her until the guard had counted us and moved on. Then we lowered her gently on the ground until whistles were blown and we could disperse. During the night she tossed and turned and shivered although we had collected four blankets to cover her. In the morning she was so ill, not even black tea would stay down. She had not been able to eat her rations for the past three days.

I left her with a very heavy heart. Up to this day we had filled our baskets with nettles in no time at all and then sat down in the grass doing nothing, preserving our strength for things to come. Even with double rations we were beginning to get thinner and weaker. Still, in comparison with the other prisoners, we looked fit.

Always good at relaxing and doing nothing, I just could not sit still today and time did not seem to pass. When another Capo with her commando came by and yelled at us to get up and work, it was a relief to put out my tongue and tell her to mind her own business. "Leave my girls alone," I called over at the top of my voice, looking at her group of poor skeletons who could hardly drag one foot in front of the other. "We are not all murderers. My girls are going to be alive when you have to answer for all you have killed."

The Capo shook her fist at me and one of our guards said, "Now you've done it. Can't you count your blessings and keep your trap shut? That one is the most notorious Capo in Birkenau. She'll report you and when you return to camp, you'll lose your armband and I'd be surprised if you are still alive a week from today. We will probably go on extensive exercises, if not the Russian front, for allowing you to be lazy."

I was too worried about my mother to listen and did not care, but, right enough, when we reached the gate in the afternoon, a voice shouted, "Berlin Commando halt! . . . Capo, fall out!" I stepped out and an SS woman tore the band off my sleeve. To the accompanying guard she said, "No. 51459 gets no rations tonight. Report to her House Capo: no sausage, no margarine, no jam for three days. Half bread ration only and two weeks hard labour. Berlin Commando, march!"

The guard handed me over to our Blockova with his instructions and I slipped past her before she could open her mouth to see my mother. But my mother wasn't there. Her blankets were neatly folded on her bunk and there was no sign of her anywhere. I ran back to the Blockova. "Blockova, where is my mother?" Like the guard earlier, she said, "Now you've done it, you stupid B! Don't you know when you're well off? Your mother is all right, she'll survive you now. She has been chosen to go to the sewing room in SS staff quarters in Auschwitz. They have tiled bathrooms there, single beds, good clothes, and plenty of food from the SS kitchen." I did not believe her.

The SS had a well-known trick. From time to time they went through the camp after workers had left to take weak and sick prisoners to "Block 24." That dreaded and notorious barrack was the collection centre for the gas chambers. There the condemned were kept up to two weeks until the required number was complete. Once here, there was no hope of escape. The victims were fully aware of their imminent end and their demented screams haunted our dreams at night.

Most prisoners who were left behind in the camp now hid

under straw mattresses or in the eaves of the roof as soon as SS approached. Therefore, in order to find as many victims as possible with a minimum delay and fuss, SS administration had developed a new system. They produced a list of vacancies at other, better camps, desirable posts in factories or staff quarters, ordered the Blockovas to find prisoners to fill these vacancies and left. Needless to say, there were many volunteers, and when the SS returned half an hour later, their required number was waiting. It took a long time before the truth trickled through and a rumour went round that these appointments did not exist and that all volunteers had ended up in Block 24, and subsequently "gone up the chimney," the expression used by the SS and hardened camp personnel for those gassed and cremated. There was no way of finding out for sure whether my mother had shared their fate. It was no more possible to enter Block 24, a barbed-wire stronghold within the camp, than it was to fly to the moon. The condemned were completely isolated and no word or note ever found its way out. Nothing mattered to me after that. I had brought this fate on my mother. If she was dead, I had helped to kill her!

The girls tried to press some of their rations on me that night, but the mere thought of food choked me. The following day I went out with the hard labour corps. We worked from morning till night carrying rocks and digging trenches until we dropped. Night after night we carried our dead back with us. If twenty went out in the morning, no more than ten returned. The weakest died and the rest were assisted in dying by unmerciful kicks and beatings handed out by brutal guards and Capos. I learned much later that no more than half our number were supposed to return to camp at night, and if not enough died of their own accord, the guards had a last resort. They dropped their caps or drinking bottles some distance from our place of work and sent a number of prisoners off to retrieve them. As soon as the poor wretches had gone a few yards, they were shot down like clay pigeons, or worse, torn to pieces by the dogs. At the gate the guards reported that three, four or five prisoners had tried to escape and had to be killed. I found out too that the guards of these hard labour commandos got a bonus for every dead prisoner they returned to camp, a day added to their annual leave and an extra cigarette ration.

Apart from the odd kick, nobody ever touched me, probably because I was still the strongest of our sorry lot. At night I dropped into my bunk and slept, too tired to even collect my half bread ration. Often in the morning, I found crumbs of sausage and margarine almost devoured by rats, remains of rations my friends had left beside me. In that short period of hard labour, I had grown indifferent to rats, comfort or discomfort. I functioned like an automaton whose clockwork was slowly running down.

My punishment ended on the morning of 19 May 1943 after exactly two weeks. At the gate I was called out and the labour leader asked me if I had learned my lesson. There was no need to answer. He returned me personally to our Blockova with the instructions that I was to have a hot bath, delousing, clean clothes, and double rations once again. I was to have the day off and rejoin my group the next morning. We were to be incorporated into an "elite commando," the White Caps, so called because of their white headscarves. They were detailed to sort out clothes and belongings of all newly arrived transports.

So far, this commando had consisted of the prettiest girls from Eastern Europe who had been in the camp a long time. They held all the key positions and regarded prisoners of all other nationalities with contempt. They were physically much tougher than most prisoners from western countries. They had become used to a hard climate and harder conditions and they had survived many ordeals. They had, by now, lost almost all scruples and conscience: we newcomers had not. For that they despised us and exploited our vulnerability.

The steam bath and delousing was a great ordeal this time. I was very weak, and more than once nearly fainted. The Sauna Capo again turned off the water before I got a chance to wash off the soap and I no longer saw any humour in her pranks. The palms of my hands and my arms were grazed and raw from carrying rocks and the strong carbolic soap burned and irritated my skin. For the third time since my arrival barely a month ago, my hair was shaved and my scalp felt sore.

When I walked out into the blinding sunlight, I experienced for the first time a sensation which was to repeat itself many a time. All feeling of despair and exhaustion left me suddenly. I felt weightless, no longer earthbound and had the sensation I could fly if I wanted to. At the same time, an urgency I did not yet understand drove me to rush back to our barrack. It was nearly midday. The sun was high up in the sky; the camp was quiet and deserted. There was no sound.

The Blockova was waiting for me with double rations. She inspected my clean dress, apron, and white headscarf and said, "You look a bit of a scarecrow, don't you? You'd better start eating again if you want to keep up with the White Caps." With unexpected friendliness she added, "Look here, you just have to be smart if you want to survive. That dress is too long. I'll pin it up for you and give you some cotton. You can shorten it before the others get back."

I wondered vaguely where she managed to get such treasures like pins, needles, and thread, but I was restless and she kept telling me to stop fidgeting. I felt there was something I had to do, and suddenly I knew. Almost like a third person, a surprised observer, I heard myself say, "Leave the dress just now, please. I must get to the sauna to see the new transport from Berlin." I did not tell the Blockova that my husband and child were with that tranport, but I knew.

She looked at me with a mixture of contempt and fear. "Have you taken leave of your senses? There is no new transport today. I would be the first to know. Blockovas are always given a few hours' warning to make room for new arrivals." I said nothing and spent the rest of the afternoon turning up the hem of my dress with shaking hands.

My rations remained untouched; I could not eat. Innumerable times I felt a compulsion to jump up and run to the sauna but all that afternoon I fought that impulse. As the day wore on, my certainty grew but the Blockova was watching me in such a way, I was beginning to doubt my sanity.

The girls of my transport came back from work and, immediately surrounding me, shook my hands, and kissed me. They had not changed. Still full of hope and vitality, they told me I would soon be strong once more. They would see to that, and we would go to Palestine soon. Then they buzzed off to get their food rations and only my two bunkmates stayed with me, their arms round my shoulders. When we were alone I told them of the new transport and added that my husband and child had arrived too. Like the Blockova, they did not believe me and Susan said gently, "As far as I know, there is no transport today but even if there were, Daniella, your husband might be with it but not your child. Haven't you told us your baby is safe? You know that better than we do. Come on, pet, eat your sausage and calm down. Two weeks' hard labour was no joke but it is over now. Please, for your own sake and for the sake of your mother, you must eat. You know your mother would have died happily if she knew you were going to live. You owe it to her."

I made an effort but still could not eat and the whistles for roll call stopped all further attempts. As soon as roll call was over and the girls were filing back into barracks, I slipped away and ran all the way to the sauna. The doors were locked and there was no sound. I waited and waited. Susan came looking for me. She put her arm around me and told me to come back with her to our bunk. It was getting dark, she said, and it was time to go to sleep. I hardly listened, and eventually she shook her head sadly and went back to her younger sister, alone.

It was quite dark and the camp was floodlit when the sauna doors opened and the new transport came out. Among the first were the two girls I had met in prison in Ludwigshafen. Shaved and branded, their spirits were, nevertheless, as high as ever. When they recognized me. they fell round my neck and cried, "Are you still here, Dannie? Do you know the layout of this dump yet? We'll have to get out of here smartish like. We'll make plans tomorrow. If we three can't escape, nobody can."

They suddenly sobered and Hannie looked round and asked, "Where is Frau Unger? She said she was your teacher at Domestic Sciences in Berlin and you were her favourite pupil. Have you not seen her yet? She took your child from your husband before the men and women were separated and promised to bring her straight to you. She felt we women could look after the children better than these wretched men. Frau Unger had your daughter and her little stepson by their hands. An SS man demeaned himself to carry her luggage. Then we lost sight of her somehow, but ours was such a big transport. I think she must have arrived here with the first batch of women and children."

The last words I heard as if through a thick fog. I turned and ran, ran, and ran: To the electric wire, to peace, oblivion, death. Oh God, the gas chambers are belching smoke and I am enveloped by thick, black clouds of it. The acrid stench of burning flesh is choking me. Let me get out of it, please, just the last stretch! But there was no end to this long road, no kind God to take me by the hand and lead me. I did not make it. The world reeled and vanished in absolute darkness. I fell and knew no more.

# CHAPTER 16

The awakening was slow and painful. Susan and her sister Lorna were bending over me, pouring hot tea down my throat. I swallowed greedily and couldn't remember what had happened to me. The Blockova came along and fed me with small pieces of chocolate, undreamed-of luxury. Somebody said, "Get up, lazy bones. You've slept through and missed roll call already. Time to move out with the White Caps. We are going to work in Canada."

The Blockova anticipated my incredulous query and shrugged her shoulders. "Why is it named Canada? Probably because of the barrack's multi-racial contents or perhaps workers have such soft living conditions there. She drove the girls out in her usual rough manner, although she had given up hitting us and even seemed to have some affection for the prisoners in her care. When I passed her, she pulled me back into her room, a cubbyhole she had all to herself, and said, "Listen, Daniella, I have sent word to the men's camp to have your husband taken to the barracks where you are going to work. This is your first day there, so be careful. If you have the Dutch SS woman as a guard, you'll be all right and can spend some time with your man. She'll turn a blind eye. But should the guard be changed today for some reason, you'll have to give it a miss and try meeting him tomorrow. My sister will keep you right. She is in the Canada Commando too. Another bit of advice: Organize some decent clothes for yourself and your husband. My sister will give you number tapes and red paint to fix his number and the red cross on the back of the jacket. The chances are he will get a better kind of job if he is well dressed. I'll explain the system some other time. Get out now or you'll be late." Only when she mentioned my husband did the events of the previous night come back to me; but something had changed. My heart was hard and heavy like the rocks I had carried but I did not want to die any more. Suffering would come later. Now, I moved out with the others like a machine. At the gate we were told by the labour leader that he would deal personally with any one of us who looked or spoke to any of the men we might see around the barracks we were to work in. He made it clear that an ordinary death was too good for a prisoner who had any dealings with the other sex.

A tall, fair SS woman strode alongside us and we moved off through another gate into the men's camp of Birkenau. The road into that camp was lined with male Capos waving and leering at us. It was surprising to see that nobody seemed to take the slightest notice of the warning we had just been given. The old core of the White Caps gaily waved to the men who threw packets of cigarettes, sugar, and chocolates which the girls in front of us caught and quite openly stuffed into their apron bibs and dresses. The SS woman laughed and joked with the male prisoners, calling them affectionately "lazy Bs" and "filthy pigs" and graciously accepted a large box of cigarettes and a bottle of French perfume from the tallest prisoner. He was a German criminal with an armband inscribed *Lager-Aeltester*—Camp Senior—on his sleeve. She received a few more packages which she handed over to some of us to carry for her as those in front of us were already loaded with presents of their own. We realized that the privileged male prisoners paid her well for keeping her eyes and mouth shut. Once she had her dues, she hastened to drive us into the huge barracks, loaded from end to end with mountains of clothes, shoes, and suitcases.

The Capo explained we were to sort out men's and women's clothing. Once separated, we had to make parcels of different items—shirts, trousers, socks, underwear, ties, dresses, blouses, skirts, stockings, etc. We were to look for valuables, money, jewelry, cigarettes concealed in the clothes and hand them over to the SS woman. In a low aside, she murmured, her lips barely moving, "If you know what's good for you, you give them to me."

So, our work began. All these things, stacked to the barrack roof, were to be bundled, packed, and readied for dispatch to Germany by the afternoon. If the target was not reached, there were threats of punishment ranging from overtime and reduced rations to transfer to outside or even hard labour. All that did not worry me. I was completely indifferent, but remembering the words of our Blockova, I immediately set out to find suitable clothes for my husband.

There was one corner at the far end of the barrack that was almost completely cut off from view by heaped bundles of clothes and stacked suitcases. The Capo soon disappeared behind them. "There is a small door there," one of the girls who had worked here before said, following my glance. "That's where our boyfriends come in. As long as the SS woman and the Capo get their share of the loot, they don't molest us. The men bring us all kinds of food from their camp kitchen that ordinary prisoners never see and we give them clothes in exchange."

In no time at all, the bundles were separated and I had no difficulties finding the right size of shoes, socks, underwear, shirt, and sweater for Freddy. There just remained a suit and that was more difficult. He was tall and most of the pants and jackets seemed too short in the legs or sleeves. And then I found them: his own sports jacket and flannels. I recognized the handkerchief with his initials first. These clothes were all from his transport. These were the belongings of all the men and women who'd entered the gates of Birkenau yesterday and were freezing in their miserable prison rags while their good, warm suits and dresses were being sent back to Germany's Nazis for their *Winterhilfe*—Winter Aid.

As soon as Freddy's outfit was complete, I found our Blockova's sister. She showed me where to paint the red cross all over the back of the jacket and where to sew on the number tape with a red triangle. The number itself would have to be filled in with indelible ink once I got it from my husband. She also gave me a packet of cigarettes, matches, and a bar of chocolate to put in his pockets. Turning away to hide her tears, she said gruffly, "I haven't done much good to anybody so far, but you are the first woman lucky enough to have her husband alive in this camp. Do you know what that means? Men are even weaker and more helpless than we are and if you can't pull him through being in this commando, may you rot in hell! I know you are a Jaecke (a name of contempt given to German prisoners by those from Eastern Europe) and probably as stupid, stiff-necked, and scrupulous as the rest of your crowd, but I can tell you now: If you don't learn to steal, cheat, lie; if you can't walk over dead bodies physically and metaphorically and learn that damned quickly, your next port of call is the gas chambers. Now get on with your work till you are called."

She folded my bundle of clothes neatly and took them behind the wall of clothes and suitcases at the far end. She told me where to find them later and went on with her own work. We all continued sorting and bundling quickly and automatically. One or the other of the old girls kept vanishing at the far end to have a smoke, and I discovered for the first time the calming effect it had on my nerves and I smoked until it made me feel faint and dizzy. At noon, prisoners from the men's kitchen brought huge containers with steaming food and everybody got a good helping of meat, potatoes, cabbage and gravy. For the first time since my mother had vanished, I ate properly. The Dutch SS woman had so far taken little notice of us. If she wasn't laughing and flirting with the men, she was stretched out on a heap of blankets, smoking and reading a book or combing her long, golden hair. Shortly after the noon meal, however, she called me, the first and only guard to use my name. Usually, we were just numbers. Inspecting me with some curiosity, she said, "You have a very good-looking husband. Better do something about his appalling clothes. I haven't seen him or you or anything else though, understand? Scram!" She pushed me off in the direction of the far end.

He was waiting for me behind the protective wall of clothing. In spite of his shaven head, he still looked the most handsome boy I had ever seen. He still seemed so well and strong that his pitiful rags went almost unnoticed, but something about him struck me forcefully: he stood rooted to the ground and there was such terror in his eyes that I had the impression he did not see me at all. I ran to him and threw my arms around him and could feel his heart beating wildly through his thin, torn shirt. Before his hands touched me limply, he looked round him like a hunted animal and did not speak. I assured him it was all right for him to talk to me here, and at last he looked up and stared at me.

"Oh, my darling, what a nightmare this is! I can't bear it. You look so thin and ill. Are you all right? . . . Two men of my transport hanged themselves last night. One pushed the house Capo by mistake in the general upheaval and the swine beat him to pulp. Oh God!" He put his hands up to his face and seemed to forget my presence. I pulled them down gently and shook him.

"Freddy, pull yourself together. The first night is the worst, believe me. Once you are working you will find it more bearable. You just have to believe me. I've been here a month now. Listen, I have found your own clothes and painted the cross on. Put them on quickly and I'll fill in your number. Once you are decently dressed you'll be all right and get a better job in your camp. Don't ask me why; I don't understand it myself yet. They take all your own things, yet nobody asks where you suddenly manage to get new clothes from. You'll just have to accept the fact that no normal values are accepted here." I pushed the suit at him and begged him to hurry up but he did not move.

After an interminable silence he said, "I can't do it, Dannie. You don't know our house Capo. He is a murderer, the devil incarnate. He'd kill me if I turned up in these clothes. Thank you darling, but I can't change into them." I begged and bullied him, but he was adamant and so frightened I finally gave up. I had failed him, too. The words of our Blockova's sister kept haunting me. Henceforth my soul would "rot in hell." Had I known then what I learned later, I would have bought his Capo. I should have sent for him first. I should have given him a suit better than the one I had for my husband and assured him of new clothes as he required them. Freddy would then have been all right and unmolested and, what is more, would have been well-fed and given work within the camp.

Once my husband had refused the clothes and I had given up the struggle, he seemed to feel better and cheered up a bit. He suddenly asked, "How did you find Reha? Hasn't she grown? Was she happy to see you and is your mother looking after her?" He did not know anything yet.

I hid my face on his shoulder so my eyes would not let him guess at the truth. "Yes, darling, she is all right. My mother is looking after her and both are much better off than you and I. How did she get into your transport?"

He looked surprised. "Did Mrs. Unger not tell you? Margaret's brother in East Prussia got scared because the child had no identity papers and his party leader kept badgering him about that. So in the end, after another phone call from him, Margaret had no option but to collect her again. She brought Reha back to Berlin and left her on the doorsteps of a Catholic orphanage. The nuns kept her there and looked after her well. But the Gestapo took photographs of all foundlings and took them round hospitals and other institutions to find out if anything was known about their parents. "A woman detective in plain clothes turned up at the Jewish hospital where I was with scarlet fever. She left the pictures on the matron's desk and sat down in a corner. One of the younger nurses came in later to see the matron about something, took one look at the photos and cried, 'What a lovely child! Isn't that the granddaughter of Sister Elizabeth? She is her absolute image.' Of course, the detective jumped up and soon found out who Sister Elizabeth was and that I was her son-in-law. She brought Reha to my ward. I denied desperately ever having seen the child and put my finger to my mouth when nobody was looking my way, but Reha came running to me. She climbed up on my bed and shouted with all the joy of a lost three-year-old. 'Daddy, my Daddy!' The game was up then and I took her in my arms. She was so happy that I reproached myself bitterly for ever having gone along with that crazy plan of yours to hide her. Her place is with you and even this hell is better for her as long as she can be with you and your mother. Nobody can be cruel to a beautiful child like ours."

I shook him wildly, "Haven't you finished yet, you fool? Find out where you are first and what your child has come to." I quickly checked myself and apologized for my lack of control. The future was bleak enough for him and he would find out all too soon. Why could I not keep my mouth shut and leave him with his illusions and an incentive to live for a little longer? He did not appear unduly upset by my outburst though, and said tenderly and humbly, "I was a beast, darling, complaining of hardships when you have already had such a time of it. It can't last forever though. Just keep your chin up and we'll soon be together again and I will look after my family." Just then the SS woman poked her head round the corner and told him he'd "better buzz off." He kissed me and left. All

I had managed to force on him was the bar of chocolate, cigarettes and matches. I went back to join the other girls with the knowledge that I had failed them all, my mother, my husband, my child. I had believed myself to be strong and intelligent when all I had been was vain, arrogant, immature, and cowardly. I thought my heart would break with the pain of the immense vacuum that was my future.

At our return to the gate that night, our guard made a great show of examining us for loot. We all had to step out one by one and raise our arms. She slid her hands down our hips, fronts and backs and found nothing, although some of the girls were so obviously bulging that I trembled in case somebody noticed it. In the end she put her hand in one girl's apron pocket and pulled out a packet of cigarettes. With the labour leader and all other SS officials and guards watching, she slapped the girl's face, called her a filthy B and worse, and announced the girl was to go on half-rations for two weeks. That, in our commando, was a farce. Through the men and the clothes she could smuggle into our camp and exchange for food, she would not have starved had she been given no rations at all.

I did not see my husband again for a long time, but he managed to send me a note nearly every day and I sent him cigarettes, extra bread rations, margarine, sugar and onions, sometimes even chocolate for which I had exchanged clothes. He still would not hear of taking a good suit but he would accept clean underwear and socks. He was working on rail repairs, and although the work was hard with long hours, his notes were cheerful and optimistic. The days were warm now and with the extra rations he kept up his strength. Our days went by with regular monotony, but that did not worry us unduly. The chemical in the bread was achieving its objective. It not only prevented menstruation, but also dulled our senses to such an extent that we no longer felt much initiative or desire for action. Even fear and pain were dulled and blunted. There remained just a dumb instinct to survive.

New transports arrived day in, day out. If we left the barracks empty in the afternoon, they were stacked full again with fresh loads in the morning. By the quality, texture, and colours of the women's dresses more than from labels, we could tell where the transports had originated. There were well-made dresses of good, solid material from Holland; smart and beautifully tailored French models; lovely embroidered blouses and fur coats from Slovakia and Hungary; light, flimsy flower-printed frocks from Greece; and headscarves, aprons, and shawls in glaring colours from Gypsy transports. Hundreds of men and women of all these nationalities entered the camps every day. How many more had perished in the gas chambers?

The chimneys were smoking day and night. It was no longer possible to see the sun in daytime or the stars at night. A thick blanket of smoke enveloped the camp and the horrible smell stung our eyes and nostrils even if the wind carried the smoke away from us. But the days were bearable. Engaged in this futile, depressing work I was at least surrounded by my friends who tried with infinite patience, love and tenderness to instill some hope and purpose into my almost demented mind. There was the incentive of keeping my husband alive. The nights, however, were terrible. I could not sleep. The barking of dogs and the SS shouting and often shooting off rifles round the gas chambers were enough to drive even the sanest person crazy. The smoky stuffiness of overcrowded barracks was unbearable. Susan and I, when her younger sister slept, sometimes crept out in the middle of the night to try to get some fresh air but there was no fresh air anywhere. If eventually I fell into exhausted, fitful sleep, I always had the same dream: I saw Mrs. Unger coming towards me, carrying Reha and leading a little boy by the hand. She smiled and called out to me. I ran towards my child who stretched out her arms, but as soon as I came near enough to almost touch her, the road became a fast-moving conveyor belt and carried them away from me to a brick building with a huge iron door and a tall chimney. They vanished through the door and when I caught up with them at last, the iron door closed in my face. I heard my child's faint cry, "Mommy," as the door banged shut and then silence and no sound other than my fists battering and my feet kicking against the door. My friends who shared a bunk with me always woke me up then for I was hitting and kicking them cruelly.

Such was my state of mind when, one evening after roll call, the Blockova asked me if I would like a change of scenery. A new working group, the Shoe Commando, was being formed. If I wanted her to put my name on the list, I would be loading shoes into wagons outside the staff headquarters in Auschwitz and could, maybe, see my mother. At the same time, I could do her a favour and contact her sister who was Capo of the SS laundry there. The last time she had heard from her, over six months ago, her sister had promised in a note to arrange a transfer to the staff quarters. Since then she had heard nothing. I did not believe my mother was alive but I felt this was my only chance to find out what had happened to her. When my friends promised to look after my husband for me and carry messages between us, I volunteered.

# CHAPTER 17

The SS women's staff quarters was a large, square building standing isolated in the barren landscape near the small town of Auschwitz, about twenty minutes' march from Birkenau. There were a few trees around the house, but at the back, railway tracks ran immediately below the iron-barred basement windows.

The first day I arrived there, the whole length of the building was cut off from view by an immensely long freight train. On our side of it were mountains of shoes ready for loading into the gaping doors of the wagons. The shoes must have been collected from many, many transports of prisoners.

A guard ordered me to get inside the first of the trucks and stack shoes the other girls threw in. All day we loaded and by evening the mountains seemed barely diminished. Yet we had filled six trucks to their roofs. A few times I tried to slip behind the train to get a look at the basement windows but the guards and their dogs were on alert. One step away from the allotted place of work and the nearest dog let out a deep, low growl, lifting his massive head and baring his teeth; the SS man relaxed his grip on the leash and released his rifle's safety catch. By evening we had not even a glimpse of a single prisoner inside the staff quarters. For three days we worked and loaded the train and at last it was full and moved off slowly to make room for the next. There was our chance. The barred basement windows were full of excited faces calling out to us, asking for relatives in Birkenau, shouting out names I had never heard. My mother was not there. Our guards relaxed and looked the other way when we edged nearer to the windows. At last I got close enough to a girl to ask for my mother, making two or three attempts before my voice was audible, fearful of the answer.

"Sister Elizabeth? Yes, of course, she is here. She has just been summoned to give an SS woman a massage. She had hoped to get news of you through her. Why didn't you answer her notes?" the girl asked indignantly. "Don't you know your mother was wearing herself to a shadow thinking something had happened to you?"

I had never received her notes. Just before the guards whistled for us to line up for the march back to Birkenau, I managed to say, "Give her my love. Tell her I am quite well and I'll be back tomorrow and every day now till I can see her." Then I remembered to ask for the Blockova's sister. She was at the window and told me she was still trying to get her sister over to the staff quarters and hoped, with my mother's help, to get her soon.

For the first time I felt alive again. My mother was really alive and well and even seemed to be in a position to do something for prisoners in Birkenau. How or what I did not yet understand, but I would soon see her and find out. The march back to camp was nothing; there was hope After roll call, I gave the Blockova her sister's message and got double meat and fat rations as a reward and ate them. My friends were jubilant when they heard about my mother. It was almost as though she was the mother of them all and the whole of our barracks celebrated. We sat on our bunks, even the Blockova, and pooled our resources. There was even a whole cigarette for each of us.

The next day I saw her. The guards were a more decent lot and didn't appear to notice if we slipped between the trucks to the basement windows. My mother was pale like the others for want of fresh air and sunshine but well-fed and clean and her lovely black hair was growing again. The privileged prisoners of the staff quarters did not have their heads shaved.

My mother told me she had volunteered that day so long ago, convinced she would end up in the gas chambers, but she was determined I should not see her die a slow and painful death. All other prisoners had gone into hiding and she was the only one that could be found. There had been a long argument between the SS that day about whether they should take her, the poor, sick apparition that she was. In the end they decided they must have somebody quickly to mend silk stockings. For once, the "job offer" was not a hoax. Now tears were rolling down her cheeks, but she was so happy to see me, words failed her.

In the staff quarters' basement were housed not only prisoners who worked in the SS laundry and sewing room but also female prisoners employed in the so-called "political department" of Auschwitz. There the SS kept records of all people who entered the various camps in that area. Furthermore, with typical Prussian thoroughness, they listed the names of those who entered the gas chambers too. The women working in that department were sworn to secrecy and any leak of information was sufficient to justify their deaths. However, when they heard I was coming to see my mother they had prepared her. So she knew that my husband was in Birkenau and knew, or guessed, what had happened to our child. As always, she was stronger than I and talked to me about Reha, about Freddy and our extreme youth and our chances for the future. I could see her heart was breaking, yet I greedily absorbed all the love and hope she held out to me, and as usual, could give little in return.

One morning as we were marching out, my husband entered the women's camp. I had a note from him telling me he had been given carpenter's work and that his next job was to roof a block of latrines in our camp. In passing he threw me a kiss and his enchanting smile and whistled a few bars of several songs. Knowing their lyrics, I understood something was happening in Italy and Russia. We didn't get any news, but occasionally something leaked through by word of mouth from prisoners picked up in France, Holland, or other occupied countries.

Freddy was thin but cheerful, as straight as a rod and taller than any of his fellow prisoners. When I had heard he was coming to our camp, I had arranged with the Blockova to keep me back for house duties soon so I could meet him. But I didn't want to stay the first day because I knew my mother would get a terrible fright if I suddenly did not turn up with the Shoe Commando. I hoped to explain to her why she would not see me for a day or two and I did get a chance to talk to her that day.

"Be very careful, darling," she warned me. "Don't risk your life or his unnecessarily when you talk to him." She ended up by saying: "You don't know, sweetheart, what terrible consequences your meeting could have if you don't watch out. I won't be happy again until I see you back here."

The words and tone of her voice so reminded me of that far away day in Denmark after she discovered me on top of a sand dune in the arms of a young Danish student. The memory of that first, very harmless kiss made me momentarily forget where I was and I broke into helpless laughter. "You shouldn't let him kiss you," she had said on that beautiful summer holiday when I was twelve years old. "You don't know the terrible consequences your secret meetings might have. You are much too young. Why, you might even have a baby." She had never been able to bring herself to talk to me about sex, but even then I knew it was pretty safe and certainly wonderful to be kissed. However, I did not get a chance to explain what I was laughing about and later on I forgot. She must have thought I was out of my mind.

My heart was pounding from the time I woke up at dawn.

The roll call seemed endless. Today I was going to see my husband, speak to him, bury my head on his shoulder and, if only for a moment perhaps, kiss him again. The longing to be held, to feel small and protected, grew unbearably. Our Blockova had given me to understand there would be no difficulty in getting him alone. The men's guards were usually too busy with German prostitutes during working hours to worry about the prisoners. They knew that escape from within the camp was a physical impossibility. Once more I was going to persuade Freddy to wear good clothes. My friends would get them for him and we knew the ropes by now. Surely now he had more experience of camp life, he would accept them and better his chances for survival.

At last the roll call came to an end and the working groups moved slowly out of the gate. Susan had supplied me with a new headscarf and apron; others had given me chocolate and cigarettes for my husband. To pass the time until the men arrived, I helped the regular house staff straighten blankets and sweep the barracks until the Blockova came in to say the men had started work. I dashed off in the direction of the new blocks toward the sound of sawing and hammering. Creeping round the last corner, I found their guards were nowhere to be seen and I could go right up to the men. The new buildings kept me from being seen from the watch-towers. About ten prisoners were working there but my husband was not among them. An awful fear gripped me, and the longing to see him became an unbearable necessity. I recognized the boy who had walked beside him when they passed me yesterday and I went up to him. "Where is Freddy Raphael?"

He glanced at me casually and said, "He was gassed last night, poor chap. We had a big selection yesterday and everybody who was underweight or looked ill, or otherwise didn't come up to standard was taken to the gas chambers. Freddy had a sore throat and his voice became very hoarse towards roll call time. When the

SS walked through our ranks and asked him his number, he croaked in reply. That finished him. They killed over a thousand of our men during the night."

The ground seemed to rock under my feet and I instinctively covered my face with my hands to ward off the blow. The boy looked at me and asked gently, "I say, are you a relation of his?" I could not answer but pushed the chocolate and cigarettes at him and ran blindly back to my bunk. There I pulled the blankets over my head.

The girls working in the men's camp had already heard of the night of terror. Those of my friends who had passed notes between me and my husband knew that he too had been swallowed up by those insatiable monsters, the crematorium's huge ovens, serving their bloodthirsty masters, the SS. Susan and her sister sat with me till the early hours of the morning. Nobody spoke but their nearness and comradeship was the last saving grace. It preserved my sanity.

We now had new guards in the morning but all caution went overboard. Prompted by the need to see my mother and hear her soothing voice, I did not even wait to be detailed for work but jumped straight across the fenders of the train between trucks to the basement window. My mother and many other prisoners were waiting for us and Mom threw me a loaf of white bread through the bars. We had not seen white bread since our days of freedom. But before I could speak to her, I felt a tearing pain in my left leg and turned my head to see a fierce German Shepherd with his fangs buried in my flesh. Across the fenders, a rifle barrel was staring at me. "Catch her, Ralph, catch her! Good dog, tear her up, make mince-meat of the bitch! Good dog!" snarled the guard.

I saw my mother's white, stunned face and against the impulse to tear myself away and run from that brute of a dog, I heard Ruth's low, patient voice, "Don't ever run if an SS dog is after you. Stand still even if he has got his teeth in you and he'll let go." The voice faded away but the pain endured. However, I didn't move. The dog, as if surprised, let go of my leg and moved away from me.

The guard shouted, threatened, hit out at the dog, told it again and again to catch me; but the dog, tail between his legs, did not touch me again. The SS man pulled me roughly across the fenders, hit me over my hands with his rifle, and the beautiful white loaf dropped into a puddle of mud. He trampled it into the ground, but that was hidden from my mother by the train. That, at least, she did not see. The pain in my torn leg obscured the pain in my heart for the rest of the day. Freddy was well out of it. How long would he have suffered? A long hour perhaps, knowing he was going to die? Five minutes in the gas chambers? If anybody had given me a choice, I would have taken death and peace. Now and for many a day to come.

The day came to its logical conclusion: Report at the gate, sentence to starvation rations, and hard labour for an indefinite period. Then I had to kneel on sharp stones for two solid hours, and at last, deep, exhausted sleep with legs drawn up to ease the pain of the dog bite and knees bloodied by stones.

# CHAPTER 18

This time, hard labour consisted of digging trenches, standing up to the hips in stinking, stagnant water, and hacking away rock-like soil from the embankments. The sun burned pitilessly on our bare, shaven heads; our backs creaked with the unaccustomed work. My leg was festering and suppurating where the dog had bitten me. Again I was too tired at night to eat but thirst, accumulated during the heat of the day, never left me. We were not given anything to drink from morning till night. The women around me died like flies from heat-stroke, exhaustion, fever and often because they no longer wanted to live. At first the dead were carried back to camp at night, but as their numbers grew to more than fifty percent of our daily contingent, we had to dig a mass grave at the side of the trenches and there the bodies were thrown every evening, covered with a thin layer of lime. Day in, day out, the mountain of bodies grew and with it the ghastly smell of death and decay. Still the grave was left open to receive yet more and more dead.

I lost track of time. One day followed the other in killing, back-breaking monotony. The sensation of weightlessness, detachment and unreality I had first known the day my husband and child had arrived, returned. Hunger and pain I no longer felt; only thirst plagued me beyond endurance. One day, when I thought I could stand it no longer, a group of gypsies passed our trenches. Each woman carried a bowl of water and I begged them for a drink. One of them gave me her bowl. The water looked crystal clear and I drank it to the last drop. "Do you know what you have drunk, my girl," asked one of our grinning guards. "That water comes from the swamps near the crematorium. Swamps make excellent graves. Hope you enjoyed it. Prosit."

I did not want to believe it and didn't care anyway. No water had ever tasted so good. Curiously enough, once hunger had ceased to worry me, I felt less tired and more energetic. I could sit up at night and talk to my friends; only the food they continuously tried to make me eat nauseated me. Their friendship and concern still cheered me tremendously until, one night, we sat cross-legged, ten of us, on my bunk. Ada, a fourteen-year-old Dutch girl who had joined us lately, said something quite trivial but incongruous with her age. I looked up at her and saw her eyes. It is difficult to explain what I saw. Her light brown, childish, trusting eyes had changed. There was something opaque, yet tranquil and far away in her gaze. I knew beyond any doubt that Ada was going to die. This discovery frightened me more than anything I had so far experienced and I did not want to believe what I saw. After all, she seemed strong and healthy enough sitting there, chewing away at a crust of bread. However, before the end of the week she was dead. There was no illness. She just refused her rations one night and was found in a coma next morning. She never woke up again.

One Sunday, we only worked three hours to give the guards a rest. Without thinking, I exchanged my bread ration for some green apples some prisoner had stolen somewhere. Susan chided, "Now, what did you do that for, Dannie? You need your bread. These apples will only give you a sore stomach."

"The apples are for my mother. She is in hospital with a fever and this was the only refreshing fruit I could find. She wants apples anyway," I said defensively.

"Did you get a note from her?" asked Susan, very much

upset. "Why didn't you tell us? We could have visited her this morning and taken her something. She must be very ill if they sent her back from staff quarters to Birkenau. For Heaven's sake why didn't you tell us?"

"Susan, this is something you won't understand. I don't understand it myself. I didn't get a note, nor has anybody told me my mother is here. I just know it and only realized it when I bought the apples."

She only looked at me in much the same way the Blockova had done when I told her of the newly arrived transport from Berlin. Susan too seemed to be doubting my sanity but she did not want to question me further, simply took my arm in her friendly, casual way and, together, we went to the hospital barracks. We entered the isolation block and asked the first prisoner we met for my mother. We were led to a bunk near a window. There she was shivering, her face yellow and pinched, her eyes enormous and abnormally bright. Her face lit up when she saw me and she took the apples, ate one greedily and asked, "Darling, how did you know I was here? I have been lying here for the past hour thinking I'd give anything for a fresh apple and there you are, anticipating my crazy longing."

Susan pinched me and said carelessly, "Somebody from the hospital came along and told us you were here, Elizabeth. What is wrong? Anything serious?"

My mother shook her head. She had been diagnosed as having malaria. A transport of malaria patients was to be sent to a so-called research station where doctors experimented with human guinea pigs. "Don't worry," my mother said. "The SS woman in charge of this transport has given me anti-malarial tablets, and as soon as the fever is down, she is going to take me back to the staff quarters."

Already, her index card had been removed from the rest and the only reason she was here at all was that the SS doctor happened to see her when she had an attack and demanded she be sent to Birkenau. He would see her on his evening round but would not be present when the transport left in the morning and would never know she had not gone with it.

I was satisfied and knew she would be all right although Susan was still worried and doubtful when we left. My mother had noticed that I had become very thin and her last words to me were, "I'll do everything possible to get you to the staff quarters. I don't give massages and mend silk stockings for nothing. Frau Brunner, the commanding officer of all SS women in Auschwitz, has promised me she would get you over. She is a real Prussian, strict but just, and never breaks a promise. She doesn't fit into this place and treats prisoners with some consideration." My mother did not know I was condemned to hard labour and we did not enlighten her.

One evening, shortly after my mother's brief stay in Birkenau, I began feeling exceptionally light-headed and dizzy. We did not get back to camp till roll call and as usual there was no time for a wash. Afterwards it would be dark, the washrooms would be locked and again I would have to wash in a bowl of tea, the dark brew I would now much rather drink. Still, there was no shortage of tea and my friends who were not so desperately thirsty would give me plenty.

Susan and her sister, inseparable, were the first to greet me, and when I looked at the younger girl, a cry escaped me I would have given anything to choke back. In Lorna's blue, normally sparkling eyes was the same expression I had seen in Ada's not so long ago. She too was going to die. A tall, strapping, fair girl now, she would be dead in a very short time. What would Susan do without her?

The girls took my arms and led me outside for the unavoidable roll call, asking me repeatedly if I could stand up and if I was feeling all right. Apparently I had turned ash grey and was shivering. They held me up throughout the parade which must have lasted much longer than usual. We were still waiting long after dark. Most of the time I drifted through clouds of blankness, until a sharp, rasping voice penetrated the vacuum. "Elimination Tests."

A gasp of terror went through our ranks and somebody's arm tightened protectively round my shoulders. "Daniella, you'll make it. Don't think at all, just jump if they tell you to. There is nothing to it. Don't collapse now, there'll be plenty of time afterwards," a voice whispered in my ears. It seemed miles away. Slowly we moved forward and, one after another, the girls in front of me took a short run, jumped, and were swallowed up in the dark, starless night.

Suddenly, I was all alone and the rasping voice said, "Next one: One, two, three, jump!" He shone a bright torch first into my eyes, then in front of me onto an open drain and a heap of sand behind it. My legs were heavy and useless and refused to move forward. I must have jumped though, for a second later I had fallen into the ditch and collapsed in utter darkness.

Torrents of icy water were splashing over me when I next opened my eyes. I was lying under a cold shower. Shivering, my teeth chattering like castanets, I crawled slowly and painfully away out of the range of that stinging downpour. But no sooner did I feel safe when a pair of rough hands, aided by a well-aimed kick, shoved me back. Too weak to struggle or resist, I tried again and again to escape on hands and knees but to no more avail than a drowning kitten might try to get away from strong hands that held it under water, hands that know no pity or concern for another creature's suffering.

Mercifully, even tormentors grow tired of their games. Every ordeal is bound to come to an end. The first thing I knew was that I was in a single bunk-bed with white sheets and thick blankets. On a stool beside me was a small, white loaf, jam, and a mug of water. The food did not tempt me, but oh, how good it was to stretch burning, aching limbs under those clean, cool sheets. I must have slept off and on for hours for when I woke again it was dark and the naked bulbs with their glaring light made my head hurt unbearably. Patients were called to get up and stand to attention, and from beds round about me shadowy figures struggled to stand barefooted on the brick floor of the hospital ward.

Dr. Mengele made his round followed by a retinue of SS and prisoners in white coats. I did not even attempt to get up. My legs felt like rubber and just the effort of moving my head made me squirm and cry out with pain. A nurse pulled down my sheets and blankets and opened the coarse shirt over breast and stomach. Under half-closed lids I could see the doctor and his followers shrink back and, squinting down, I saw bright pink, round spots all over my exposed stomach.

"Typhoid," the doctor said, "immediate isolation. What crackpot put her in here?" He moved on and two prisoners, so-called assistant nurses, dragged me between them over the cold brick floor, out of the ward into another barrack which reminded me of our first night in Birkenau. With its smells, darkness, and tormented screams, it only differed in that this hut had three-tiered, single wooden beds instead of bunks.

Once accustomed to the gloom, I found myself staring up to the top bed into which I was told to climb. The two nurses hoisted me up and, to my horror, I found the narrow bed already occupied. When I mentioned it to them, they said, "What do you think this is, a sanatorium? Get in." They shoved me up with a jerk that landed me right on top of the sick girl already there. She received me quite kindly and moved over but I soon found my weak apologies were not understood. The burning, dark eyes in a narrow white face belonged to a Greek, and all the girl understood was Greek. However, she motioned me to the foot of the uneven straw mattress and covered me carefully with half of her blanket. Somehow we passed the night, both of us shivering under the impact of fever.

At dawn we were wakened by wild shouts. "Get up, you filthy Bs, get up for delousing." Helping each other, we got down from our top bed and shared a bowl of cold water for a wash. Needless to say, there was no soap and no towel. While we were trying to wash our hands and faces and keep on our feet, an assistant nurse whipped down the straw mattress and blanket.

She said quite regretfully, "These have to go for fumigation and we've got no replacements. So you better get on your bunk and warm each other. Send your complaints to the management." The Greek girl did not understand a word, but prodded, she struggled back up and helped me too. We sank, arms round each other, feet intertwined, onto the bare planks, no covering except our short, rough shirts.

Nature can be kinder than humans, though. I went into a deep coma and nothing penetrated, neither the hardness of the wood nor the cold, not even the feverish struggle of the Greek girl who, another patient told me later, raved throughout the night.

I don't know how long I was unconscious but when I woke, it was with a feeling of iron bands around my shoulders and legs holding me down with a firm, cold grip. It was daylight again. I tried to move but was so weak I could barely raise my head. When I looked at the girl beside me, I screamed. Her head had fallen back, her mouth was wide open, and she stared at me with glazed, unseeing eyes. She was dead. What had felt like iron bands were her cold, stiff limbs still gripping me in her last effort to get a little warmth. Poor child. What she must have suffered coming from her gay, sunny Greece to this prison camp where she found only cold, calculated murder. To her, more than to those who had been gradually prepared, this must indeed have been hell on earth.

My screams were heard. Shuffling, indifferent footsteps

approached my bed and stopped. I called out again and the well-fed face of a prisoner, a sick-bay attendant, appeared over the side. My bed-mate's body was soon pried loose and, with one hard pull from the attendant, the corpse plunged over the side of the bed and crashed down the three tiers onto the brick floor. The head and two greedy hands popped up again and found yesterday's bread ration on top of which the Greek girl had died.

"That's always good for the black market. It will bring at least two pieces of soap or a margarine ration. White bread is a luxury we can't afford to throw away with the dead. Still," said the head to me, "when you snuff it, do me a favour and keep your bread at the foot of the bed and don't squash it. After all, I have to carry your body out of here. That deserves a bit of consideration, don't you think? Meantime, you can wallow in luxury and have the bed all to yourself. I'll try not to put anybody else in with you." The head was in an expansive mood and talked on and on, but in the end I heard only a far-away murmur and must have fainted again.

Again, somebody was talking, far away. It might have been the same voice, but no, there were two voices and they came closer. I tried to cling to the peace of the unconscious but something penetrated. "She is dead. No pulse, no heartbeat. You can put number 52 in her bed. Dump her on the floor. She won't feel anything." I saw the Polish woman doctor, a prisoner herself, and a nurse bending over me and then moving on to the next patient. True enough, I felt nothing until, in an aura of white light, I seemed to be looking down from a great height and saw my own body on the brick floor in the darkest corner. A huge rat was darting out from behind a corner post to settle down on my bare legs. The light vanished and all of a sudden all of me was back on the ground again. Shock and horror must have given me superhuman strength. I rolled along the floor and crawled towards a bed near a window. How I got up on to the top bunk, still without straw mattress or blanket and unoccupied, I'll never know. Once that objective was achieved, I fell into a deep sleep and when I woke up, I felt well. The fever had gone and with it all the pain. Only weakness remained, but the will to survive was there again and I immediately began to scheme how to get out of the sick-bay and back to my friends. When the SS doctors visit was due, I had made up my mind. Sick prisoners were forbidden to address the doctor unless he spoke to them first, but I was determined to appeal to him. After all, Dr. Mengele, although known as the "Angel of Death," had saved my mother in one of his rare humane moments. I could see him before he came near my bed. He glanced at his chart and asked the prisoners senior nurse, "What have we here? I thought that bunk up there was empty." He pointed at me. "Who or what is that apparition?"

The nurse was not tall and she climbed onto a stool. "Who carried you up there?" she asked with her deep, almost masculine voice.

"I came by myself. I did not want to die in that corner.

She slapped my face hard. "You are a liar. You could never get up here by yourself. You were all but dead." She slapped me again. The SS doctor stood by and watched the scene with obvious interest and amusement. This was my chance. I ignored the nurse and sat up as straight as I could. It cost me all my will power. My back muscles hardly supported me.

"Sir, there must be a mistake. I am perfectly well and have no fever. Would you please release me and let me get back to work?"

The nurse, stunned into silence for a moment, hit me so hard my nose began to bleed and would have gone on hitting me had the doctor not kicked the stool from under her feet. She rolled on the floor and, getting up slowly, brushed the dirt off her white apron. She was frightened and cowed.

Dr. Mengele came nearer my bed and shoved a thermometer into my mouth, looking at me steadily all the time. He removed the thermometer and said, "Where have I seen you before, you miserable skeleton? You have beautiful eyes . . . Wait a minute, weren't you the nurse who came with the Berlin transport in April? I thought I had sent you to Dublinka or somewhere with a malaria transport."

"No sir," I said quickly, "that was my mother. Please, will you let me get back to work?"

Again he looked at me closely. "Well, I like your courage and your eyes. Report to me when you are worth looking at again, but if you return here sick I'll kill you myself." He scribbled a note, handed it to the nurse and told her to take me to the sauna for delousing before returning me to my barrack in the labour camp. I was to have double rations and light work for two months. I was released, but the following night all remaining patients, without exception, were taken to the gas chambers. For days, the "nurses" scrubbed and cleaned the sick bay, and the fumigated mattresses and blankets were returned to the empty, silent wards.

My friends were indescribably happy to see me back. They fussed over me, offered all kind of tidbits, even shredded chicken on fried bread. The chicken, I learned later, was really frogs' legs, the only protein prisoners occasionally caught in the swamp.

Now I found out how weak I really was. The girls had to hold me up during roll calls and even the few steps from our hut to the assembly ground was too much. They carried me to and from work and during the day heaped up clothes in the barrack of the men's camp where they covered me and left me to rest, sorting my quota of clothes between them. They were very good to me.

Susan's sister was dead. She died the night before I returned from the hospital. Susan, whose courage I admired tremendously, cared for me more than anybody else. I often marvelled at her great and generous heart. She might have resented my release, physical and mental wreck that I now was in comparison with her attractive young sister. Not her. She nursed me with infinite, saint-like patience, humouring, supporting, giving hope. She re-taught me elementary knowledge forgotten during my illness. My memory failed and often I did not know who I was, where I was, and why I was there. Years of my life had vanished somewhere along the road of disease and misery. As far as she could, Susan filled in the gaps, but it wasn't until years later that my past came back to me and events gradually fell into place.

In spite of the girls' love and attention, I didn't seem to gain strength. It wasn't for lack of will power because I was as determined as ever to survive, especially in my more lucid moments. I tried hard to walk and stand on my own but my muscles simply refused to obey my will. Nor did my brain function normally. Later I was told that I had had long conversations with Lorna, Ada. and other girls long since dead. Sometimes I started singing in the middle of the night, mostly cradle songs to my baby. They told me I pleaded with Freddy to take new clothes and to let me wash his old ones. I don't know how many days or weeks this continued. We had not had an elimination test for some time.

Inevitably, after a lull between transports from Germany or occupied countries, they started again, and one afternoon we were assembled and taken back to camp very early. As we approached the gate, we saw that all commandos had been recalled. We had to wait a long time to be counted and recounted before we finally reached our barrack. There, we were immediately lined up outside for a roll call. It was hot and I felt tired so I let myself drop to the ground and fall asleep. My reactions were those of a small child or a senile mind. Any urge or need had to be gratified at once and no amount of reasoning, pleading or threatening would have kept me on my feet and awake at that moment. I woke up when the Blockova kicked me and hit my face and the girls on either side pulled me up. It was too late.

The SS doctor had gone through our lines and had not missed me. Before I was fully awake, I was dragged away from my friends and joined a handful of other poor, tottering creatures. "Block 24," somebody said. A heart-rending wailing started up all around me. Within seconds we were surrounded by armed guards and their dogs but we did not move as yet. I suppose we were to wait until our numbers were complete. Again I slipped to the ground, unable to stand any longer. Nobody seemed to worry and the guards took no notice of me. Though I was weak, my brain seemed to have cleared, and once more I was able to observe with complete detachment.

One woman near me screamed abuse at a guard until she was hit over the head with a rifle and collapsed. Another fell on her knees and with outstretched hands pleaded with the guards to let her go back to the workers. She said she was too young to die and that it was all a ghastly mistake. Over and over again she repeated that she had been pretty and that she was still strong. The guards turned their back on her, nobody listened, but she went on pleading. Some prayed to a god who was deaf and blind and had forsaken them long ago. One stuffed a piece of bread into her mouth and ate it greedily as though her salvation depended on it. Mostly they cried, some quietly, others noisily with sobs that tore at their wasted bodies. There was little dignity among us and I could not bear it.

I got up and found I could stand and even straighten my back. I took the hands of two women next to me and said softly so the guards would not hear and make fun of us, "Let's make an effort and die decently. There isn't really any fun in living, is there? My husband and child were killed not so long ago and I'll be in good company. There is no future for me. How about you?"

"My parents were gassed and I don't know if my brother is still alive," said one. "My father was shot and my mother and five-year-old twin brothers were gassed," said the other. "My fiancé died in Sachsenhausen. You are quite right although it seems hard. I am only nineteen." We talked for quite a while and gradually we got others to talk and it helped. Most of the women calmed down. Only the girl who was pleading with the guards was still on her knees and would not be distracted; there were two Greek girls who did not understand us, but they, fortunately, did not know where they were going and probably wouldn't know until the last minute.

We were still talking when I heard my name being called. I did not move or answer. What more could they do to me? The guards opened their ranks for Dr. Mengele and Frau Brunner, the commanding officer of the SS women's staff quarters. They went past us, peering into each prisoner's face, arguing wildly. The doctor was shouting, "Now look here, I let the mother into the camp against all rules and regulations. I allowed the daughter out of the hospital after one of the worst cases of typhoid I have ever seen. She was a Muselman, fit for nothing but the gas chambers. In fact, she should never have been in hospital in the first place after failing elimination tests. But again I made an exception because of the mother. I promised myself and her I would see her dead if she ever came to my attention again because of ill health. Now she can't even stand through roll call any more and you come along and demand her release for your staff quarters? Have you gone off your head? Do tell me, do you intend to turn Auschwitz into a sanitarium or a holiday camp for physical and mental wrecks?"

The SS woman strode past me, turned and stopped, pointing her whip at me. "You are Elizabeth's daughter, aren't you? Same eyes, same mouth. Why don't you answer when your name and number are called?" Before I could answer, she turned to the doctor, fixing him with cold, steel-grey eyes. "I want to take this girl for the SS laundry and I want to take her now. I am not interested in any promises you gave yourself or a lousy prisoner. You know, I have full powers to demand any woman I need. The camp commandant and the labour leader have authorized me to transfer her to the staff quarters, and if you have any complaints, you'd better lodge them there."

Without taking any further notice of him, she handed a note to one of the guards, told him to get me into the sauna and out of it as quickly as possible as she was waiting to take me to Auschwitz.

The doctor turned on his heels and stormed away. My guard told me to get moving and I went under the envious, hostile, and pleading eyes of those others condemned to death. What a fraud and a coward I felt and how I wished the ground would open up and swallow me. Only a few minutes ago I had asked the others to die decently and with dignity and now I was walking out on them. Once more I had cheated death at the eleventh hour. It was becoming a habit. The guard had no patience with my indecision and reluctance to move. He prodded me along at the point of his bayonet.

All the way to the sauna, on the long, painful walk to the staff quarters, and up to this day I have asked myself if I had not perhaps known I would be saved again. Could I have died decently? Should I not have insisted on going with the others to Block 24 and faced the ordeal? The knowledge of one's own selfishness and perhaps cowardice is very hard to live with.

# CHAPTER 19

Through a haze of fatigue I saw white faces pressing against the iron bars at the bottom of a staircase. Many hands stretched out towards me and I heard my mother cry out among a babble of voices. SS Brunner strode ahead and told me to stand back. With her strong, clipped voice, void of all emotion, she ordered the prisoners to go to their dormitory immediately and stay there till she told them they could move freely again. Underneath that hard shell she had a heart, however, and she was just. She explained that disease was rampant at Birkenau, that I was probably crawling with lice, and that nobody was to come into contact with me until I had had a bath and clean clothes. She added that anybody who caught lice from me would get their marching orders back to Birkenau. She could and would not risk infection being carried to the staff quarters.

Within seconds the gate was cleared and all prisoners had vanished except the Capo of the laundry who was told to stand by with fire tongs to take my clothes and burn them immediately. This vexed me. At the transfer to the staff quarters I had been given a new dress, new, clean underwear, and stockings. How many in Birkenau would have felt the richest people on earth had they been given the chance of wearing them? Now they were going to be burnt. But I was too tired to object, and what, after all, was a set of clothes compared with the millions of human beings who had been burned in this death camp?

The long run from Birkenau had been one of those nightmares one never gets used to only, contrary to most nightmare marches from there, mine ended in what appeared to me to be heaven. All the way, the SS woman had pedalled slowly ahead on her bicycle. Like a dog, I had run and stumbled after her, always afraid that should she get out of sight, the mirage of the staff quarters and my mother would vanish again, as unattainable as survival seemed at that moment. Behind me, the guard had pushed, prodded, and kicked me on. "For goodness sake, woman, can't you do better than crawl? Do you want to spend the night on the road, you miserable B? Get moving." To me it seemed I had never run so fast for so long. My sides were aching with every breath and every step, but like any other, this road, too, came to an end. It was a miracle I could make it at all when only a few hours ago I could not stand for any length of time.

Now I was propelled into a warm, heated shower room. I could hardly trust my eyes: I was in a small anteroom leading to the bath; both were white tile to the ceilings, the floor was tiled, there were two wooden benches on either side, clothes hooks and a mirror on the wall. The SS woman stayed outside and left the door open for the laundry Capo to take out my clothes. Etta was the sister of our Blockova in Birkenau but she was her sister's opposite. Homely, small, and plump, she did not aspire to beauty. Her head was set deep between broad shoulders as though nature had forgotten to give her a neck. But how kind she was.

Her gentle voice was infinitely soothing when she asked me to undress and have a warm bath quickly so I could see my mother soon. "You know, Daniella, your mother has been a mother to all of us here but she has never been at peace. I wish you could have seen her face this morning when Frau Brunner said she was going to Birkenau to get you." With those words, Etta whisked away my clothes, careful not to touch them, SS Brunner closed the door behind her after dropping a towel and soap on one of the benches.

A person who has never been in a prison camp cannot imagine what it is like to be alone for the first time: the luxury, wonder and happiness of privacy and solitude. Nobody can appreciate what it is like to be jostled and pushed every minute of the day and night, never to have a moment of unobserved peace; to be lying like a sardine, wedged in at night, trying not to stir, trying to avoid the clammy contact of other bodies; washing and undressing in a crowd; working and standing in crowds all day long. Until this first solitary moment, I had barely been aware of my longing to be alone.

I turned on the shower and the cascade of pleasantly hot water that didn't disappear washed all exhaustion and despondency off me. The soap was real, scented toilet soap, not the evil-smelling concoction made of human fat we had on rare occasions been forced to use in Birkenau. I washed and soaked and washed again. Nobody rushed me, nobody pushed me. Eventually, Etta knocked at the door and brought in a heap of new clothes, the summer uniform of the staff quarters: a black and white cotton dress with white collar and cuffs, a white apron and headscarf, new, clean panties, and white socks. She said apologetically, "I'm afraid there is no brassiere yet. We didn't know your size but we'll fit you out in the sewing room tomorrow. The girls there will alter your dress too, if need be."

What utter bliss: a Capo who was considerate enough to knock at the door before coming in, who worried about a missing brassiere and the appearance of my dress. She left me alone again after promising to take me directly to my mother when I was ready. I turned off the tap. It seemed a lifetime since I had felt so clean and warm, but before dressing, I could not resist the temptation of the mirror. Since our deportation in April I had not had the chance to look into one.

This bathroom mirror was so high up on the wall, I could

barely see my face in it. The closely cropped, sprouting hair on my head showed a round, white spot the size of a teacup. I knew about that white hair. Susan had told me. It had turned white the night my husband and child had arrived in Birkenau. However, I was not prepared for the rest.

I climbed onto the bench and what I saw made me shudder. I had the face and body of an old woman, wrinkled, grey, and sagging. I looked like Ruth, my first acquaintance in Birkenau, and so many, many others who had died or had been gassed so long ago. I resolved that my mother would never see me undressed and appreciated all the more Etta's kindness for not having remarked on my appearance. It must have shaken her, having lived so long among the healthy, well-fed, isolated prisoners of the staff quarters. I dressed quickly. Dress and apron, although a small size and too short for my height, were hanging loosely around my emaciated form. Etta pulled the apron bands tight and tied them in front to give an appearance of neatness. She then took my hand and led me to the dormitory. SS Brunner had gone, locking the entrance gate and leaving us alone.

It is impossible after so many years to describe what it was like to embrace my slight, slender mother who seemed so much bigger and stronger compared with the feather weight I was at that moment. Let it suffice to say that we talked and talked about everything and nothing. I don't think I told her how SS Brunner found me, but she must have guessed how close to death it had been. There must have been other prisoners around, but they tactfully left us alone to get over the first joy and shock of our reunion.

The dormitory was crowded with two-tier bunk beds, and how wonderful it seemed to me to have clean, white sheets and pillow cases, and thick, woolen army blankets on every bed. Pipes which supplied the SS women's central heating upstairs kept it warm. But it was the cleanliness of the room that made it so striking.

My mother tried to make me lie down. Prisoners were not normally allowed to go to bed before the evening meal unless they were ill, but she was sure she could make an exception. I was too excited, however, to relax and we talked on and on until, at dusk, the front gates were unlocked and prisoners brought in loaves of bread, heaps of margarine, sausage, jam, and two large containers of steaming hot tea.

Only then did the other girls turn up, clamouring to be introduced. I met them all, the women from the sewing room, the laundry, and later those who worked in offices. The latter were extremely lovely girls, chosen I think for their beauty rather than their knowledge of office routine. There were one or two, in fact, who were semi-illiterate. Curiously enough, they were the ones who looked down on washing and sewing women and kept very much aloof. On the whole, the prisoners of the SS staff quarters were a confined, artificial community, a caricature of a purely feminine society with all its snobbery and prejudices. The "upper class" was represented by the office staff, the "lower class," with all their ready kindness, willingness to help, and their enjoyment of gossip, by the sewing room and laundry women.

All this I learned gradually, but one thing was obvious from the start: the prisoners here were civilized human beings. Probably due to their softer living conditions, they could afford to respect each other's privacy and individuality. There was no fighting or pushing for food. Everybody waited patiently in line until their turn came. The Capos did not take the best part of the others' rations. There were no arguments over beds, blankets, and the rotation for baths. Everything was arranged justly and without friction and one never awoke to find a bread ration or other treasure stolen.

It was strictly forbidden here—as it had been in Birkenau—for prisoners to own any personal property but it was amazing how much was collected just the same. Every girl owned a small bag made from remnants in the sewing room which contained everything from a little, cracked mirror and broken combs, to last year's diary and stubs of pencils found in the SS women's wastepaper baskets. Prisoners who worked as chars upstairs brought them down. Every girl owned at least one handkerchief and a table napkin. During the day, such treasures were hidden in the straw mattresses and at regular intervals were found during the meticulous searches by the SS women on duty. Yet within a few days everybody had managed to replace their lost possessions.

How delighted I was to find a bag of red and white gingham on the bed allotted to me next to my mother's. It contained a small mirror, a comb with only one tooth missing, a handkerchief, and a toothbrush. I had no hair to comb yet and did not want to look into a mirror ever again, but the very knowledge of owning such treasures made me feel rich.

My mother made me some dainty tidbits from our evening rations. Laid out on a napkin, white and clean as fresh snow, were paper-thin slices of bread with finely cut pieces of sausage and small triangles with jam. The tea was hot and sweet. Safe and contented, I felt hungry for the first time in weeks and wolfed down my delicious supper. There was plenty of everything left and I asked for more but my mother knew only too well the danger of overeating after a long period of starvation.

For the first time in her life she refused me food although it was there. I behaved like a spoiled child, pleading and begging for more and refusing to take no for an answer. Fortunately, the whistle for roll call interrupted her agony and my further disgrace. What a different affair the roll call was here compared with Birkenau. All we had to do was to line up in the warm passage outside the dormitory. We were quickly counted by the SS woman on duty and told to go to bed. The whole affair lasted barely three minutes.

My mother tucked me up in bed as though I were a small

child again. My stomach was still rumbling but I was so warm, clean, and comfortably drowsy, I no longer minded the hunger pangs and fell asleep within seconds. In the morning I awoke refreshed. Fresh air and sunshine entered through the open windows, only iron bars casting shadows on the floor. Birds were singing in the trees outside. It was the sweetest music on earth. Although we were confined to the basement and never got out for exercise, I was perfectly content for the moment just to be there. Compared with Birkenau, this was peaceful and luxurious living.

Breakfast had been prepared for me and my mother had not only managed to toast the bread somewhere before I woke up, but also to produce a cup of real, hot, sweet cocoa like a magician whisks a rabbit out of a hat.

After breakfast we were counted again. The office staff had already left but we did not have far to go. Just along the passage was the sewing room which contained a few long tables, wooden chairs and some old, decrepit sewing machines. In spite of the open windows, it smelled dusty and it was rather dark. My mother and the others turned in and I just had time to see a heap of silk stockings in front of my mother as she sat down, her dark head barely showing over the top.

The laundry was a long room further on. There were three large boilers and three long, wooden troughs with washboards. There was also a small tub where the best of the laundresses washed the SS women's daintier clothes separately. Etta detailed me to one of the long troughs and to a washboard somewhere in the centre on the far side, my back to the window. "That's the best place for you meantime," she said. "You can sit on a stool till you get stronger and get up if an SS comes in without being noticed. If you can't cope with your allotted washing, pass it on to your neighbours. They'll do it for you." She must have noticed me wince for she added kindly, "No need to feel ashamed, Daniella. We were all weak when we first came from Birkenau. If we had not been helped to start with, we wouldn't be here now. Just take it easy and you'll be surprised how quickly you'll pick up." She went off to stoke the fires under the boilers and distribute the day's quota of work.

Etta was one of those rare Capos, non-existent in Birkenau, who worked as hard as any of her girls and didn't mind helping out at the wash-tubs if we did not manage to complete the ordered quota. We had to do the washing of all SS officers and guards from Birkenau and Auschwitz. The SS women's washing was only an infinitesimal part of our duties. The male guards' shirts and underwear were so dirty you would never have guessed they had once been white. Etta grabbed them with the fire tongs, as careful not to touch them as she had been with my clothes yesterday. After mixing lots of soap powders in the boilers, she dumped everything in, closed the lids, wrinkled up her nose in disgust and said, "Well, that's that. Filthy swine, this master race." She then distributed the men's long underwear, pants, vests, shirts, grey tunics, and socks as well. Although these had been boiled the previous day, they were still unbelievably dirty. With soap and scrubbing brushes, all severely rationed out, we were to get them clean and spotlessly white again.

Every night our finished washing was inspected and if there was the slightest dirt mark still visible, they were thrown back at us with threats varying from withdrawal of rations to transfer to Birkenau. The girls told me nobody had so far been sent back except for serious infection. Whenever a transfer was ordered because of complaints on the work, SS Brunner always overruled the orders since she had the last word. However, you could never trust any SS woman, and one day she too might be in a bad mood and let us down. The threat and fear of Birkenau hung forever over our heads.

The whole of that first day, I don't think I managed to clean even three shirts. Towards early afternoon, after a good lunch of stew and potatoes, the other girls had reduced their heaps of washing to almost nothing and mine was still as big as ever. Yet, my back and arms ached unbearably, and in the end tears started rolling down my face and I just couldn't stop crying. My neighbours at the trough grabbed the rest of my washing quickly and divided it up and down the line. In no time at all it had vanished.

The Dutch SS woman, who had been in the men's camp with us in Birkenau, did the evening inspection. She hardly looked at our efforts and said to Etta, "Everything finished, Capo? Have you done my blouse and undies today?" Etta lifted a bundle of pressed, neatly folded clothes off a stool behind the boilers and handed it to her. The SS woman gave us a bright smile. "Thank you girls, have a good night." Before she left, she came over to the trough, gave me a curious, compassionate look and asked, "Are you Elizabeth's daughter? How do you get on with the washing? You don't look strong enough."

My neighbour on the right poked her elbow in my ribs and answered quickly on my behalf, "She is doing fine, Aufseherin (Overseer), she finished her whole quota. She is much stronger than she appears to be." The SS woman shrugged her shoulders, grinned doubtfully and disappeared.

The day's washing was collected, hung up in the drying room, and we returned to the dormitory, supper, roll call, and bed. My mother told me later that the Dutch SS woman was the best of the lot. Mom had massaged her once for a stiff neck and mended her stockings and ever since hardly a day passed that she didn't come down to bring my mother something to eat. Today she had left a bar of chocolate and three cigarettes. My mother didn't smoke so I shared them among the few girls who did. We had half a cigarette after supper, enough to make me light-headed and dizzy again.

The Dutch woman's story was the old one of a beautiful girl from a poor home who fell in love with a good-looking SS officer in

Holland after the German invasion. Her father kicked her out when he learned of the affair and so she had followed her lover to finally end up in Auschwitz. Unlike others, she never got used to cruelty nor did she herself take to the perversions usual amongst the SS. Naturally, she did not like what she saw in Birkenau, but she was a superficial, fun-loving creature, popular with men for her good looks and gaiety. She was always given the best and healthiest commandos of women prisoners and on the whole managed successfully to close her eyes to the horrors around her. Very occasionally she had black moments of despair. When she did, she sent for my mother under the pretext of needing a massage for a sprained ankle or knots in her shoulder muscles, and then she almost cried her heart out.

Unlike us, who were afraid of the present, she was afraid of the future. She was intelligent enough to see the way the tide of war was turning. "Elizabeth, what am I going to do after the war? I can never go back to Holland. Where else could I live? Would anybody anywhere ever believe me that I did not kill or torture prisoners? Elizabeth, you are a nurse and know about drugs. Tell me the best way to kill myself. Shall I do it now or when the war ends?" In that vein she talked on and on. It was a monologue and did not really require an answer. My mother felt sure the young butterfly would not kill herself and did not take her very seriously. Contemptible though she might have been, she was one of the very few, if not the only one, of our guards who was kind to us and treated us as individuals. I had done her an injustice in Birkenau when I had thought she was keeping her mouth shut about our meeting men because she was well paid. She accepted presents as a tribute or flattery, but was perfectly capable of deep affection for a prisoner like my mother who had nothing material to give.

# CHAPTER 20

The office staff returned for their evening meal and brought back with them the latest gossip from the outside world and from the other prison camps their offices administered. "The war is nearly finished," they said. How often we heard and how often were still to hear this prophecy. Here, in the staff quarters, we could afford to be a little more patient. The prisoners in Birkenau could not. There, the daily ration of hope, dealt out by a few courageous men who tried to keep up morale with facts or fiction, had ceased to mean anything to desperate people. Nobody knew whether they would live a few more months or merely hours.

However, in the winter, when the tide in Russia really turned, we were jubilant. Big or small, every event brought to us from the outside world was magnified. Sitting on our beds at night, we debated every development. We arranged the affairs of the world for the next century to come. There was no doubt in our minds that the few who would survive the terror of this decade could convince any government on the globe of its past and future mistakes and so prevent their repetition in the lifetime of our children. In our analysis of the news, we broke through the restrictions of imprisonment, and the barrier of years and confinement was, temporarily, less irksome.

Preoccupied though we were with the future, our first aim was to get as many prisoners as possible transferred from Birkenau to the staff headquarters. With the Shoe Commando, passing prisoners, and the office staff came many desperate messages pleading for help. Our chance came eventually, but first these comrades of ours had to face yet another winter under inhuman conditions—a winter in Birkenau that demanded a heavy toll of lives.

As the German offensive in Russia came to a standstill and then turned into a fast retreat, there were more and more reprisals on the helpless, suffering inmates of the concentration camps. Many new transports arrived, mainly from Hungary, escorted and handed over to the SS by their own Hungarian militia and police. Theresienstadt, the camp in Czechoslovakia where distinguished families from Germany had been sent because of their past services to Germany and had lived under bearable conditions, was dissolved and the inhabitants evacuated to the gas chambers of Auschwitz. So ended the lives of our most famous contemporary scientists, doctors, musicians, university professors, and other distinguished men and women who had been too loyal, too old, or like my father, simply incapable of believing the Germans would condone mass murder.

This journey in cattle trucks from Czechoslovakia to Poland was Germany's return for a lifetime of faithful service. After they were all gassed, they still brought a last, involuntary service to their beloved fatherland: their gold teeth, rings and medals, even their hair were removed from their bodies and sent back home.

Every setback in Russia and North Africa was marked by mass eliminations and the gas chambers again worked day and night. There was a rumour, later confirmed, that gas and room for this planned genocide were in short supply and people were burned unconscious but still alive. By order of our camp commandant, gas was no longer wasted on babies and young children. They were thrown alive into the ovens of crematoria and open bonfires.

I recovered quickly. In a very short time I filled out and

grew strong again under my mother's loving care and supervision, helped by ample food. Soon I not only managed my daily quota of washing but could help others as my neighbours had helped me. The day came when I risked another look in the mirror and found that I looked young and pretty again. My hair had grown nearly two inches and was standing up like the prickles of a hedgehog, but with patient combing and brushing it settled down silky and boyish.

Early in winter, a rumour that we were soon to be moved to a new camp at Auschwitz was confirmed by SS Brunner. She said it was a very nice building and a great improvement for us. However, proposed changes in a concentration camp were always dreaded. So many promises and false hopes had been dangled in front of prisoners' eyes and had ended in misery and death. A deep depression settled down on us, and as the days shortened and the sun no longer penetrated into our basement abode, we appreciated more and more how snug and warm and comparatively safe we had been here. The Dutch SS woman cried when she learned of the impending move and that did not help to reassure us. As it turned out though, she cried because she had come to rely on our company in her darker moments of fear and on the comfort of having her clothes cleaned, mended, and looked after without having to exert herself.

The day before my birthday, on 27 December, our dormitory was again searched and raided and all our little possessions disappeared from under the mattresses. We had just been given half of a Red Cross parcel each for the first time. So far, everything sent for prisoners by the International Red Cross had gone to the SS. My share had contained, among a few other things, a can of sardines and some chocolate biscuits. I had kept them unopened with the intention of giving a birthday party on the 28th. They had vanished with my other treasures. So I sat on my bed and cried. The girls laughed at me. They had been there long enough to know they would soon replace their losses, but I was still new and the things taken were my first possessions since my arrest. What hurt me the most was that I was now unable to do something nice for my comrades who had been so good to me. Nobody else had had sardines in their parcels and everybody's eyes had popped out of their heads when we unpacked them. Gone!

My mother was called upstairs again after roll call to massage the Dutch SS girl. Some of my friends said, "Don't go, Elizabeth. Punish her and say you are not feeling well or something. She only wants to cry on your shoulder. Rub it in that they have taken all we had, even Daniella's Red Cross parcel." But my mother went upstairs just the same. I was asleep when she returned.

She woke me with a kiss and said, "It's your birthday, my darling. You know, all the things I wish for you but, more than anything else, freedom and happiness." Before I was completely awake, I was hugged and kissed by everybody. I rubbed my eyes. On a stool at the side of my bed was a tray with twenty-one burning candle ends and, laid out on my mother's already neatly made bed, were presents: a new bag embroidered with my name, a comb, a hardly used toothbrush, a handkerchief and a napkin with my initials, a bar of chocolate, ten cigarettes, and a can of sardines.

The girls stood back to watch my reaction. I could not help it; I broke down and wept. No presents in the past or in the future have ever touched me the way this unexpected surprise did. During the night, after I was asleep, the girls had sat down to sew and embroider the bag, handkerchief, and napkin after raiding the sewing room for material. The comb and toothbrush came from a girl whose bed in a corner had been overlooked in yesterday's raid. She would now do without till she found new ones. The candle ends were stolen from the SS women's Christmas tree by prisoners who had cleaned upstairs, and the chocolate, cigarettes, and sardines were a contribution from the Dutch SS woman after my mother had told her of my distress. "A twenty-first birthday is a very special one," somebody said. "You have now reached the age of discretion and can use your inherited fortune as you please without asking your mother's special permission. You are free to do with your life whatever you want. Use your freedom wisely. Bless you."

We all burst into helpless laughter and the day was the best I spent in a concentration camp. Working hours passed quickly and in the evening we all sat cross-legged on the beds and celebrated. The candle stumps were lit again and we each had a square of white bread with a sardine, a piece of chocolate, and half a cigarette. Chocolate and cigarettes had been augmented by the office staff who had "organized" some during the day. Never had a can of sardines stretched so far and given so much pleasure. About thirty of us were sharing my bounty. I was rich.

Sometime in January, SS Brunner took the Capos of the sewing room and laundry to look over the new camp and work rooms in order that they could assess the number of prisoners to be asked for from Birkenau and what additional equipment was needed. Both Etta and the other Capo had recently managed to get their sisters transferred to us and the two sisters took over for the day they were to be away on their inspection tour.

Our ex-Blockova couldn't curb her deep, commanding voice and hearing her shout all day brought back unpleasant memories. It also made me realize what a fine person Etta was. However, the sister's bark was worse than her bite. On the whole, she had changed for the better. She soon learned that she no longer held power over life and death and that she had to behave herself if she did not want to be ostracized. Her sister had a calming effect on her too, but she still never learned to share equally in our working life; she gloried in her position as second-in-command and was never popular. If Etta was ashamed of her, she only showed it by working harder and helping us more, and hid her distress even when she was nagged by her prettier, younger sister. Our ex-Blockova was by no means the worst, but to a certain extent the SS had achieved their objective in making her a tool, an almost incorrigible camp product.

The two Capos returned radiant and full of good news. Sitting in our usual position, cross-legged on our beds in the evening, we listened unbelievingly to their reports. They had decided on the way that Magda, the sewing-room elder Capo, would tell us first about the living quarters and Etta would then take up the story and tell us about the new place of work and her proposed requirements.

Magda' s smiling, dancing eyes were infectious. "Listen girls," she said, "try to imagine a newly built, two-storey house with lots and lots of large windows, no iron bars, and a staircase in the centre. Downstairs, a large common and dining-room on one side, tiled showers and toilets on the other. Upstairs, two big dormitories on either side of the stairs, each containing well-spaced-out, double-tiered beds, tables and chairs. Believe it or not, there are woven mats on the floor around the tables and each bed has sheets, pillow cases, blankets, and an eiderdown quilt."

Here she was interrupted. "Stop kidding, Magda. We'd swallow the story about the beds and tables, but when it comes to floor mats and quilts, we draw the line. Come on, be fair." But she insisted there really were eiderdowns on each bed. We let it pass and presumed fresh air and unaccustomed walking had gone to her head. She was a quiet, not easily excitable Hungarian in her thirties.

She went on raving about this new building of ours, one of four identical ones, surrounded by similar houses which were, at the moment, vacant. Later, they were to house passing army troops on their way to the Russian front. There was no electric fence and no watch-towers round the new camp, only a single, ordinary, wire enclosure. My ears pricked up.

The four houses reserved for prisoners were going to be shared out as follows: House No. 1 for prostitutes to keep SS, army, and privileged German prisoners amused, and No. 2 for office staff working in the so-called "political department" and camp administration. No. 3 was intended for laundry and sewing room personnel. "No. 4 is a mystery," Magda frowned. "It is a house just like the other three but completely surrounded by barbed wire, a camp within the camp." SS Brunner had said we were not permitted to go near the barbed wire of No. 4 and anybody caught speaking to the inmates there would be sent back to Birkenau immediately. We were allowed to visit prisoners of Houses 1 and 2 although No. 1, she hoped, would not be frequented.

We debated for a while who the prisoners in No. 4 would be, but as nobody had any likely solution, Etta took over from Magda to give us an idea of our future working conditions. The laundry and sewing quarters were about a mile from camp but it was a pleasant mile through fields and tree-shaded avenues. Etta wasn't quite sure but she thought it was outside or just at the perimeter of the watch-towers, very near the town of Auschwitz. The buildings must once have been a small factory. They were built around a cobblestone yard and there were stables and administrative blocks on one side. The laundry was huge and would easily employ fifty to sixty girls. There was a drying room, large enough to warrant at least two or three permanent attendants. The place where clothes were pressed and mangled would require another twenty workers and the sewing room about thirty. At the moment, the laundry and sewing rooms together employed only about twenty-five prisoners and that meant we could safely ask for the transfer of eighty to one hundred girls from Birkenau. "Write out a list, girls, of any friends you still have there and I'll present it to SS Brunner tomorrow." We cheered with joy.

"There is one more thing that might interest you. There are

men from Auschwitz, mainly trusted old prisoners, working in the stables and administrative buildings of the factory. They drive horses and carts into the town with only one guard and trade for food for the SS kitchens. We didn't get a chance to speak to any of them today. You know SS Brunner and what a stickler she is for proprieties and ladies' decorum." Etta grinned. "No doubt we'll get the chance to make our neighbours' acquaintance. Now get on with your lists of likely transfers."

I waited until everybody dispersed. There were things you didn't discuss in the presence of office staff employed in the "political department." Two of them we suspected of being planted spies for the SS. That was never proved beyond doubt, but one of them had been at one time the most notorious Capo in Birkenau. She was killed at the end of the war by a few survivors she had maltreated there. While she lived with us in the staff quarters, she was always trying to be friendly, too friendly, and nobody trusted her or spoke to her more than was absolutely essential. The other was her right hand—to her, subservient, to the rest of us, arrogant. We feared and disliked these two.

As soon as they were out of sight and hearing, I went after Etta and asked her what had been uppermost on my mind. "Etta, what are the chances of escape from the factory?" Maybe she was not the right person to approach on this subject. She was rather more timid than the rest of the Slovaks. The laundry was now her life and I often suspected that, in her zeal to do well, she forgot who she was working for. Escape had certainly never crossed her mind. Nevertheless, her answer to my question was sensible, much as I disliked hearing it.

"If we were in Czechoslovakia or even Germany, Daniella, I'd say go ahead and try if you can bear the thought of reprisal and torture on the wretches you left behind. However, as long as you are in Poland, you haven't a chance in hell. You know what happened to nearly all the Jews who escaped through the sewers of Warsaw? The Poles will hand you over to the SS without batting an eyelid. You haven't money or jewels to try and bribe them, although they'd probably take that and still return you. Only if you want to commit the most horrible and painful kind of suicide imaginable should you try to escape from Auschwitz." She put her hand on my arm. "Have a little more patience. The war is bound to end soon and, judging by the standards of our new camp, you have every chance to survive."

A week or so later we moved, once again losing most of our collected treasures. We were not allowed to take anything from the staff quarters save the clothes we had on. Most of us concealed combs and toothbrushes in our bras, risking the possibility of being stripped. We were not and this time got away with it.

It was a beautiful morning when we marched out of the staff quarters for the first and last time. Just the same, hearts were heavy, for this building had been shelter for a long time and the future was frightening. Even prisoners are creatures of habit and we were frankly afraid of any change.

# CHAPTER 21

We arrived at our new quarters and a united shout of joy soared into the still, blue sky. Lined up in front of the house were our friends from Birkenau. Etta had given SS Brunner our list and since then we had heard no more about it, but here they were, Susan and many others. They were ghastly thin, pale, and shivering in spite of the sun. Many faces were missing, but those that were there were so happy to be away from Birkenau at last that I felt bitterly ashamed for our reluctance to leave the staff quarters. We were immediately allowed into the building and nobody very much regretted the departure of the office staff into the adjoining house.

Inside, it was just as Magda had described it, bright and airy, with mats on the floor and eiderdowns covered with satin in matching colors on each bed. Unbelievable luxury. For the girls from Birkenau who had, all this time, slept on bare wooden or brick shelves, it was an even greater change and surprise. Many of them wept with joy. The excited chatter stopped and for a while there was utter and complete silence when everybody thought of our many friends who had not survived the last bitter winter in Birkenau and the forsaken thousands who still existed, doomed and without hope, in the death camp. Nobody had said "three minutes' silence." We were so adjusted to our common fate and tuned in to each other's thoughts that it was seldom necessary to make an announcement.

About lunchtime, the prostitutes moved into house No. 1.

They were a lot of beautiful young women in gay, colorful coats, a noisy, chattering crowd. Few wore make-up and, had we not known who they were, they could easily have been mistaken for students and factory girls which, of course, many of them had been in their former life.

Later in the afternoon, the last house behind barbed wire was occupied. We walked around it, curious to find out something about these confined neighbours, but SS guards drove us indoors. We did see, however, that they were all young Jewish women whose hair was neither cut nor shaved and that one of them had a little boy of perhaps four years of age with her. He was the first young child I had seen since I entered Birkenau.

Just before roll call, one of our girls got a chance to speak to them. They were the human guinea pigs we had heard about, women who were subjected to the most cruel experiments since the Middle Ages. Some were sterilized, others had animal sperm implanted, many were operated on without anesthetic or pain killers of any kind. German "doctors" performed bone and skin grafts on them and transfusion of incompatible blood groups. Some were submerged in freezing water and given large amounts of salt water to drink while the "medical team" watched to find out how long it took them to die. The resulting knowledge was intended to aid naval rescue. The woman and her child, Peter, had come with a fairly recent transport from Berlin. Because of her beauty, she had been given the option to volunteer as a guinea pig and so save her child. She had not hesitated, although she was probably the only one who knew what she was letting herself in for.

Most of the occupants of this "research laboratory" were newcomers whose trials and tortures had only just started or were about to begin. Those of their group who had already been experimented on and who were of no further interest to the SS doctors had been taken to the gas chambers of Auschwitz.

Susan and a few others sat on my and my mother's beds that evening. They were not in as bad a state as I had been. To the last they had been fortunate enough to work in the storehouses of the men's camp, but even there food had become scarce during the winter and they now greedily ate the sandwiches we made for them.

The news they brought from Birkenau was terrible. Since the first rumours of Allied victories in Russia and North Africa, the SS had doubled and tripled their extermination program. Again, the gas chambers were working around the clock while transport after transport was fed into their gaping doors. Any time there was a short pause between arrivals, Birkenau had to provide the numbers to keep them going, and elimination tests had become increasingly more frequent. The SS made no secret of their intention to exterminate every single prisoner should Allied victories continue.

Meantime, we learned that our new camp had been erected as a showpiece to the world. Its gates were to be thrown open to the Red Cross for inspection. Hence the eiderdowns, the mats on the floors, and the luxurious, tiled shower room.

At 9:00 p.m. the lights went out, and soon the dormitories were quiet except for the regular breathing of the sleeping inhabitants. I lay awake thinking over the reports from Birkenau and marvelling at some of the girls who had joined us today. I had seen them praying before going to sleep. How could they still pray after all they had just seen? I envied them their steadfast faith and trust in some divine justice.

Eventually, I too felt drowsy and was just dropping off to sleep when I felt a small hand glide under my blankets and rest on my breast. A voice whispered, "Daniella, darling, you are beautiful, beautiful." I got hold of the hand and, careful not to waken my mother and my neighbours, climbed out of bed and dragged the hand and its owner to the window. In the faint light of the moon, I recognized a fourteen-year-old girl who had been in our transport from Berlin. Frozen to the ground, she looked up at me terrified.

"Don't hurt me, please don't. I can't help loving you. I was so longing to touch you." I took the little thing by the scruff of her neck and shook her, but soon under her lack of resistance my first unintentional fury spent itself and I let her go.

"Don't ever do that again, you silly thing. Learn to control yourself and don't corrupt others." I steered her back to her bed, tucked her in and went back to my own, shaking with repulsion, but I soon learned that some of my best friends had become lesbians in Birkenau. Their attachment and love affairs with other girls were their only escape from reality and the terrible strain of existence in the death camp.

The little girl who had come to me had been seduced by older women before she had had a chance to know a normal life and real love. Once I realized this, I tried to talk to her and help her sort out her mixed-up feelings and desires, but I don't think it did any good. My initial disgust and brutal reaction had frightened her so much that I could not penetrate her defensive attitude.

Prisoners—men—were walking in and out of the new laundry. Nobody stopped them, nobody questioned their business. The guards and their dogs who had escorted us to the "factory" had departed and the Dutch SS woman sat with a book in a warm corner of the sewing room. The men brought us some of their washing wrapped around packets of margarine, salami sausages, sugar, or pieces of cheese. They seemed to have plenty of time for they talked to us for as long as an hour. Soon, friendships developed between them and the girls and the same man always brought their washing to the same woman. Of course, there weren't enough men there to supply all the girls with washing and I was glad nobody had singled me out yet.

I felt shy all of a sudden and had forgotten how to talk to a man. At least I thought I had, until one day a man arrived at my trough and spoke to me. He was a gorgeous creature, tall and good looking, witty, friendly, and polite. He talked to me for a long time and only then asked if I would do his washing for him.

"You are a great lady; I hate to ask you for this service, Daniella," he said with old-fashioned and, under the circumstances, ridiculous courtesy, "but you know how hopeless and helpless we men are. Anyway, if you would do this for me now, I promise you will never do a washing again in your life once the war is over. You'll have servants and all the luxuries you were surely accustomed to before the war. "He was a fast worker and I had a proposal of marriage before the day was done.

The sad truth was, however, that this charming man sometimes thought that he was Siegfried the dragon-killer sometimes King Louis XIV and sometimes Napoleon. On days he was Louis, his personality was the most delightful and intriguing. I always looked forward to his French days. He spoke the language fluently and pretended he didn't understand German. It helped to brush up my French and was great fun. The peculiar thing was that he never appeared ridiculous, and in whatever role he happened to live he was a gentleman. All the girls adored him and nobody made fun of him. He must have been about twenty-eight or thirty years old and had been in various concentration camps for more than ten years. His way of escape was enviable and his personality so commanding that not even the SS molested or ridiculed him.

We had far more work than we ever had in the staff quarters even though there were now so many more girls. Now that we had more personnel, more space, and more equipment, the SS piled it on. Previously, we had washed for officers, SS women, and a few privileged guards; now we got the washing of all guards stationed in Auschwitz, Birkenau, and round about—truck loads full of the filthiest clothes imaginable. Our food got worse. In the staff quarters we had received leftovers from the SS; here it came from the camp kitchen of Auschwitz and was often as bad as it had been in Birkenau. Again, rations were kept back by the Blockova, a German political prisoner, and her house service staff. By the time they reached us, they were reduced to the most minute portions. The long, brisk march to and from the factory and hard work made us terribly hungry. Therefore the food wrapped in the men's washing was more than welcome even though it meant scrubbing all day long without a break, even through lunch hour. It was hard living, but in comparison with Birkenau it was still heavenly.

Not all girls from our commandos were fortunate enough to get the washing of prisoners and I know many were so hungry they sold their bodies to the men for a piece of bread. There was plenty of opportunity for them to slip out into the stables whenever the Dutch SS woman was with us and that was most of the time. Thus most men had two girlfriends: one who washed for them, another as an outlet for their desires. They were going to marry both after the war. Among the girls there was jealousy and pathetic fights over their lovers. The men, of course, told each one what she wanted to hear. To the one washing his clothes he would say, "Because I love and respect you too much, I could not bear to touch you until we are married, but you must understand the needs of a man. You are too innocent, darling. As long as some women can be bought, that innocence will be protected from our baser desires." To the other: "I love you more than anything in the world, but a man has to get his washing done, don't you see?" These affairs were parodies of the eternal triangle behind barbed wire. I don't know whether my Louis XIV did the same, but then I did not imagine myself to be in love with him and was quite disinterested in his amours.

During the day, I hardly saw my mother, but at night we shared what rations I had managed to earn with the extra washing. Women in the sewing room did not see much of the men and had less opportunity to work for them. Once their clothes were torn, privileged German prisoners got new ones and did not bother to have them mended. So I was very surprised when my mother brought back a whole liver sausage one night and I teased her unmercifully. When she did get a word in edgeways, my surprise was even greater.

This welcome contribution to our scant rations had come from Otto, the men's Capo. We all knew him by sight, but he was the only prisoner who never entered the laundry or spoke to any of us, although he always gave us a friendly wave when we arrived at work in the morning or late at night.

Now he had unprecedentedly strolled into the sewing room and sat down on the table in front of my mother, swinging his long legs. He had asked her where she came from and complimented her on her youthful appearance. He told her he had been in concentration camps since 1933 for his part in a street brawl with Nazi troops before Hitler came to power. The murder of two SS men could not be pinned on him but, as he was a communist, he was arrested as soon as Hitler was prime minister. Somehow, somewhere during those years, the reason for his original arrest was forgotten. When prisoners were classified into political and criminal groups, he preferred to wear the green triangle of the criminal on his sleeve. He thought his chance of survival in that category was greater.

Before he left the sewing room, he pulled the liver sausage from his jacket, dropped it in my mother's lap and asked her to share it with me. He was gentle, intelligent, and kind and called her "mother." She got to like and respect him tremendously. It was difficult to guess at his origin since he hardly ever talked about himself or his background; however, she said he had a great reserve of wisdom and knowledge and when he was near her, he gave her a feeling of protection and peace. They became friends and when he asked her one day if she would allow him to talk to me, she said she would have had no objection had I still been a child and needed her permission.

One day, he arranged with the Dutch SS woman to send me over to his office with a message. She wrote a note containing a short list of items she wanted him to purchase for her in the town of Auschwitz, handed it to me, and told me to take it to the men's Capo. Otto was waiting behind a large desk, got up the minute I entered and, taking both my hands, pressed them warmly. He pulled up a chair and asked me to sit down.

"If only you knew, Daniella, how long I have waited to talk to you," he said, pacing up and down and then seating himself again behind his desk. "This is a very great honour, young lady."

My mother was right, he did inspire confidence and trust. With his hawk-like features, intelligent grey eyes, and his hair turning white at the temples, he looked like a wise politician. In spite of his striped prisoner's uniform, he had none of the furtive, nervous or cowed characteristics of the long-term prisoner. He was neither shy nor afraid of anything or anybody and he was remarkably easy to talk to. I realized almost immediately that he was the first person since my father had died who made me feel safe, precious, and protected.

The gist of our first long conversation was that he was confident we would soon be free but, should the war carry on much longer, he would escape if my mother and I would go with him. He asked me to trust him to work out a plan and said that he would not attempt anything foolish. Unless he found a way that was at least ninety-five percent safe, he would not risk our lives. I did not commit myself, of course, but I trusted him implicitly and from then on met him for a few minutes every day. And every day he went to see my mother and told her what he had discussed with me. He looked after us, brought us food, clothes and luxuries from his trips to town, and never asked for anything in return, nor did he ever speak to any other woman prisoner beyond a friendly "good morning" when he entered the sewing room.

He never spoke of his past, only the future, and in the beginning I could not understand why he had singled us out from all the others. It was soon obvious that he loved me deeply and revered my mother. He was wise to the dangers and pitfalls of concentration camp life and knew instinctively which guards and SS women could be bribed to turn a blind eye. When he looked aloof and turned his back on us when we arrived at the factory, we knew that a dangerous guard was on duty and that it would be a day we could not talk to each other. How I missed his considerate, loving kindness on these days. Yet, I never imagined myself to be in love with him and in any case knew too much about the dangers and heartbreaks of love in a concentration camp to easily permit myself the luxury of feelings.

One day he showed me a pouch. It had been concealed between the false bottoms of his desk drawers. It was brim full with uncut diamonds. "These will buy our freedom soon, little Daniella." However, his plans to escape did not materialize. He contemplated many different ideas, but in the end was always defeated by Polish hostility towards Jews. Escape from the factory would have been easy enough. All we would have to do was to hide until the workers had left at night and then walk out as soon as it got dark.

Occupied now with their own fears and problems, many guards had become careless and often we were not even counted before returning to camp. At roll call, somebody could have answered for us when numbers were called and it might have been possible to deceive the SS until the more thorough counting in the morning. Otto could easily have escaped on his own. He was a German but spoke Polish fluently and was, unmistakably, not a Jew. However, my mother and I would have had little chance to get even as far as the German border. We would have had to travel by day as well as by night; for by morning our escape would have been discovered, and unless we had moved a considerable distance, dogs would track us down with the ready co-operation of the Poles. We pleaded with Otto to take his chance and go alone, but he would not be persuaded and was determined to see us through.

# CHAPTER 22

Winter turned into spring and spring into summer. The fields we passed on our way to work displayed their poisonous green. Even the trees had none of the tender colours of spring you see anywhere else in Europe. What was there about Auschwitz that turned even nature into something ugly and deadly?

Time passed quickly enough. We were working harder and harder. I was now posted to the drying room where it was hot and comfortable, but as it had no windows I worked in artificial light all day and hardly ever saw the sun. I could not work for my favourite prisoner any more either. Otto kept us well supplied with food, but I missed the delightful conversations with King Louis XIV.

Through Otto we heard of political developments, but we could not really rejoice as every Allied victory cost thousands of lives in Birkenau. The nearer Germany moved towards ultimate defeat, the greater the lust for mass murder.

The barracks surrounding our buildings were now fully occupied by soldiers passing through to the Russian front. On their return they rested there for a week or more. There were wounded; we got their washing too, and often the water in our troughs turned red from the blood caked on their uniforms. We now worked day and night shifts. More women were transferred to us from Birkenau. All ex-staff quarters prisoners worked night shift and slept in the daytime.

In the summer of 1944, we saw Russian bombers passing over Auschwitz for the first time and then heard the rumble of explosions of bombs dropping on the nearby town. We learned from Otto that the underground workers of the Resistance had passed on detailed maps of the layout of concentration camps in the area to the Russians. They had a secret transmitter operating somewhere in the men's camp. Otto now stayed behind in the evenings and talked to us for a while every night. I don't know how he wangled this extra time at the factory, but I suppose diamonds were sufficient persuasion if paid in the right quarters.

One lovely summer day, I could not sleep and sat on a window sill sunbathing. At the window in the barracks opposite were a few soldiers. One was playing an accordion and the others sang, mostly wistful tunes of home. I closed my eyes to listen and basked in the warm sun. From time to time the soldiers stopped singing to shout to me something like, "Hello, beautiful, this is a request program. Any songs you would like to hear?" I ignored them and did not answer. So they just continued with their music.

A sweet, sentimental song was interrupted suddenly by a mighty roar in the sky and, looking up, I saw it was black with low-flying bombers. It was like a bad dream when their flaps opened to emit small, oblong, black shapes. A carpet of bombs fell towards me.

It can only have been seconds between the time I saw them and the blast. One minute I was sitting on the window sill in the sun, the next I was flung against a bed post; everything was black with clouds of dust and breathing was almost impossible.

When the dust settled, I glanced out the windows. The sky was clear and blue again and there was not a single airplane to be seen. But the soldiers' music had stopped. Where their barrack had been there was a deep, gaping hole and a heap of rubble. With all these bombs, only the one building had been destroyed, but in the fields and yard around it there were innumerable craters.

My mother and most of the other girls had been sound asleep when the force of the explosion threw them out of bed. They got up, rubbed their eyes and shook the dust off their clothes. They looked as though they had been dipped in flour. Somewhat late, the air raid alarms went off and everybody ran down to the cellar for shelter; that is, everybody except my mother and I.

A few minutes later we heard the planes roaring overhead again. This time I did not wait to see their flaps open but dived into my bed, pulling the blankets over my head. Muffled, through my covers, I heard my mother pleading with me to come down to the cellar. "You go down if you feel safer, Mom. I prefer my bed. We can only die once, and I'd much rather stay where I am."

She left me and walked towards the staircase when an explosion rocked the building. A tremendous weight settled on my chest and I choked, but a few minutes later I risked pulling down my blankets. There was a deadly silence and the sun hit my eyes at an unusual angle. As soon as I got accustomed to the bright light, I saw why.

My bed, which had been near the centre of our dormitory, was now the last in a row. The outside wall of our house had collapsed down and inwards, and I was lying on overhanging floor planks, open to sun and wind. The top bunk of my bed had partly broken down on top of me, but otherwise I was all right. As I carefully crept out from under the debris, I saw my mother limping towards me. The blast had thrown her down the stairs but she got away with bruises and a slight shock. When she saw me alive, colour returned to her chalk-white face and she smiled with relief.

Only then did we hear screams from the cellar and raced downstairs. We had to break in the jammed door. It was a sorry sight that met us. Just a few of our girls were standing near the inner door. Bloodstained and shocked, they scratched away at the rubble of bricks and beams that had fallen on the rest. With our bare hands, we worked and dug and carried away the debris to uncover a few more of our comrades who were badly hurt but still breathing. Two hours later we had finished. We found ten dead and many of the others so badly injured they had little chance to survive. There were many more with broken bones.

Those of us who were not hurt worked on and on, and with superhuman effort carried the injured out into the fresh air and as far away from the building as we could. The dead we left behind. When the next wave of bombers approached, we broke though the single strands of wire fencing and ran into the open field, panic stricken and without thought of consequences.

Not a single guard or SS man was anywhere in sight. Squadron after squadron of Russian bombers passed over, dropped their loads and disappeared again. By the time they had finished, there was not a single SS or army building left. They were razed to the ground but, except for the one stray bomb that had hit the wall of our house, the prisoners' houses were untouched. The Resistance workers' plans of the prison camps and the SS barracks had been accurate.

During the lull in the attack, we carried our wounded into the field and there we sat or paced about unmolested for at least an hour after the last raid was over. Then, slowly and cautiously, SS guards appeared at the skyline of the field. From behind trees and bushes these heroes approached, their guns pointed at us. From a safe distance they shouted at us to line up and raise our hands above our heads. We did, except for the wounded who could not get up or lift their arms. From an easy shooting range, the SS fired at our injured and we ran back through the fence to our damaged building, dragging with us those unable to walk and not yet dead. From then on we were locked in the terrifying cellars during air raids, but since all SS targets in our immediate neighbourhood were already destroyed, we were never under direct attack again.

Exhausted after this eventful, sleepless day, our decimated commando was marched out to work at night, and when we arrived at the factory, Otto was waiting on the steps of his office, his face white and strained. The news of our dead and wounded had already spread to the men.

He did not even wait until the SS woman had vanished to her place in the sewing room, but raced through the laundry into the drying room. Without bothering to shut the door, he gripped my shoulders so hard I thought he was going to crush my bones. For once this cool fearless man lost all control and cried like a tormented child. "If anything had happened to you and your mother, I would have killed myself." It was the nearest he ever came to actually saying that he loved me. Unlike the other men who tried to tie girls down, he never asked for promises or emotions, although he was ready to risk his life for me.

By early October 1944, there was no longer any doubt about the final outcome of the war. Through Otto we got all the information received by the Resistance on the movements of the Allies. It was now just a matter of time until the Allies would meet on German soil. But if outsiders thought Germany would realize its defeat and capitulate, we knew better. After eleven years of Nazi terror and nearly five years of war, not even the enemies of the Nazis realized they were dealing with unpredictable madmen. We, their victims, knew only too well.

The wildest rumours circulated among us: the whole of Birkenau was going to be liquidated; the last transports were arriving and after the prisoners were gassed, all traces of the death camp, the grave of millions of Jews, Russians, Poles, Czechs, Hungarians, Greeks, French, Dutch, Gypsies, and Germans, was to be obliterated.

Otto gravely confirmed these rumours, but he was convinced that, this time, the SS would not succeed in carrying out their plans. The Resistance, now very strong in most camps, would save the prisoners of Birkenau. So we were not surprised when the word passed that prisoners of the *Sonderkomando* —special commando forced to gas, cremate, and bury the victims—had revolted at last and blown up the gas chambers with bombs smuggled in by partisans. Before they exploded, rumour said, the prisoners threw into the vaults as many SS guards and dogs as they could get hold of. We all had come too far to think of possible reprisals. Without reservation, we rejoiced in the knowledge that the tortured prisoners of Birkenau were at last free of these monstrous, smoking death chambers and that men had, at last, fought back and refused to kill their own people.

Two days later Otto brought the terrifying news that something had gone wrong and only one of the gas chambers had actually been destroyed. The SS had sent reinforcements as soon as the explosion was heard, and all existing Sonder Commandos had been gassed. The revolt had failed. The murder continued on a larger scale than ever before.

Smaller revolts continued for a while. The bloody, scorched and bullet-holed uniforms of SS guards sent to us for washing bore witness to the courage of desperate prisoners. But those fighters were doomed from the start. Contrary to regular German army units, the SS could still draw on almost unlimited reserves. Reinforcements flooded into Auschwitz to carry out reprisals and put down any spark of resistance. Even our guards were increased and became watchful and vicious once more. We were counted and recounted innumerable times every day. The men could no longer stroll into the laundry and bring us their washing, and even Otto rarely managed to talk to us.

At the end of November he appeared in the drying room. His face was drawn and tired. He had bribed one guard and made the other so drunk with illicit alcohol that he would be unconscious for the rest of the day. Nevertheless, his voice held tremendous urgency.

"Daniella, this is the last time I can talk to you. All German prisoners are going to be transferred back to Germany tomorrow. We have the option of volunteering for SS or the army. The latter means the Russian front. All my men have volunteered, but I prefer to stick it out to the bitter end as a prisoner and will probably be sent to Dachau. All that, however, is beside the point—just for your information. I want you to listen very carefully to what I have to say. Your life and your mother's may depend on your memory. All healthy prisoners, men and women, will soon be evacuated. You will most likely be sent to Belsen. I shall try to tell you what is probably going to happen.

"You will get five minutes to assemble and, surrounded by guards and dogs, you will be marched out of camp. Soon, on the main road past Auschwitz, you will be joined by endless columns of prisoners from Birkenau and other surrounding camps and more and more SS. The march will be very fast because the Russians will be close at your heels. It is winter and it will be bitterly cold. Now I am coming to the points you must remember if you don't want to die within sight of freedom and victory. Don't let your mother get out of your sight, no matter how hard the pressure from behind. Keep to the centre of the column, no matter how fast you are made to walk. Never get to the front or sides. When prisoners get tired and slow down, the guards will shoot and club to death anybody within their reach in the front and flanks.

"You must promise to stay somewhere in the centre, will you? No matter how tired you are, don't fall behind. Push on and grit your teeth.

"If the pattern of previous transports I have been in is followed, the women will have a cart in the rear to carry those unable to walk. Don't feel tempted to get on it and don't let your mother get on even if you have to carry her. Those on the cart will be killed somewhere along the road.

"I don't know how long you will have to walk. It might be only hours; it might be days; it might be weeks. Remember what you have been through already, and don't give up so near the end. No matter how weary you are, Daniella, go on."

I stood mute as he took my face tenderly between his hands. "Daniella, I have never asked you for any promise. I have never asked you to love me and to marry me. I'll see about that when I find you free after the war, but now I am asking you to live. Will you promise me? If I never saw you again in my life, I could not bear the thought of a world in which you and your mother did no longer exist. Promise me, Daniella, promise, please."

"I will live," I promised.

"All right, pet, let's presume you saw a chance to escape the first night. Don't try it on Polish soil. You know what happened to the others who tried it, and don't feel tempted to make your way to the Russians either even though the front may be very near. My sympathy has been and always will be with the Russian struggle for survival, but the Russian fighting forces are a rough and mixed crowd, brutalized to a point where rape and murder are everyday events. You don't speak Russian and couldn't even explain where you came from, should they wait for an explanation from a beautiful young girl, which is unlikely.

"Curb your impatience until you get well into Germany. Then make a break at your first opportunity. The chance will come your way, and when it does, don't hesitate. Believe me, I have thought about the wisdom of giving you this advice through many a sleepless night. I know it is dangerous, but Belsen is worse. You may survive even that notorious camp, but your mother would not. If she got as far as Belsen, she would look so old and frail from the hardships of the journey, she would be sorted out and killed on arrival. She would not be allowed even to enter.

"Can you remember all I have told you so far? It is vital." He repeated it all and asked me to tell my mother everything except the necessity of our escape. He thought that would worry her and frighten her so much it might sap her strength before we even started.

"Keep that extra burden and responsibility to yourself and take the initiative when the time comes without unnecessary explanations. Your mother will follow you wherever you go.

"As soon as I have gone tomorrow, you must go to my office. I have arranged with the Dutch SS woman that you are to collect some papers from my desk. Under a loose floorboard behind the door, you will find a pair of fur-lined shoes for your mother and skiing boots for yourself. You will need them. Wear them from now on so that they are well worn and comfortable when you are evacuated. There is also a pair of long, warm trousers there. Take SS sweaters, warm underwear, and another pair of slacks from the drying room within the next two weeks and wear them under your striped prison garb. See you get a complete and very warm outfit for yourself and your mother because you will have to take off the striped uniform.

"Your mother told me once you have friends and money in Berlin. Get there as quickly as you can and always keep close to the crowds of German refugees who are bound to be on the road fleeing from the Russians. Don't stay in Berlin either. There will be a lot of bombing and fighting before the final crash. Make your way to the West and wait for the Americans and British. They won't be long.

"This advice is all I can do to help you. I could give you some diamonds, if you want them, but I would advise against your taking them. You and your mother are so damned honest, any ape could read in your faces that you carried something valuable. Also, you have neither the experience nor the mentality to bribe the right people at the right time. You would be far better to join the stream of refugees, destitute as most of them will be. Look after your mother, you sweetest girl in the world." He turned and almost ran out of the drying room and laundry. I did not see him again as a prisoner. The following day the factory was deserted. All German male prisoners had been evacuated. Their transport had left Auschwitz by train early in the morning.

It was lonely after he had gone, so terribly lonely. And I was again terrified of the future and my responsibility. Only then did I realize how much I had come to depend on and lean on Otto. He was wise and kind, at least twenty years older than I, and for the second time in my life I felt I had lost a father and the first security and protection I had known in years of struggle and misery.

There were other changes too. The German Blockova had been evacuated and replaced by a prostitute. Food got scarcer and no extra rations came our way. The Dutch SS woman who had been so kind to us left with a transport for Germany and we had a succession of cruel, sadistic women. SS Brunner still protected us and took an interest in our welfare from a distance so guards were forbidden to beat us, yet we got kicked and slapped in the face for crimes as insignificant as an unwashed SS handkerchief.

On return from work, we were locked up in camp and could no longer walk around the yard or talk to girls from the other buildings. All that was bearable. We knew it would only be a matter of time until something happened. We waited.

Many of the girls hoped the Russians would liberate us overnight, before we could be evacuated. I did not. I was afraid of the Russians and even more afraid of being killed by the SS before we fell into the hands of their enemies. And, curiously enough, in spite of all that had happened to us, I was homesick for Berlin as I had never been before.

Years ago, when the Gestapo had finished with me, I had fervently hoped I would never see that accursed city again. Now I was breaking my heart with longing to get home. I never mentioned it to my friends for they were all Zionists. For them, Palestine was home. I wanted to share their enthusiasm for I knew full well that I could never live in Germany again, and I was afraid that for the rest of my life I would be a stranger wherever I went. I hated everything German but loved the soil and the beauty of the country with all my heart.

Only days after Otto left, I stole a pair of navy blue, woolen slacks and a brown pullover from a line in the drying room, put them under my striped uniform and rolled up the trouser legs. I looked and felt somewhat bulky. For days I was frightened, waiting for enquiries, but the clothes were never missed. Emboldened by my success, I stole more every day. Once I took a blouse belonging to an SS woman still on duty, but when she came looking for it, I quickly returned it the next day and said it had been overlooked. I got my face slapped for that but it was worth it.

Gradually I acquired civilian clothes not only for my mother and myself, but for all my trusted friends. I could not get shoes for them but at least they would all be warm and have a chance to escape in civilian clothes when the time of transfer came.

# CHAPTER 23

January 1945: we woke up to the steady whining of shells and the crackling of machine gun fire not far away. It was very exciting. Never did we dress so quickly and carefully. Both my mother and I put on two sets of woolen underwear, blouses and sweaters, two pairs of stockings and woolen socks. Fortunately, Otto's boots were large enough to be still comfortable.

It was bitterly cold, snow had fallen inches thick through the night and as we lined up in the yard for the usual roll call our breath froze and tiny icicles formed on our noses. A large number of SS guards carrying full marching kit and armed to their teeth turned up with the dogs and we knew before we were told that the time for the dreaded exodus had come.

The SS women did not take time to count us, and as Otto had predicted, the first group of one hundred prisoners marched out of the camp within five minutes. We were assembled in lines of four and told to wait. We waited and waited. One of the SS women used this time to search the prisoners in front. With fear and shock, I saw her tear off clothes we had so carefully collected, and the heap grew of pullovers, slacks and warm underwear she took off the shivering girls. The SS woman hurled insults as well as her whip at the unfortunate prisoners in the front who stood all but naked, defenseless under her assault.

She had almost reached us in the centre of the column when

a messenger arrived with a note. She nodded and said to the messenger, "All right, thank you." Then she turned to us, lifted her whip and broke it into small pieces, grinding the remnants into the snow with the heel of her boots. Putting her arms round the shoulders of two prisoners nearest to her, she addressed us.

"Girls, I just got a message. We are too late to be evacuated. The Russians are very close and we are more or less surrounded. We are now all in the same boat and have to make the best of it. I was forced into the SS and did not want to come to Auschwitz. When the Russians arrive, I want you to confirm that I have never been cruel to you and have only done my duty.

"You will do that, won't you, my dear girls? Oh dear, what am I thinking of, leaving you out in the cold so long, you poor things. Quickly, get back into the house and warm yourselves. Put extra coal on the fire. We might as well wait in comfort."

As we filed in, she went on talking to us individually, pleading with us to help her. In return she would demand food, clothes, and money for us from the Russians. I saw with glee that the heap of warm clothes she had taken off the prisoners had vanished and all were dressed as before. We pressed round the stoves and nobody listened to the continuous whining of the SS woman deploring her fate.

Half an hour later though, a second messenger turned up with another note. Unbelieving, we saw that wretch take up the handle of a broom to hit out at the girls near her. "Downstairs, you pigs. Line up in marching order and be quick about it. I'll show you what's what, you filthy Bs. We are going back to Germany."

To escape the swinging broom handle, everybody rushed downstairs and out of the building, but before I could take my mother's hand, the beastly woman lifted her booted foot and kicked her so hard in the back my mother rolled down the stairs head first. Rushing after her to help her up, I swore to myself I would kill that

SS woman with my own hands if I were ever free.

This time it took only seconds to line up and we were out of the gate and on the road before we fully realized what was happening. My mother was not hurt by her fall and that was a blessing for it wasn't a march, it was a run. In our warm clothes we soon felt too hot and were sorely tempted to take some off. For half an hour the guards whipped us on. Then we came to a short halt on the main road to Auschwitz where long columns of prisoners were plodding along, blocking the road. We bypassed them across a field. Already many of the prisoners were faltering and falling behind, and some of their dead were lining the road. The living were hit, kicked, and pushed by their guards and some stretched out their hands to us, begging for bread. But we had not been given any rations this morning either and couldn't help.

Soon we left them far behind. We had the advantage of being a smaller group and physically fit. After another half hour or so, we passed a deep ditch and a gasp of horror went up from the girls on our right flank. My mother and I were in the centre of the column and did not see anything, but those who did recognized some of the first hundred prisoners who had left our camp earlier this morning among the dead bodies filling the ditch. They were mainly from the house behind barbed wire, the guinea pigs.

When the message had reached them that Auschwitz could not be evacuated, their guards had lined them up along the road, shot everyone and fled.

Was that the end we were coming to? On and on we marched; we left the sound of front-line fire far behind until it diminished to a distant, low rumble. Gradually our pace slowed down and the first moans were heard. Some girls had sore feet, others were getting hungry. At least we did not suffer from thirst. There was plenty of snow. All day we marched without break or rest until it got dark. Then the guards herded us into a deserted barn.

They were too frightened of partisans, said to be hiding in the forests, to drive us on in the dark.

The barn was full of straw and comparatively warm. Exhausted, we sank down against the stacked bales. So far, our group had no losses but many had feet that were so swollen their shoes and boots would not come off. Somebody asked me if we should try to escape in the night. There was a small trap door at the side of a bale of hay where we might be able to squeeze through. Remembering Otto's advice, I refused to consider it, but two Polish girls got away while we were asleep. As we were no longer being counted, the guards did not notice their absence.

At dawn we were again driven out. If anything, it was even colder than yesterday. None of us had any food. We stuffed our mouths full of snow; snow was our breakfast, our lunch and our supper. That day we had our first casualties. Some girls had not been able to get their shoes on again in the morning. Their feet were swollen beyond recognition. They wrapped rags round their feet, but this was no protection against the deep snow and icy road. Soon their feet were bleeding and they fell behind.

The road led through deep forests and the SS were hysterical with fear of partisans. Every time a twig snapped or a load of snow tumbled off the tall pine trees, they let off wild shots and started shooting into our ranks to speed up this nightmare march. In front, at the flanks, and in the rear, prisoners slumped down, shot in the back. Closing the ranks, others stumbled over their bodies.

Again we were on the road all day, and when it got dark we were driven into an open field, fenced in by barbed wire. There was no house, no barn anywhere in sight. My mother told everybody to keep on their feet and walk around, but mostly the girls took no heed. They were too tired to care. My mother went from one to another trying to rouse them, but in the end she gave up and concentrated on me, for I too had reached that state of exhaustion when

I dropped off to sleep against my will.

The snow was soft and inviting and I curled up in it. The next moment my mother gave me a stinging slap in the face and brought me back to my feet and to my senses. I, who had promised Otto to look after my mother, was ready to give up, and my mother, with superhuman strength and energy, kept me awake. Throughout that endless night she told me stories, rubbed my hands, slapped my face and back, and made me run up and down the length of the field. Only a few of our closest friends stayed awake with us. When at last a pale, wintry sun rose behind the forests, those who had gone to sleep in the snow were dead. Hundreds of prisoners from Birkenau had marched throughout the night and caught up with us that morning to swell our ranks, but from our camp only a few survived.

Once more we walked all day. Many a time I would have fallen behind or dropped down had my mother not pulled me forward, her small hand round my wrist like an iron band. Hungry and tired, we stumbled over our own feet, fell in snow drifts, and went on without conscious thought. My mother's unbreakable will and wiry strength kept me and a handful of friends alive.

Finally, on the evening of the third day, we reached a railway siding and were loaded into open coal wagons, a hundred women to each truck. There was no room to stretch or even sit down. Two guards and their dogs occupied more than a third of the truck. We crouched close against each other as best we could, and with rumbling stomachs and frozen limbs, watched our two guards settle down under thick blankets and warm furs.

Each SS man took a long drink of brandy from his flask and ate chunks of bread and corned beef. Under our hungry eyes they stuffed themselves and then threw bread and meat they did not want over the side. The train moved slowly, stopped again and then chugged along steadily until, perhaps an hour later, at the German frontier, the guards' identities were checked and they received new rations of bread, sausages, and alcohol. Some prisoners begged for a drink or a piece of bread, but the border guards ignored their pleas. The guards emptied their bottles in one short session and rolled under their blankets, covering their dogs as well.

Crouching there, I fell into brief spells of fitful sleep. Every few minutes somebody tried to extricate an arm or leg from the general entanglement. It was agony, but after a few hours, moving my aching legs, I woke my mother. It was almost pitch dark except for a faint glow from the snow on either side of the rails. My mother tried to move and everybody else woke up. Some cried with pain, cold, and hunger; others cursed and fought desperately for a little bit of room. The guards snored noisily under the blankets and the dogs did not stir. Slowly the train rumbled through snow-covered land.

"We must be very near Kattowitz," my mother whispered. "I know every inch of this country, I was born near here. Little did I think I would ever travel through it under these circumstances. I'd give anything to be free and see my parents' house once more. Do you remember our garden, Daniella? You played hide and seek behind the hedges when you were a little girl."

"Why not, Mom?" I whispered back. "We'll get off the train here and visit your old home.

"Don't joke, darling." The guards did not stir. They were dead drunk and sound asleep. I got hold of Susan's hand and squeezed it. "Sue, my mother and I are getting out of here. Come with us." I whispered to some other friends, "We are going to my mother's home. Will you come?"

Tears were streaming down my mother's face. "Don't take any notice of her. She has gone out of her mind, my poor child."

Somebody cried out in despair and agony, "Stop pushing, I can't stand it any longer." I clouted her lightly over the head and said, "Will you be quiet, you goat. Don't you understand, I am going to make room for you now."

Susan was the only one who understood I was in dead earnest. She pushed and rammed herself to the side of the truck, pulled me after her, and I in turn pulled my mother over the crouching bodies. "Climb on my back, Dannie," Susan breathed quietly. "Climb out first and I'll help your mother once you are out. I won't come, but thanks for the invitation. You are better off on your own. There is no safety in numbers. Good luck."

I climbed on her back, swung myself over the side and jumped off the slow-moving train, landing softly in a snow drift. I waited, immobile. Almost immediately my mother followed, but she was stiff and above the noise of the train I could hear her feet clanging against the metal siding. If the dogs started barking, the game would be up.

The loud beating of my heart drowned out all other noise for a moment. In the milky glow of the snow in a foggy dawn, I saw my mother jump. She fell and rolled down a gently sloping embankment a little distance away. I ran to her, got hold of her hand and we raced over a short expanse of snowy field into thick, dark forest. We ran and stumbled through thicket and undergrowth. We fell into holes and scratched our faces on low branches and went on running till we both dropped down in a hollow.

From the direction of the train came weird noises. The engine whistled and puffed to a halt. Brakes screeched, dogs barked, SS guards cursed and shouted. We could hear it all echoing through the silent wood. I closed my eyes wearily. They were after us. There was no point in running any further. If the dogs were loose, they'd catch up with us. Our only chance was to sit quietly and motionless and hope they would not pick up our scent. The shouting grew louder, prisoners screamed and shot after shot was fired. I was paralyzed with fear. Suddenly all was silent again; a complete and utter silence. The engine of the train snorted and puffed and soon the wheels rattled noisily on, westward into Germany.

We did not move until the last, distant rumble was swallowed up in the early morning mist. Then we jumped up, fell into each other's arms, laughing and crying at the same time. We were free, free, free. There and then we tore off the striped prisoners' uniforms, buried them under two or three feet of snow, and walked away in civilian clothes through the calm, glistening winter wood. Our hearts were so full, we did not speak, just plodded on, the pale, rising sun on our backs.

"Wait till we get to the next village, Daniella. I'll be able to tell you then where we are exactly and which way to go.

"Do you really want to go to your old home, Mother?" I asked. "People might recognize you. If you could bear to bypass it, we could get back to Berlin sooner. I think we should go there as quickly as possible." She agreed and admitted it was just a dream and she did not really want to see her house again. Her parents were dead and it was just as well to forget the past.

Out of the forest, we came into a small Silesian village. We were afraid to enter in case we were questioned, but after nearly four days without a bite to eat, we could not afford to walk past. For a long time we looked at the snow-covered thatched roof of the nearest farm. All the houses seemed dead. Not a wisp of smoke came from any of their chimneys, no dogs barked, there was not a soul to be seen anywhere. As we cautiously approached the farm, we heard cows mooing and rattling in the byre, but it was not the gentle sound of happy, contented animals. The noise they made was savage, full of fear and agony. I opened the gate and went in. There were only three cows and we could see at a glance they had not been milked for at least a day. Their udders were swollen to the bursting point. We found a dirty bucket and I went into their stable and milked them unskillfully but effectively. The cows seemed to appreciate my efforts. They stood quietly and nuzzled my hand in a friendly way when I had finished. We drank some of the fresh, warm milk and then went into the house. Nobody answered our knocking. The farmhouse was deserted, but on the table in the kitchen we found bread and butter, cheese and jam, and dirty dishes. The owners appeared to have left in a hurry. We sat down and helped ourselves to some food, made a few sandwiches, and wrapped them in a newspaper that was lying around, its headlines still promising final victory.

We opened the gate of the cow shed and untied the animals in the hope they would find relief if they were free to roam. The whole village was the same: cows chained and unmilked, houses deserted, untidy and uncared for. We came to a small railway station. It was locked but a notice in the entrance proclaimed, "All train services for civilians to Berlin and West Germany will cease to function as from 2:00 p.m. this afternoon, the 25th of January 1945."

We had lost track of time, but eventually we worked out that the 25th was yesterday. We had escaped on 26 January 1945. Seven years before, on the same day, my father had died. It seemed a lifetime ago. My mother thought of it at the same time for she went on looking at the notice in that railway station and said quietly, "If I had known seven years ago all that would happen to us, I would not have grieved so much. He could never have survived Birkenau-Auschwitz. He had a wonderful escape, too."

# CHAPTER 24

The silence in the deserted village was shattered by distant explosions and even while we were listening, the noise of shell fire and cannons came closer. We had escaped from the SS, death marches and concentration camps for the time being, but we were only at the very start of a long road to freedom. We had many, many weary miles to go yet. We plodded on, following signs to the west, through vast forests, deserted villages, and frozen fields, with the low rumbling of the Russian front in our rear.

Toward late afternoon we saw the first signs of life and soon we caught up with long treks of refugees. Cart after cart blocked the road. A few were pulled by tired horses but most were pushed by men and women. The carts were loaded high with furniture and household goods, and on top of these perched small children and very old people who could not walk. These people were too preoccupied with their own plight to ask us questions, and I spoke to some of them to find out where they were going and what they thought their future was going to be.

The general feeling was that of despair, disillusionment, and fear. They knew, at last, the war was lost and they had lived too close to the Polish border to have much hope of returning to their homes and farms. A few had relations in the West, but the majority were bound for Berlin where they had been told they would find shelter and soup kitchens.

It was not necessary to ask them what they thought of their "Thousand Year Reich" now. These arrogant Germans had come a long way indeed.

Unhampered by luggage, we left the trekking families behind, and at nightfall reached a large village where people were pushing toward the station. We were told there were still trains running from here and soon we joined an orderly line outside rows of ticket counters. Repeatedly the crowds were addressed and reassured through loudspeakers, "Keep calm, keep order, don't panic. Everybody will be evacuated."

Closer and closer we moved to the ticket office and it occurred to me that we had no money for the fare when a woman in front of us cried, "I have no money. I don't know where my husband got to. I lost him in the crowd but he said he'd meet me in Berlin should we get separated. I forgot to ask him for money and papers. What am I to do?" She was quite hysterical until a stationmaster put his hand on her shoulder and told her to stop worrying.

"There are hundreds like you without money and documents, old girl. We'll see you get the train all right. If you don't find your husband before then you will be given money and accommodation on arrival in Berlin. The trip is on the house. Don't you think we have deserved a little joy ride?" he said flippantly.

We finally arrived at the counter. I dabbed my eyes and cried too. "Mother and I have lost our money. I don't know where my father got to. Can you help us?"

"Sure girlie, don't you fret. Here is your ticket. See you get something to eat before you get on the train. You look hungry. It might take a day or two before you get to Berlin, conditions being what they are."

We moved on to the platform and another line-up. Grey-clad women ladled thick, steaming potato soup into big mugs. We drank our soup greedily. It seemed ages since we had anything hot and it was years since we had eaten anything so good and rich.

The train we were to board had just steamed into the station and was almost empty. We sat down on adjoining seats. Gradually the compartment filled up, small children were lifted into the luggage racks and people sat on the floor and on suitcases all along the corridors. Doors slammed and the train moved out. My mother, I knew, was thinking as I was of the thousands of starved, frozen prisoners from Birkenau and Auschwitz travelling through the cold, dark night in open trucks, towards yet another concentration camp that few of them would survive. There was no pity left in my heart for these dispossessed members of the master race now travelling with us on this comparatively comfortable train. My eyes closed. With the rhythmic singing of the wheels, "Going home, going home, free, free free; going home, going home . . ." I fell asleep, my arm around my mother's narrow shoulders.

It was broad daylight when I finally woke up. We were travelling through flat country. We fought our way to a washroom. Water was scarce, but there was enough for a drink and to wipe our hands and faces.

"Should we be asked our names and where we came from," my mother whispered behind the locked washroom door, "say the name is *Doverg* and we came from Kattowitz. There are lots of Dovergs there. It's a very common name in Silesia. We'll stick to our Christian names and our own birthdays so we won't have too much to remember. Should we be asked what Kattowitz was like before we escaped from the Russians, let me do the talking because I know the town well and heard a bit of what was bombed there last night from some refugees."

We returned to our compartment to share the sandwiches we had taken from the farmhouse yesterday, but the packet, wrapped in newspaper, had vanished from the seat. Somebody had stolen them and there was no point in asking the refugees. Whoever had taken them would have eaten them by now. We were hungry, but life in Birkenau and Auschwitz had gradually conditioned us to take losses in our stride.

The train was desperately slow. It stopped every few miles for no apparent reason. Often we seemed to go back the way we had come, and many a time we had to be shunted back and forward onto a different line to avoid craters blasted into the railroad during recent bombing. Late at night, the train pulled into Berlin. I strained my eyes for familiar landmarks of the city that I thought was like none other in the whole world. But it was under complete blackout and I saw nothing.

The station from which we finally disembarked could have been any station. In gloomy semi-darkness we could see just the bare skeleton of what were once walls of glass.

Again, crowds of refugees were channelled quickly and efficiently into orderly lines and again we were met by grey-clad women handing out mugs of hot soup. The soup eaten, we moved on to another woman who wore a big swastika badge and was asking the people ahead of us for their identity cards. My heart was in my throat, but I heard a number of them say they had lost or left behind their documents in the rush to get away.

Our turn came, we told the same story, the woman nodded and filled in temporary cards for us: "Elizabeth Doverg, born 1 January 1902, refugee from Kattowitz" and "Daniella Doverg, born 28 December 1922, refugee from Kattowitz."

"Have you any money?" she asked in a monotonous, disinterested voice. We said we hadn't and she gave us twenty marks and told us to report to the nearest labour exchange the following day where we would get more until employment could be found for us. "There is plenty of work clearing rubble," she confided, before passing us on to a housing officer.

"Have you anywhere you could stay in or near Berlin?" was

the next routine question.

"Yes, we have relations who are expecting us," I lied.

"Thank God for that," sighed the woman. "You are lucky. Most of these people will have to sleep in bunkers and air raid shelters. Do you know how to get to your relatives?"

"Yes, thank you." We were dismissed. Outside the station were a few battered, old taxi cabs, all driven by women. We tried three, but were refused when we admitted we could not pay with food. Many refugees had brought something edible from their farms. "Well, if you can't give me butter or meat—even bread would do, or flour—you'd better walk. Money is no good to us these days." In the end we found one driver who asked how much money we had. "Twenty marks? It will cost you all of that. Twenty marks don't even buy half a pound of butter now. "

We agreed to give her all we had and she drove us to the district where Margaret lived. We stopped and got out a good mile from her house to make sure we were not being trailed.

It must have been in the early hours of the morning when we rang the bell on Margaret's door. "Who is there?" she asked cautiously through the keyhole.

"Open up, Margaret, please, Elizabeth and Daniella here." The door flew open and closed behind us. Margaret, in an old-fashioned flannelette nightgown, danced round us like a buzz saw. She asked no questions. In no time at all she had set the table and was feeding us royally. She gave us the first cup of real hot coffee we had tasted in years. While we ate and drank, she made up two beds with our own sheets and eiderdowns she had kept for us, warmed with hot water bottles.

"Get to bed, children, you look like you need your sleep. Your story will keep till the morning and we'll discuss your future then. Have a good rest first. Oh God, I didn't think I'd ever see you two again." She laughed and cried, but all the time she was busy making us comfortable. She tucked us in like children and, with exhaustion and the comfort of a warm bed, I slept at once.

In the morning I heard whispers. "Elizabeth, where is our baby and what has happened to Freddy?"

"Dead. Don't mention them when Daniella wakes up. She has suffered enough, poor child." But I was awake and tears started running down my face. I buried my head in the soft pillow, trying to sleep again and pretend everything had been a bad dream. It was no use. I had to get used to the facts and face the future, no matter how bleak and empty it appeared.

My mother had saved my life over and over again. I owed it to her not to break down now. I waited till Margaret had regained her composure. She had genuinely loved my child and had risked her life trying to save her. It was not her fault her plans had failed. I pretended to wake up and Margaret ran a bath for me. After I had wallowed in it for half an hour she called me for breakfast. In spite of shortages, she had everything—fresh coffee, eggs, sausages, bread and butter, marmalade and jam.

Nothing had changed in her house. Our carpets on the floor and all the furniture I had given her before my attempted escape were just as I had seen them two and a half years ago. It was good to be in a real home again, but I realized that we could not stay here. I had left all my personal clothes with Margaret too, but she had sent them to East Prussia to save them from the bombing. The Russians would probably find all my lovely dresses, coats, and shoes. Still, we had lost so much, what did it matter?

Margaret suggested we call on a very good and trusted friend of hers before we discuss our next move. That friend had lots of relatives in the West and might be able to help. I longed to see our old home, and leaving my mother to tell Margaret something of our experiences, I went out for a walk.

The house of my husband's parents was only a few blocks

away but, although I had found Margaret's home in the dark the night before, I did not recognize a single street.

I walked in the direction of my own home, which had been taken from us in 1939. Black ruins and heaps of rubble blocking road after road were all that was left of a once-prosperous area. Taking many a wrong turn and climbing over mountains of stones, I eventually found it. The walk, which before the war would have taken no more than fifteen minutes, took me nearly two hours.

I don't know what I had expected to find, but when I faced my home, reduced to a hill of bricks and boulders, two of the hall's marble columns still sticking out of the rubble, I cried. I was crying not for the house, but for what it represented to me—my lost childhood, the ruins of my past. It made me realize how truly homeless and rootless I now was.

My school opposite the park still stood, undamaged. It looked grey and tired. Against my will, my feet carried me over to its ancient portals, and as I gazed up at it, the school bell sounded as it had rung for me so many times only a few years ago. Children came running out and skipped down the granite stairs. I could not help staring at them. With an aching heart, I wished the clock could be turned back and I could be one of them again: innocent, free of the dreadful knowledge of death and destruction, free of the memory of their fathers' guilt and crimes.

One of the senior girls stopped and asked me if I was waiting for someone or if I had lost my way. I shook my head and said, truthfully enough, "I was just looking at your school. I knew a child who had been very happy here once." The girl gazed at me uncomprehendingly. "How could she have been happy in this ghastly, antiquated dump? I wish a bomb would drop on it. The people are fighting for their destiny and still we have to go to school."

I did not wait for more slogans from this teenager. I made my way back to Margaret's. There were few people on the roads, and those I met were all women, drab and tired, scuttling like grey mice through the ruins.

My mother was frantic with worry when I got back. I had been away so long and I had to promise not to go out again on my own. Charlotte, Margaret's friend, was already there. A slender, attractive woman, about thirty years of age, she wept bitterly when Margaret told her briefly of all that had happened to us.

"Oh Germany, Germany," she cried in genuine despair, "we have deserved everything and more that is coming to us." However, as soon as she got over the first shock of Margaret's revelations, she got down to discussing with us our immediate future.

"You have to get out of Berlin as soon as possible," she said. "There are so few houses left standing, you might be discovered in the routine searches for accommodation. Also, the bombing goes on and on. If these madmen continue much longer, we will be living under siege. No, you two have suffered enough. Get out while you can. Now, let me think for a moment."

Charlotte stared out of the window for a while and nobody spoke. "I have got it," she said at last. "I am going to send you to my cousin Mahlmann in Mecklenburg. She is the stupidest female you have ever met and a great Nazi to boot, but if I give you a letter and tell her to take you in, she will. I'll say that you, Elizabeth, are my best friend and that I used to spend many happy holidays with you in your grand home in Kattowitz. I'll tell her she owes you all the hospitality she is capable of giving. You wait till I have written that letter. Cousin Mahlmann will be in tears when she reads it and will beg you to come in and make yourself at home. I have other relations in the Rhineland, but there you might get mixed up in the fighting. I think Mecklenburg is the safest place at the moment. Gadebusch is a small village, they have plenty to eat and there won't be any bombing."

She immediately sat down and wrote to her country cousin,

chuckling as she concocted imaginative inventions about our fictitious past and her great friendship with my mother in Kattowitz. She gave us the letter; with tears in her eyes she wished us luck and asked us to remember her after the war should she still be alive.

Margaret was on night duty in a hospital and soon left after an early supper. She promised to find out what time the train left for Mecklenburg the next day, and warned us not to open the door to anyone or to answer the telephone while she was away at work. Everybody knew she was working and any callers might be spies or Gestapo. We went to bed after she was gone, read for a while and slept. For the second night there was no air raid. Margaret said at breakfast the following morning, "I wish you didn't have to leave. You brought me luck. We haven't had a single night without bombing for ages. The Allies must know you are here and are sparing you."

She packed some clothes for us, made sandwiches, gave us some of our money she had in safe keeping, and took us to the station. We protested, thinking she must be tired after a long night on duty, but she insisted, "I would not have a moment's peace if I did not see you onto the right train."

# CHAPTER 25

A few hours later we arrived at the little station of Gadebusch. Charlotte had sent her cousin a telegram and she was expecting us. But Charlotte had been over-optimistic when she thought Frau Mahlmann would beg us to enter her house; she took us in very grudgingly. She was, so far, the only woman in the village who had not yet been allotted a family of refugees and would have to take some in sooner or later. She commanded her little daughter to show us to an attic room.

The stout, gruff, ugly woman did not have the slightest family resemblance to her pretty cousin in Berlin, nor did she know Charlotte's compassion and will to help. Her first question was, what were we prepared to pay for board and lodging. She fixed a rather steep rent and we paid for three months in advance. Not entirely dependent on charity, we felt better for having paid.

It was no pleasure living with the Mahlmanns. From the day we arrived until the day of liberation, no mealtime passed but that we got a lecture on the glorious Hitler regime. The woman was sure the leader had a trump card up his sleeve as well as a secret weapon and that it would just be a matter of time until the tide turned and the war was won. She never lost her firm faith in victory until the Americans actually took over. She made it quite clear that, in her opinion, refugees were foreigners wherever they came from, and that they would be deported once the war was over.

Frau Mahlmann's unfriendly attitude was heartily supported by her older daughter, a plain, ardent Hitler Youth member, and by her oldest boy, a precocious ten year old. Both made us feel uncomfortable and often afraid when they added their pinpricks to their mother's open hostility. The father was away, a soldier at the Russian front, and the only one of the family who was consistently kind and thoughtful was the little girl who had first shown us to our room. She feared her mother and sister's vindictiveness and had enough imagination to suffer with the homeless and displaced. She was only eleven years old, but she asked us more than once, "Why doesn't Mother understand that it could happen to us tomorrow? If we were driven out of our village, wouldn't she hope for people to be kind and helpful?" She asked many questions we tried to answer as truthfully as possible without giving ourselves away.

The child was suffering under the treatment we received from her family, and to make up for it she introduced us to their neighbours, the Schlees, a kindly old couple, too wise to believe in the myth of a secret weapon. The old man, conscripted into the Home Guard, was put in charge of French and Italian prisoners who worked in a preserve factory next door. His prisoners had a wonderful life. His wife cooked for them and looked after them like sons. Except at night, they were not locked up, and I often met them strolling through the nearby woods. None ever attempted escape for they knew that would cost old man Schlee his job if not his life. They adored him and his wife and were quite content to sit out the war with them.

It was this old gentleman who warned me one day in February that all refugee girls under twenty-five were to be mobilized to join one of the German fighting forces unless they had regular and essential employment. He quickly found me a job before anybody else in the village knew of the recruitment drive. He arranged with the foreman of the jam and preserve factory for me to work with the prisoners because, as it turned out, I was the only person in the village who spoke French.

The foreman was delighted at first as he could not get the prisoners to do their work properly, presumably because they did not understand what he told them about the machines. However, I soon got into trouble with him because I would not translate his foul language, his continual threats, and his lectures on Nazi doctrine.

He threatened to have me before a disciplinary committee of the Party, to have me thrown into a concentration camp, or sent to the Russian front. He didn't know, of course, that I had already been there and back again.

One day he hauled me before the boss for disobeying his orders and for assisting the prisoners in their "sabotage." The head of the factory was an understanding and more enlightened man. When the foreman had left the office, still raving at me as he went out of the door, he said kindly, "Look here, Miss Doverg, I am perfectly satisfied with your work and I shall prevent the foreman from taking you before a Nazi committee, but why don't you try to fool the crazy blighter a little while longer? Pretend to translate anything he says. He wouldn't know if you repeated the words "honey bunch" a hundred times in French. In a few weeks the war will be finished. You are too young to fall by the wayside at the eleventh hour." I took his advice, pretended to translate, and the foreman was satisfied.

And so we waited for the end of the war. My mother helped in the Mahlmann household as much as she could, but as she never could please Frau Mahlmann, she spent more and more time with the Schlees, helping Frau Schlee to mend the prisoners' socks and wash their clothes. In the factory, I got two proposals of marriage from a French and an Italian prisoner who were hurt and blamed each other when I politely but firmly turned them down.

No more news came from the capital. Charlotte had written regularly, but now her letters stopped. Berlin was under siege and soon we heard the rumbling approach of the front line. April was nearly at an end. Spring had come early that year. The sun was hot and everybody wore summer dresses. Our long-sleeved sweaters became conspicuous, but we didn't dare leave them off because of the tattooed numbers on our arms. Frequently now the Mahlmanns asked if we didn't feel hot, and while the sweat was pouring down our necks, we pretended to shiver and said we always felt cold.

I forgot one day and rolled up my sleeves to wash my hands in the kitchen. Fortunately, only the little girl was there, but she was observant and immediately asked what the number on my arm stood for. I was terrified but answered quickly, "Poppet, can you keep a secret? Promise not to tell your family?" She nodded. "Well, when I was a little girl, I ran away with gypsies and they tattooed this number on my arm so that I'd be one of their family because they all had numbers. My mommy fetched me back, but to this day she can't bear to be reminded of it because she was so terribly upset when I had vanished. That's why I asked you not to talk about it. Your family would never let her forget it and they would make my mother cry again."

The child said she understood perfectly and she would never do or say anything that would hurt Aunty Liz; she loved her far better than her own mother. I worried for a while but I needn't have. That child could keep a secret and she never mentioned what she had seen to a soul.

On the second day of May, old man Schlee was called to the Western front to fight. It was only a few miles away. "What," he said, "leave the wife in charge of all these prisoners? I'm blowed if I'll go fighting at my age. Why don't they send that young gutter-snipe of a foreman? He managed to keep out of the war success-fully." The old man was well over seventy and had lost two sons in

Russia. He told the factory foreman what he thought of fighting a lost war at his time of life. The foreman was furious. Had the Allied troops been delayed, this bit of plain speaking would have cost Schlee his life. But nothing now could stop the German defeat. There was no opposition left in this part of the country. Old men like Schlee and young children were expected to hold back the mighty surge of the victorious armies. They were overrun, often without a shot being fired.

On 5 May 1945, early in the morning, the youngest Mahlmann children rushed into the house, out of breath and full of excitement. "The Americans are here! They are marching through the village!"

Already the one main street was echoing with the noise of tanks, armoured cars, jeeps, and marching feet. We hung out of the windows, eager to get a first glimpse of our liberators.

"Aren't you ashamed of yourselves to be seen looking at our enemies?" asked Mother Mahlmann angrily. She pulled her two daughters from the window and tried to get my mother and me away too. I turned on her at last.

"They may be your enemies. They are not ours. Leave us alone." My blazing eyes must have intimidated her. She asked no questions.

The first Americans passed under our window and we waved and shouted with joy. They waved back. So that was what a victorious army looked like. Sunburnt and dusty, heads high and backs straight, an expression of pride on their faces that I'll never forget as long as I live.

With dismay I suddenly discovered the young Mahlmann boy aiming a shotgun out of the next window. Pushing my mother aside, I flew at him, hit the gun from his hands and slapped his round childish face hard. His mother gathered her howling offspring in her arms and screamed at me, "What do you think you are doing, you traitor? You wait till we have chased those bastards out of Gadebusch. I'll see you hanged for this! Get out of my house!" The younger girl tried to calm her mother but got only abuse for her efforts.

"Don't worry, Frau Mahlmann, we are getting out of your house now. We had no intention of staying longer than we absolutely had to." I pulled off my sweater and showed her the tattoo on my arm. "My mother and I are escaped prisoners from Auschwitz concentration camp, if that name means anything to you. I'm sorry we had to deceive you, but for us it was a matter of life or death."

The woman turned ashen and trembled. For the first time since we had come to her house she was speechless and frightened. Her little daughter threw her arms round my mother's neck and cried bitterly, "Auntie Liz, you poor, poor Auntie Liz! What have they done to you?" She hid her head in my mother's arm. "Whatever happens, I'll always love you. Will you take me with you if you have to go? I don't want you to leave." My mother gently stroked the child's long, fair hair as I went out of the door into the glorious, warm May morning.

Even before the victory parade was over, a civil administration had been set up in the mayor's office. The armed guards outside did not stop me. The number on my arm opened all doors for me now. Within minutes I was taken to the new town-major's office and got a royal welcome when I revealed my true identity.

"Haven't you grown since I saw you last. You are a woman now and a lovely one at that," the major said in perfect German. I thought for a moment he had gone crazy or, later, that he had mistaken me for somebody else. Neither was true. He had, in fact, gone from Berlin to America when Hitler came to power. The son of a well-known Christian family, he had befriended my oldest brother at Heidelberg university. He had known my parents well and me as a small child. Our world had become a small place.

Busy though he was setting up his administration, he immediately delegated his duties to a subordinate, packed me into a jeep and drove to the Mahlmann's house to see my mother. They had a long talk, and in the end the major asked if I would care to join their intelligence corps as an interpreter.

"We have a big job ahead of us hunting down SS who are presumably hiding in this neighbourhood. You could be of tremendous help, if you would." He almost pleaded. Why, wasn't this what I had dreamed of and waited for all these years? I just nodded. "Can you come with me now?" he asked. My mother's serene, happy face made the sun seem brighter.

Frau Mahlmann had stood by all this time trembling. She did not understand English and had no idea what we were talking about. The major now turned on her and said in German, "Until we find better accommodation for Elizabeth and her daughter, you will give them your best rooms. If you fail to obey my orders, I shall have you and your family evacuated. Is that understood?" The woman promised to make us comfortable and apologized for her early morning temper. But my mother refused and said we were perfectly happy in the attic in the meantime. She need not move out of her rooms. The major frowned. "You are too soft with these people, Elizabeth, but have it your own way.

"Come along then, Daniella, we have a lot of work to do." First we went to the Schlees to free the French and Italian prisoners. They embraced the major, who was somewhat bewildered by the many kisses he got on both cheeks in typically Latin fashion. He told the men they could go anywhere they liked, of course, but it would take a little while and some organization to get them repatriated. Asked what kind of treatment they had received, they had nothing but good to say for their warden and his wife. Therefore the Schlees were instructed to continue looking after their charges until they could be sent home.

We returned to the major's office where I got my own desk, and for days sifted and translated intelligence reports. A few Jewish officers were attached to our unit and they treated me as though I were highly breakable porcelain. I was not allowed to walk alone anywhere. Wherever I went, at least two guards trailed behind. Guards were placed in front of the Mahlmann house and I was given a jeep for my own use. Every afternoon after work, I was taken home and a few officers and some of the ex-prisoners invariably assembled in the house to chat with my mother and me. We received American rations, chocolate, cigarettes and clothes.

My family was informed of our survival and my cousin, who was an officer in the US forces stationed in Bavaria, was rushed to Mecklenburg to see us. The tremendous pile of work on my desk stopped me from thinking too much, and the consideration, kindness, and respect we received from the occupation forces was heartwarming. For the time being, I was contented and almost purring under the unaccustomed freedom and friendship we were given.

Reports of SS hiding in the forests near our village began to trickle in and office routine was interrupted. I was bundled into a jeep and off we went on an exciting hunt. Many a time it turned out to be a wild goose chase, but often we were successful in tracking down individuals or groups of straying SS. What a despicable lot they were. Cringing, subservient, begging for their lives, they were a far cry from the vain, strutting tormentors we had known in Auschwitz. The clock had turned full circle. Now I was no longer the hunted but the hunter. I felt all the glory of freedom and revenge, until one day the difference between us and our ex-masters was brought home forcefully.

Two captains, a lieutenant of the 7th American Army Intelligence Corps, and myself were combing the woods for SS who had been reported in the vicinity. Some SS women were said to be with them. Troops were covering every move we made.

At the age of twenty-three, I was still young enough to thoroughly enjoy the exhilaration of the chase. The new town-major had tried to stop me from taking part in these manhunts, but I felt I had survived for this and that I deserved the satisfaction of catching at least some of our murderers. The Jewish captain under whose direct command I now worked, managed to persuade the major that my presence was justified when arrests were made. The major acquiesced. Actually, there was little danger involved. Not one of the cornered heroes tried to shoot it out; probably they had run out of ammunition long ago. Mostly they had thrown their revolvers away before they were captured.

For hours we patiently covered every inch of the woods and had almost given up hope, when somewhere above our heads a branch cracked and broke. My captain jumped back and pulled me behind a huge oak tree for cover. Like an overripe plum, a woman dropped to the soft mattress of dead leaves. She wore the dreaded grey uniform of women guards, minus her revolver belt. She tried to break away and run, but before she moved more than a few yards, the captain and two soldiers pinned her down, turned her towards me and asked me if I had seen her before. Had I seen her before! She was the woman who had begged for our help when she thought Auschwitz was about to be taken over by the Russians and who had kicked my mother down the stairs as soon as she had orders to evacuate us. I told the captain of that incident and how I had hoped to meet her again after the war.

The SS woman whined and cringed and insisted she had never heard of a place called Auschwitz. The captain turned her over to a couple of guards and instructed them to take her to my office. Without being asked, the woman revealed the hiding places of five SS men and another two women before she was led away. We picked them up on the way back to the village.

In the woman's pocket were found photographs of the entrance gate to Auschwitz and pictures of a hanging. She said she had never seen these pictures before. Somebody must have planted them on her. The tall guards brought her into my office and then stood outside the door. The captain opened a desk drawer, pointed at a small revolver in there, put his hand on my shoulder and said quietly, "For your protection. She is all yours. Do you want me to stay?" I shook my head and he too went outside.

The woman continued to deny she had ever seen Auschwitz. I showed her the number on my arm and she turned a pasty grey. I reminded her of the day of our evacuation, of her breaking her whip after taking the clothes off the prisoners and leaving them standing half-naked in the snow. I reminded her of the broomstick she had beaten us with when the order to evacuate had come through.

She slumped forward against my desk, tears streaming down her face. She pleaded for her life; she offered me money, a house, anything I would ask for, and she was a disgusting sight. I picked up the revolver. How often had I promised myself to kill her? In those early days immediately after the war there was a time of rough justice. Nobody would have turned a hair if the revolver had gone off and an SS woman had been shot. For a moment I aimed the weapon at her. It was impossible. I could not kill in cold blood, not even a murderess.

I slipped the revolver back into the drawer and got up. The woman whined and bubbled out a full confession and the captain, who had quietly come in again, took it all down. Still she continued to plead with me to let her go. She had not missed my weakness and was leaning hopefully on my desk. Recoiling with disgust at her and myself, I shouted at last, "Stand up, don't touch that desk or anything else I come in contact with!" She shrunk back into a corner and the captain called for guards to take her away. She did not escape. On her own confession of all the murders she had committed, she was hanged shortly afterwards.

Two weeks after this encounter, our work in Gadebusch was finished; the civil administration worked smoothly and we were posted to a larger town. A jeep took my mother and me to a delightful house that had been requisitioned for us. The brigadier in charge was there to welcome us. He handed the house keys to my mother, invited us for dinner, and left. My mother opened the door, we went inside and gasped. The sun was pouring in the windows. In every room were huge bowls of white and purple lilacs and the whole house was permeated with the lovely scent. Everything we could possibly want was in the house. There were cigarettes and chocolates, a bottle of wine and glasses on the table. In the bedrooms, both our dressing tables were loaded with perfume and cosmetics. The larder and kitchen were well stocked. In the bathroom we found scented soap, bath crystals and soft, white towels.

I stood at the window gazing out into the sunny garden with its flowering shrubs and spring flowers.

"This is what I have wished for you, my Daniella. My dream has come true," my mother said softly. "You are young enough to start a new life and be happy again. This beauty is only an interim. You will not always be spoiled and treated with so much consideration. But I could not think of a lovelier springboard for a new start or for a better place to rest for a while. If ever you look back in despair, remember this day and remember that, in the end, there were, after all, people who fought for us. There will be a new generation happy to be alive who will, I hope, never know the horrors we have seen. If we have one mission in life, a debt to all who have died, you will carry it out. You, Daniella, will see to it that young people will not ever again be persecuted for their race, colour, or beliefs."

"Yes, Mother, I'll try," was all I could say. But it sounded hollow, skeptical, and without conviction. Yet, when I realized her need to relinquish at last the burden of responsibility, I knew I had to take over where my mother had left off. Her superhuman strength had saved my own and other lives over and over again. Now it was my turn to repay the love and sacrifices I had taken for granted. That day so long ago, I promised my mother, my murdered little family, our six million dead, and myself that, never again, as long as I lived, would a dictatorship rob our children of their birthright, their freedom, and their happiness.

*l to r: Kate (back centre), Lotte, Gerhard, Mother and Stephan, and Eva in front, 1924.*

*Father shortly before he died January 1938.*

*Eva's first day of school, holding the traditional gift of candy, 1928.*

*Stephan outside his school where Hitler Youth threw him down a staircase and pelted him with stones, fall 1933.*

*Eva and F.H. Raphael after their wedding, February 1939.*

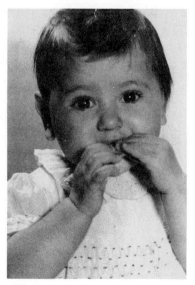

*Reha on her first birthday, July 1941*

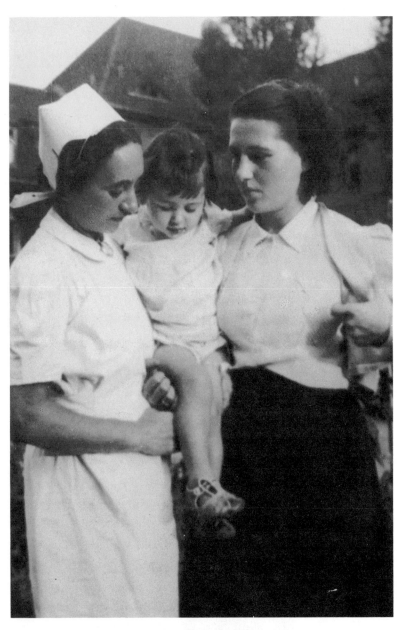

*Eva, mother, and daughter Reha outside the Jewish Hospital, 1941. Since Jews were not permitted to have any photos taken other than for identity cards and police records, Eva is preoccupied with hiding the Jewish star on her jacket*

*Ross Brewster, British Control Commission Special Branch Intelligence, 1946*

*Eva and Heidi, the dog that hated jackboots, 1946.*

*Ross and Eva Brewster with children Joyce and Jimmy, 1962.*

*Eva Brewster addressing a group of students, April 1994.*

# CHAPTER 26

Later in the summer of 1945, the 7th American Army was posted to Japan which was still at war. The brigadier I was working for by then took us to Luneburg in the British sector of occupation which he believed to be a safer place. He was afraid that Mecklenburg could still come under Russian administration before Germany's post-war borders were permanently set. Prior to leaving, he arranged my transfer to work as liaison between the Allied jurisdictions and as an interpreter for the British Control Commission in the Department of Property Control dealing with Nazi estates.

The transition from working with the 7th American Army to the British Control Commission was not easy for me. The latter's officers were no longer the front-line soldiers who had liberated concentration camps and had seen for themselves the horror inmates had suffered. The Control Commission was staffed mainly by civilians who were given military ranks and uniforms, but who had been appointed through the "old-boy's network"—not for what they knew about Hitler's Germany, but for who they knew at home. These people seem to have felt more sympathy for their defeated enemies, the German officer corps and aristocracy, than for the rag-tag flotsam from all parts of Europe now crowded into refugee camps.

Those refugees, almost all starving, did not endear themselves to the new administration by their black-market activities. My British superiors, trying to restore law and order, did not accept my suggestion that the black market was the only means by which those dispossessed, mostly stateless refugees, could get adequate food supplies in the absence of an issue of ration cards for them. At that time, ration cards were only given to Germans. Nor did my new bosses support my efforts to get clothing, food, and money to those people who had no home to go back to and who could not even get work permits or resident status which would have allowed them to move out of the overcrowded camps. Instead, to deal with the perceived lawlessness, the Control Commission employed many former members of the German police and of Nazi organizations who continued to terrorize the refugees.

The Department of Property Control was mandated to deNazify industry and business and to deal with assets misappropriated by the Nazis. My specific assignment was to investigate estates, including businesses, homes, and bank accounts which had once belonged to foreign nationals, Jews, or other political opponents of the Hitler regime and had been confiscated by the Nazis. In Luneburg and the county town of Hanover, where registries had not been bombed out or destroyed, it was easy for me to find records of former Jewish residents and other dispossessed property owners and to look into files of deeds and transactions. But to get the officer in charge of my department to read my meticulous reports and translations of German documentation and to take appropriate action proved almost impossible, in large part because I was constantly defeated and humiliated by a former Nazi who, himself, had been managing director of a large industry which had employed and mistreated prisoners during the war. Although he had not denied his past career in the questionnaire every German civilian had to complete with job applications, he had been appointed head clerk in my department because of his "management experience and acumen in business affairs." He either made my reports disappear or, if he did present them to the British officer in charge, he suggested that I had no knowledge of proper investigative procedure and methods of collecting reliable data. He also kept telling the officer that my background and wartime imprisonment would have made me vindictive enough to compile complaints against honest, wealthy German citizens "just to get even."

Our British boss, an Englishman who had never fought in the war, swallowed that line. He had been a school drop-out, starting his career as a door-to-door salesman in London. He frequently interrogated me about my education and knowledge of the German language. On one occasion he even had the nerve to say: "I understand you people only speak Yiddish, a bastardized form of German?"

For the first time since my liberation, I lost my temper; I pointed out that I had been raised in what was once German high society, that I had been educated in Berlin's best girls' school, and that I had never even heard the Yiddish language until I met Jewish prisoners from Eastern Europe. But, I informed him, while I had every qualification for the job I was supposed to do, I doubted that his experience in hawking men's socks and ties qualified him for his present position.

My impudence got to him; he'd have me fired. Ross Brewster, a young Special Branch Intelligence office, came to my rescue. At my boss's own request, he sat in during a subsequent somewhat heated interview. I had complained to Special Branch that my reports either "got lost" or were never followed up. Perhaps to justify my threatened dismissal, my boss had made a counter-complaint asking Special Branch to investigate my reliability and impartiality. Brewster had quietly looked into my list of properties that had been taken over by the Nazis and found them correct. As a result of this investigation, the former salesman was quietly sent home. The German office manager, who had thwarted my efforts, was replaced by a Dutch civilian who became a staunch ally and a good friend as did Ross Brewster.

Exactly when and why Ross fell in love with me, I never discovered. I suspected that he originally became infatuated with Heidi, a beautiful Springer spaniel we had rescued together from a trigger-happy German who was going to shoot her. Special Branch had been informed that this man, a former member of the SS, had trained German Shepherd dogs used by concentration camp guards to maul and kill prisoners. Ross Brewster was asked to investigate his activities. Because Ross knew by then that I had seen those dogs and their handlers in action, he took me with him one weekend to witness and interpret the interrogation. By the time we drove out to the well fortified compound in a forest near Luneburg, the suspect had shed his SS uniform, of course, and fiercely denied that he had ever been involved in training dogs for any reason other that his love of animals. He was now teaching young spaniels the art of hunting and retrieving. It soon became evident that his methods had changed only slightly from those used in training killer dogs. Instead of human prisoners, he now trapped and tethered live ducks, hares and deer and let the dogs loose to get at them.

According to the owner, Heidi was the only one of her litter that proved to be untrainable. While she did learn to detect tracks, spoor and to follow a trail, once she had spotted the game, her master told us, all the whipping and kicks she received could not persuade her to retrieve it. Instead, she would bite through the rope or trap to release the wild animal, yapping triumphantly when birds flew off or hares vanished into the bush. Her owner let us witness her activities to justify what he was going to do and kicked her viciously. Turning to us, he said more quietly: "A bullet is wasted on her, but that's all she is fit for."

Seeing Heidi cowering at her master's heels, flinching at

every crack of his aimlessly swinging riding crop, I felt an immediate affinity for the young animal. The man's cruelty may have been responsible for the puppy developing the life-saving instincts of a Saint Bernard and a compassion for suffering creatures of other species I have seldom seen in humans and never again in an animal.

Ross Brewster saw my distress. He told me later that he bought Heidi's life for two cans of corned beef and two hundred cigarettes to prevent me from killing the guy. And that was the beginning of a mutual friendship beyond any value in material terms. That dog didn't have a mean bone in her body, but for a long time to come she remained a timid shadow. She only showed courage at the sight of jackboots; yet she could not differentiate between those of friends or foes. Many a pair of shiny German officers' boots had surreptitiously changed owners in the black market of a defeated people. When Heidi now attacked the kind of boots that had kicked her, the men wearing them were likely to be Allied personnel. Since her sympathy was, and always would be, with the "underdog," she was as likely to lick the feet of now barefooted Nazis as those of their former victims.

The night a burglar climbed into my groundfloor bedroom window, Heidi simply rolled over, whimpering softly. I knew her well enough by then to understand that she was not afraid of the burglar, but felt great pity for his shoeless feet. Then a jeep full of military police stopped in front of my house to break up a fight between British soldiers in the adjoining bowling alley. The hapless intruder simply fled through the backdoor of my apartment without stealing anything. Heidi did attack my British boss's boots from under the dark safety of my desk. Although I felt he deserved it for the way he had treated me, I couldn't blame him for being upset. Heidi lived with us in England and Scotland, where nobody wore jackboots, for fourteen more years. She never attacked anybody again.

My assumption that our mutual love for animals forged the original friendship between Ross and me was probably correct. But as I gradually learned more about his background, I realized that this young Scottish Intelligence officer was motivated to support me from the start for different reasons. He had left university in 1940, two years before he would have graduated as a veterinary surgeon. He wanted to join the army and fight in the war, but veterinary and medical students in the UK were in a reserved position and he would not have been called up. He therefore dropped out of university and volunteered to work in an aircraft factory. Having had no technical training for that job, he knew that he would promptly be recruited for the army.

Unlike many young men of his generation who joined up for the imagined adventure, Ross knew what he wanted to fight for: the preservation of democracy and freedom. He had always been at loggerheads with his strict father's right-wing views and prejudices. His father, the youngest son of Scottish farmers, had worked his way up from apprentice in a ship's engine room to engineer and then up the ladder to managing director of Scotland's largest shipbuilding company. Although he had few personal dealings with Jews or Catholics, he hated both. He rarely missed an opportunity, such as the Orange men's parades in Glasgow, to demonstrate against Northern Ireland's Catholics. As the international representative for Fairfields, the big shipbuilders on the Clyde, Ross' father had been in Berlin in 1939, just before the war broke out, sent there to find out what had been accomplished in the German ship building industry, by then Scotland's main competition. He had met Hitler, had been lavishly entertained, given a tour through the major ports and ships built since 1933. Finally, he had been invited to join Nazi bigwigs on the stand overlooking an extravagant military parade past Hitler's Chancellery. He returned to Glasgow, deeply impressed and delighted with German discipline. Praising the

German work ethic, he had mentioned to his son as an afterthought: "If Hitler had done nothing else but got rid of the Jews, I'd admire him."

Had I known all this at the beginning of our relationship, I would have presumed that Ross was trying to atone for his father's discredited political opinions. Whatever the reason, he did everything to make both my working and private life more bearable. He augmented our meagre food rations with his own. He even risked a court martial for hunting and killing a wild boar and getting a German butcher to cut it up for us which was strictly forbidden to British army personnel. Hunting rights were reserved for Germans only.

By then, he had met my mother who was working as a nurse in the large hospital for Displaced Persons. She was as disillusioned as I was by the British Control Commission's neglect of, if not downright contempt for, the needs and rights of the Nazis' barely surviving victims. Once she had introduced Ross to her very sick and dying patients and showed him the refugees' deplorable living conditions in the camps, he immediately organized regular supplies of food and medicines through both the International Red Cross and private organizations in Britain.

Although Ross was then visiting us almost every evening, he never gave any indication that he felt more for me than friendship and respect. Heidi always grabbed his first attention and she boisterously reciprocated. My mother came next and only when they had finished discussing aid programs for the refugees and progress at the hospital was I included in conversations. Therefore, when he took me and, of course, my dog for a weekend at a hunting lodge and asked me to marry him, I was more than surprised. Obviously, he said, he didn't expect me to commit myself straight away, but he hoped I would seriously consider it before I said yes to one of the two other men he admitted he was very jealous of. The first he considered a genuine rival was Otto.

Ross had already met the former German prisoner who had helped us in Auschwitz and had advised me to escape with my mother. Otto had started searching for us as soon as the war was over and eventually got our address from the Swedish Red Cross where we were registered. He came to Luneburg hoping I'd go back with him to East Germany as his wife. Otto had already been appointed mayor of his city, Halle, by the Russians.

The other man Ross was afraid I might fall for was Flight Lieutenant Don Snipper, a Canadian Jewish fighter pilot, who had been given our names by an organization looking for survivors of concentration camps. This officer had taken me to his squadron's dances and followed up his version of courtship by flying dangerously low over the office building where I worked in Property Control next to the rooms occupied by Special Branch. Snipper, in a daily 9:00 a.m. dive out of the sky over our heads, dipped his wings, nearly scrapping the roof, to wish me a good morning. I could never persuade Ross Brewster that neither of those two threatened a serious contest although I had many reasons to adore both.

Otto, more than twenty years older than I, had been like a father to me and would have spoiled me like a child. He offered my mother and me a home, love, peace, and most tempting of all, life in what he genuinely believed to be the best of all worlds—a just and incorruptible society. But even if I had loved him as a man, I could not have lived under a Communist regime which, to me, seemed no better than the dictatorship from which we had just escaped. Not long after Otto had returned alone to his city, his best friend escaped to the West and confirmed how right I had been to distrust Soviet-ruled East Germany. Otto had been arrested and deported to Siberia. His main mistakes had been to believe in a political system that thrived on suspicions and to love his country and countrymen in spite of what they had done to him. He had therefore refused to escape with his friend through the back door of his home while the Russian secret police were breaking down the front door. They accused him of "crimes" which he had learned to be necessary for mere survival as a prisoner of the Nazis, deeds for which the Russians had actually honoured him by appointing him mayor after liberation.

His friend told us that Otto had intended to go voluntarily with the secret police because, when they started banging at the door and he realized they were coming for him, he was still convinced that he could persuade the Russian leadership to ease its harsh regime and postpone war reparations until he had rebuilt his city's industries to be able to pay its debts. The population in Halle, his totally bombed-out city, was starving. Yet, the Russians requisitioned the very first post-war harvest in the surrounding countryside for shipment to the Soviet Union. In despair, the mayor unhitched an unguarded train already loaded with flour and destined to leave for Russia in the morning. He had the flour distributed among his people in the middle of the night. A former high-ranking Nazi, who had much to gain from collaborating with the Communists, denounced him and Otto was never seen again.

After Otto's disappearance, Ross still worried about the Canadian fighter pilot who, to me, was just a reckless boy. But his lighthearted laughter and untiring admiration did make me feel young and free again. He also reaffirmed my belief that Jews in some parts of the world were able to fight for human rights and in Canada, as in the US, they could live as equal citizens. However, I needed time and more than a moonstruck dare-devil before I could fall in love again.

Still, Ross never believed that he would be the one man I'd want to spend the rest of my life with. Even after I married him and for the next forty years of our married life, he always feared he'd lose me one day to another man. April Fools' Day may not have been the most auspicious date to begin a new life, but we got married by special license on 1 April 1947. But this marriage, unlike my first, was not the consecration of a crazy teenage love affair. It was built, at least on my part, on the much more solid grounds of trust and decency. For the rest of my life my husband helped to restore my much damaged belief in the basic goodness of humanity.

# EPILOGUE

I started, almost by accident, on a journalistic career in 1971 because a few incidents reminded me of a past I had tried to forget. I also remembered at last the promise to my mother to protect our children from a repetition of Nazi persecution.

My memory was jolted by a German youth band marching in the Calgary Stampede parade. They played some tunes that had been the Nazis' favourite melodies and, more than the melodies, I remembered the blood-thirsty, hateful texts. For the first time in my life, I wrote a letter to the editor of the *Lethbridge Herald,* the daily newspaper in the city and surrounding areas. My objections to the choice of music appeared unedited on the Editorial page on 9 June, 1971, and raised an unprecedented storm of protest from the large German community. For weeks, the newspaper published letters to the editor opposing and criticizing my point of view. The furore spilled over to the other media with Germans calling radio phone-in show hosts and there seemed to be no end to it. Three weeks later, the publisher of the *Lethbridge Herald* phoned me: "Mrs. Brewster, would you do me a favour? We have to discontinue publishing those letters and they are still piling up on my desk. Can you please shut them up?" I did and it wasn't too difficult.

The general gist of the Germans' letters had been one of denial that the anti-French song I had brought up as an example had any meaning in Germany today. It was basically an old miner's tune, they wrote, and insisted that "German is the Saar, German forever" always was and always will be, the Saar's provincial anthem. The letter writers ignored the fact that the Saar belonged to France until Hitler marched in and took it over and that it was again returned to France after the war. Others wrote that the march I objected to was merely played for the tune and that words of such marches "don't mean anything to any German alive." Others said that "the German band's visit was purely and simply a 'postcard from home' for most Canadians of German origin living here." Others wrote that "if we objected to such songs, then we might as well object to Wagner's Wedding March . . . since Hitler took quite a fancy to Wagner's music." Or, "if we censor music, we might as well forget all other aspects of democratic freedom." Quite a few letters ended with the slogan "Canada stand together, understand together!"

Briefly, I "shut them up" by pointing out that having seen countless victims being marched to their death to the sound of this particular "folk song," I might be forgiven for my distaste. And I couldn't agree with the people who claimed that "words don't mean anything to any German alive" since I am one who is very much alive and could name many more who have, if not longer memories, at least a national conscience. If the German band was simply a "postcard from home," those who sent it should have ensured that the message could not be misconstrued and that there was no room for ambiguity. It seems inconceivable, I wrote in response, that of the millions who lined the routes of death marches in my generation, nobody remembers cheering and singing this song with that title and words I had quoted from the Saar to the Polish border. Is there nobody left now to tell their children and keep them from committing a *faux pas* when visiting Canada, a country that sacrificed so many lives to free the world of the very tyranny that song helped to create?

I, too, am against censorship of any kind, I continued, but I refuse to join the three proverbial monkeys to "see no evil, hear no evil, and speak no evil." Although I hold no particular brief for Richard Wagner's teutonic music or, for that matter, his well-known anti-semitism, both of which so endeared him to Hitler, I would not dream of depriving generations of young people of his Wedding March. The analogy is barely appropriate, since I don't know a single person shot for refusing to sing it. In conclusion, I said that, to preserve one's cultural background does not mean sweeping under the carpet or hiding behind slogans every painful memory or mistake of one's recent past. It is the duty of every Canadian citizen to make sure that democracy is not undermined as unnoticeably and gradually as it had been in Germany — with a rousing song here, a slogan there, a bit or propaganda written between the lines. There should be no need for censorship in a free country but, "to stand together and understand together" it is essential to exercise the maximum of tact and understanding for ethnic groups who escaped from a lifetime of persecution to this beautiful country, Canada.

We had been fighting a narrow-mindedness I had not expected to see in Canada, but the worst kind of discrimination was still to come. Before I got involved, my children, young adults by then, were the first to be faced with anti-semitism. Hoping they would never experience it, I had not wanted to burden them with the horror I had lived through or with the terror that irrational hatred of Jews could lead to. In short, I made the same mistake my parents had made: Sheltering our kids behind a wall of love and material advantages, I had told them little, if anything, about Nazi policies and had left them totally unprepared. They knew, of course, that they had a Jewish mother, but that didn't mean any more to them than the fact that they also had a Christian father. Just as I had, they too presumed that being Jewish was a religion as was being

Christian, Mohammedan, or believing in any other creed. When they first came across the theory that being a Jew meant not only belonging to a segregated race, but also a nationality, they instinctively dealt with it in their own ways. During their travels since early childhood, they had met Japanese, Indian, Lebanese, and North African Jews. All had the looks and characteristics of the country and race they had been born into, including the skin colour, shape of eyes, and hair, just as European-born Jews were often blond and blue-eyed.

Joyce, my daughter, was already in university two years before her brother graduated from high school. She was attending a convocation dinner when the conversation got round to a recent vandalism of the small Lethbridge synagogue which had been smeared with swastikas and anti-semitic slogans. The student seated beside her was the son of a former German prisoner of war who, repatriated after the war, had come back to Canada with his German wife. Thoroughly indoctrinated, the young man approved of the vandalism. "What a pity," he said to Joyce, "Hitler was not given the time and opportunity to get rid of Jews world-wide with his final solution!" When Joyce asked him if he had ever met Jews who gave him reason to hate them enough to want them killed, he told her: "I know enough about those shady characters to die rather than associate with them."

"Well," my daughter informed him, "by your definition at least, you are sitting beside such a shady character since I have a Jewish mother. Want to drop dead?" The young man laughed. He thought she was joking since she didn't fit the image of what he had been taught a Jew should look like. When he was finally convinced that she was serious, he apologized sincerely. She managed to point out the stupidity of his preconceived ideas. When she told me about this encounter and I admitted I'd probably not have had her patience and might have lost my temper, she said: "But, Mom, you taught me to be tolerant of other people's ideas and opinions. Would you really have curbed his freedom of expression and speech you always said is so important in a democracy?" Touché! I found out a few years later how right and successful her method of thoughtful persuasion had been. When the first edition of my book about the Holocaust was released and I was asked to autograph copies at the University of Lethbridge, that young man was one of the first to ask for my signature under his inscription: "To my father, Fritz . . ." Recognizing the name, I asked him: "Do you think Fritz will even read it considering his views?" Blushing to the roots of his fair hair, he answered: "He better read it if he wants to keep his son!" And then, not knowing that I was Joyce's mother, he told me of that dinner so long ago and what an ass he had made of himself until my daughter had shown him the error of his parents' teaching he had so readily accepted.

In the meantime, our son could not get admission to either of the only two veterinary faculties in Canada because they were over-subscribed. He thought of going back to Scotland to study at his father's university. But there, we were informed, he needed a lot more chemistry and science than was taught in Canadian high schools to qualify. Jim therefore entered the Lethbridge college to upgrade in those subjects of missing qualifications. At the same time, he wanted to find out about alternative careers, but didn't know what else he'd be interested in or able to get into. He surprised us with a letter and application for an interview with a high-ranking army officer, thus accepting the army's offer to give IQ and aptitude tests to potential officer cadets. To my suggestion that he'd be better to consult a civilian career counsellor since he'd probably not be very good at accepting army discipline, let alone dishing it out, he said: "Everybody tells me I need more discipline and I've worked it all out. If the army accepts me for officer training, they will pay university fees for any professional career I am suited for.

They can even get me into a veterinary school ahead of other applicants if they need veterinarians in the army. I'll try the tests."

He got his interview when the examining officer visited Lethbridge and I drove him to the recruitment office. A few hours after I dropped him off, I collected my son again. The officer who had tested him came out to my car, handed me the application form and almost pleaded that I talk my boy into completing it. Jim showed me one of the first questions he refused to answer: "What is your parents' nationality? Canadian? American? British? French? German? Italian? Jew?

"Your son's exam papers," said the officer, "are among the best I've seen in ten years. I can understand his objections to the nationality question, but he wasn't even raised in the Jewish religion. His father is of Scottish extraction and a member of the Church of Scotland. Why doesn't Jim simply state that his ancestors were British? For that matter, he wouldn't lie if he claimed that his maternal grandparents were German which they were until Hitler decreed otherwise! Mrs. Brewster, can't you persuade your son that he is throwing away a wonderful career opportunity if he refuses to compromise a little? I would recommend and approve his immediate admission to the officers' cadet school, and we could send him to medical school. All he would have to do in return would be to sign on after graduation for a three-year term as an army doctor."

Although I appreciated the officer's sympathetic attitude and apparent lack of prejudice, my husband and I were as outraged at the questionnaire as our son and did not attempt to influence his decision. That was the end of our son's army career before it had even began. He underlined the offensive question and commented in the margin: "You've lost me! I am a Canadian! 'Jew' is NOT a nationality and I will not accept your form of institutionalized anti-semitism. I therefore do not wish to join your exclusive club."

The ball was again in my court and I took it up in my newspaper columns and presented the argument directly to parliament in Ottawa. There it was debated in the House of Commons and in the end I was given the assurance that no future questionnaires would include "Jew" under parents' nationality and that the existing application forms would be scrapped and shredded forthwith. I don't know whether that was actually done, but the political decision could create a legal precedent that should hold up if any future recruit decided to take legal action objecting to this or similar official questions.

In 1981 I accepted another newspaper assignment to cover political, social and economic changes in Europe. As it happened, I arrived in Europe in April just at the time German school children were protesting publicly about neo-Nazi literature sent to their schools by a Canadian of German origin. Four high schools in Bonn, the German capital, had received batches of unsolicited hate literature from a Canadian right-wing organization in Toronto which called itself "Samisdat." Among Nazi memorabilia, it offered the sale of Nazi books banned in Germany. The kids' disgust over the Canadian letter writer's glorification of war and antisemitism was all the more thought-provoking considering the propagandist had attempted to influence them using pressure tactics bordering on blackmail. He asked for large monetary contributions and student support for his organization, and he threatened reprisals should he be publicly denounced or hear as much as one negative comment about neo-Nazism.

The young publisher of a Wagenburg high school paper had the courage to inform the German State police that "Samisdat" had tried to incite German youths to persecute minorities. He also told the authorities that the Canadian Nazis attempted direct recruitment for their organization in German schools. At the same time, the children complained to our red-faced ambassador that the Canadian

Nazi leader, Ernst Zündel, had asked for names and addresses of any Germans who owned copy machines and who could be persuaded to circulate his hate literature among young people. He also asked for names of German organizations with similar aims to support his efforts.

Until I wrote about his activities in my newspaper columns and until Zündel was brought to trial, very few Canadians knew much, if anything, about neo-Nazis in Canada. The Canadian government had swept information about their dubious actions at home and abroad under the carpet. If it hadn't been for a private citizen, a Holocaust survivor's legal action, and my articles, very few people would have known that Zündel, the leader of the Toronto-based "Samisdat", was not even a Canadian citizen. He was a landed immigrant who refused to apply for citizenship because, as he said repeatedly, "I prefer to be a first-class German to becoming a second-class Canadian." People wouldn't have known, had I not discovered it, that his own country refused to renew his German passport a year later in 1982 because of his efforts in Germany and elsewhere to unite the Nazis of the world. Yet after his trial and initial conviction for spreading hatred and false allegations against Jews, Zündel claimed that the penalty of being deported to Germany would mean "being sentenced to paradise." He added that it wasn't a punishment "being sent to a place where there are comforts, money, and supporters." It was that statement that made me continue my investigation in 1982 when my husband travelled with me to England and the European continent.

I found out then that the West German State and Justice Departments had been trying to get Zündel since 1981. If he set foot in Germany, they intended to jail him at his first attempt to publish or distribute his notorious propaganda. What's more, the German State Department confirmed that a right-wing Toronto organization had deposited 200,000 Marks spending money in a special account. Their investigation into doubtful bank deposits revealed that Zündel, whose activities were by then well-known to German authorities, had opened this account some years earlier. Our Solicitor General was informed of this man's activities and of his attempts to unite the Nazis of the world. But in spite of Canadian laws protecting human rights and outlawing hate literature, Canadian justice seemed to be unable or unwilling to stop him. To me, it was appalling that Canadians — and I was one of them — were then confronted all over Europe with "our" criminal activities abroad. It added insult to injury to be so accused by German school children who were innocent of past sins but were still trying to atone for those of their parents and grandparents.

I was so incensed over this affair that I spent the whole winter after my return debating and talking in public affairs meetings across Canada about Zündel's and other neo-Nazi organizations. For the first time, I believe, Canadians were made aware of the dangers of those doctrines I had already experienced once in my lifetime. My views were supported by the Alberta government's legal action against Keegstra, the high school teacher who had taught his students for fourteen years that the Holocaust was a hoax. He told his classes that there was a Jewish conspiracy to take over the world and that gas chambers in German concentration camps never existed. He claimed they were a Jewish invention to get a lot of money in compensation from post-war Germany. Like Zündel, he was also initially convicted. He lost his teaching certificate and his position as mayor of Eckville, his Alberta town.

However, our justice system allows so much time for appeals and counter-appeals that both Zündel's and Keegstra's cases were tied up in the courts till 1992. Both men claimed that their convictions violated their human rights and freedom of speech. Zündel was therefore not sentenced to "paradise" and his original conviction was squashed by the Supreme Court of Canada on a technicality. As I understand it, he was tried under a wrong clause in the Constitution. Already I heard that some groups and individual people he maligned intend to reopen his case under the proper permissible section. Keegstra, who was convicted a second time, said he would appeal again and if he did, the prosecution would counter-appeal for an even stiffer fine than the one imposed originally. At that time, Keegstra had run out of money for his defense, but early in 1994, he did appeal once more. I doubt I'll live long enough to see the final outcome of either these cases.

Why had it taken me so many years to realize that the only hope for a change in human attitudes rests with our very young people? I should have seen long ago the need to speak up when my daughter convinced the anti-Semitic son of German Nazis, that his hatred of people he had never met was not only wrong but dangerous. I should have realized, when our local children warmly welcomed the much maligned teenage boat people into their school, that a happier future for all children, whatever their background, depends on the new generation. Telling their parents and grandparents about their friendship with the young refugees changed public opinion in my small town.

If it is true that small Canadian towns resemble the proverbial mill-pond which, with its teeming life, is a true, miniature copy of our universe, I may have been the first person to throw a pebble into the pond. Persuading my community to sponsor the Vietnamese, I may have started the ripples, but it was the children who extended the ripples until they covered the whole pond.

All those years I had accepted invitations to discuss the issues with leaders of ultra-right-wing racist organizations, I was blinded by the standing ovations and honours I received. Perversely, I had even gained a certain amount of satisfaction from the hate-letters and vindictive comments I received from the new Nazis' followers. In a debate with the Alberta "Canadian League of

Rights" leader, a Mr. Boswell, at a Public Affairs forum in December 1977 for instance, I had little difficulty refuting his racist arguments. During the question period following that debate, a spokesperson for the League of Rights members, who had turned out in great numbers, got up, obviously irate, and said: "Our leader is entitled to freely voice his opinions and give the public the true version of history. What gives you the right to make him look ridiculous?" It gave me great pleasure to respond: "He did very nicely doing that himself. He didn't really need me to help him." This elicited a roar of laughter from the majority of the audience who got up one by one, not to ask questions, but to correct the "true version of history."

For at least another two weeks, people supporting the Canadian League of Rights called CJOC's Lethbridge radio phone-in show to complain about my attempts to "inhibit free speech." The mildest comment was probably one woman saying: "I did not know that Eva Brewster was a Communist!" The popular show host, Terry Bland, responded effectively and with some irony to even the most vicious comments. He was aided by phone calls from a great number of people phoning in from all over southern Alberta supporting him and me. I didn't have to get involved at all.

One thing became clear: The Canadian Nazis, like their German predecessors, presumed automatically that anybody who did not share their particular views had to be a Communist. However, if I had thought that this long debate would save me a lot of time and effort educating people still ignorant of recent history, I was wrong. More often than ever, I was invited to talk to school children, teachers, colleges and universities.

Young students are a joy to talk to. They are totally unbiased as a rule and open to any reasonable argument. It is almost like writing on a clean slate. But because they are so receptive, demagogues rewriting history and spreading hatred could also leave kids with a lasting contempt for different races and religions. That is precisely what happened in Germany and seems to be happening again. If I achieved nothing else, my Auschwitz Memoirs are now included in many schools' Social Studies curriculum.